Libraries and the Reading Public
in Twentieth-Century America

Print Culture History in Modern America

JAMES P. DANKY, CHRISTINE PAWLEY, *and*
ADAM R. NELSON,
Series Editors

Libraries and the Reading Public in Twentieth-Century America

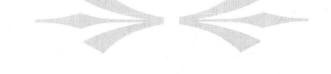

Edited by

CHRISTINE PAWLEY *and* LOUISE S. ROBBINS

THE UNIVERSITY OF WISCONSIN PRESS

027.473
Lib

Publication of this volume has been made possible, in part, through support
from the Anonymous Fund of the University of Wisconsin–Madison, the Brittingham
Fund, Demco Corporation, the Library History Round Table of the American Library
Association, the School of Library and Information Studies, and the University of
Wisconsin Libraries.

The University of Wisconsin Press
1930 Monroe Street, 3rd Floor
Madison, Wisconsin 53711-2059
uwpress.wisc.edu

3 Henrietta Street
London WC2E 8LU, England
eurospanbookstore.com

4/23/14

Printed in the United States of America

Library of Congress Cataloging-in-Publication Data

Libraries and the reading public in twentieth-century America / edited by
Christine Pawley and Louise S. Robbins.
p.   cm. — (Print culture history in modern America)
Includes bibliographical references and index.
ISBN 978-0-299-29324-6 (pbk. : alk. paper) — ISBN 978-0-299-29323-9 (e-book)
1. Public libraries—United States—History—20th century. 2. Books and reading—
United States—History—20th century. I. Pawley, Christine, 1945–
II. Robbins, Louise S. III. Series: Print culture history in modern America.
Z731.L546   2013
027.473—dc23
2012040073

Contents

Preface

Libraries and the Reading Public is a volume in the series "Print Culture History in Modern America," a project of the Center for the History of Print and Digital Culture (CHPDC) at the University of Wisconsin–Madison. This series focuses particularly on the mediating roles print has played in American culture since 1876. Its scope encompasses studies of newspapers, books, periodicals, advertising, and ephemera. Special attention is given to groups whose gender, race, class, creed, occupation, ethnicity, and sexual orientation (among other factors) have historically placed them on the periphery of power but who have used print sources as one of the few means of expression available to them. Recent previous volumes include *Science in Print: Essays on the History of Science and the Culture of Print* (2012, edited by Rima D. Apple, Gregory J. Downey, and Stephen L. Vaughn), *Education and the Culture of Print in Modern America* (2010, edited by Adam R. Nelson and John L. Rudolph), and *Religion and the Culture of Print in Modern America* (2008, edited by Charles L. Cohen and Paul S. Boyer).

Like other volumes in the series, *Libraries and the Reading Public* emerged from one of the CHPDC conferences, held biennially in Madison, Wisconsin. We would like to thank all those who took part in the 2010 conference, "Library History Seminar XII: Libraries in the History of Print Culture," as either organizers or contributors. We especially thank the following for their sponsorship of the conference and for providing financial assistance toward the publication of this volume: the Anonymous Fund of the University of Wisconsin–Madison, the Brittingham Fund, Demco Corporation, the Library History Round Table of the American Library Association, the School of Library and Information Studies, University of Wisconsin Libraries, the School of Journalism and Mass Communication, the Departments of English and the History of Science, the Holtz Center for Science and Technology Studies, the Wisconsin Historical Society, and the Wisconsin Print Culture Society. Thanks also go to Patrick B. Robbins for his careful indexing, the staff of the University of Wisconsin Press for their professionalism and expertise, and the two peer reviewers, whose knowledgeable and insightful comments did so much to improve the volume.

Libraries and the Reading Public
in Twentieth-Century America

Introduction

CHRISTINE PAWLEY

From the mid-nineteenth century forward, public organizations—free schools and libraries—played a crucial part in fostering in Americans the skills and habits of reading and writing. By the early twentieth century, government-sponsored community organizations like the agricultural extension agency, the school system, and the public library routinely provided access to standard forms of print that included informational genres, such as newspapers, pamphlets, textbooks, and other reference books, as well as literary genres, such as poetry, plays, and novels. Millions of ordinary Americans—those who lived unremarkable lives in relative anonymity—encountered officially sanctioned print, whether at work, school, church, or in the home. In terms of sheer numbers, public libraries continue to have an extraordinary impact; in the early twenty-first century, as the American Library Association reports and as historian Wayne A. Wiegand is fond of stating, there are more public library branches in the United States than McDonald's restaurants.[1]

Public libraries emerged during the antebellum period, as leaders of the Early Republic wrestled with the problem of how to foster an informed citizenry. On the eve of the American Revolution of 1776, twenty-nine "public" libraries contained a total of 45,623 books.[2] In the nineteenth century, however, these figures soared. Subscription, or "social," libraries became common in the New England and Mid-Atlantic states during the first half of the nineteenth century, and as antebellum Yankee settlers moved west, they brought with them this model for institutionalizing the sharing of books. In 1849, New Hampshire passed a bill allowing municipalities to tax themselves to set up free public libraries, and Massachusetts followed in 1851. The 1854 opening of the Boston Public Library spurred public library development elsewhere, and by 1875 all other New England states had passed public library laws.[3] In other parts of the country, too, states passed public-library-enabling laws during the later part of the nineteenth century, although legislation did not necessarily translate into actual libraries, at least in the short run. Iowa, for example, passed such a law in 1870 but five years later still had only four public libraries.[4]

Many social libraries converted themselves into tax-supported public libraries, and gradually the latter came to outnumber the former. In the fast-growing cities, reformers organized charities to save immigrant and native working-class boys and girls from the evils of the streets, believing that carefully chosen reading was an especially safe and suitable occupation for children, and later transferred this impetus to the support of free libraries.[5] Rural communities lacked the resources of big cities, though, and typically lagged behind them in providing purpose-built libraries. Between 1886 and 1917, the Carnegie philanthropic library building program spurred on the library movement by funding 1,689 public and academic libraries in the United States, many of them in small towns. States that benefited most were in the Midwest and the West, where communities were still new.[6] As support for free public libraries took hold, establishing local libraries became one of the ways influential members of pioneering communities put down roots and boosted their own value.[7] In towns and villages, thousands of women formed clubs that made support of the local library a high priority.[8] Local control of public libraries usually fell to more affluent members of the community, who served as library "trustees" (the library management board), but librarians were slowly forming themselves into groups that aimed for professional standards of management; at the state level, they set up library associations and supported the creation of state library commissions. The American Library Association began in 1876, and over subsequent decades it assumed an increasingly powerful national voice and role. The resulting tension between the exercise of local control and of professional judgment persisted throughout the twentieth century and into the present day, as several contributions to this volume demonstrate.

Studying public library activities makes visible complex beliefs and attitudes about reading that sometimes clashed with each other. Throughout the twentieth century, debates arose over the value of literature as opposed to mere literacy and of useful information as opposed to stories, over who should be encouraged and indeed allowed to read what and who should pay. Should libraries focus their efforts on adults rather than children? Should librarians accept a primarily consumerist (give them what they want) or educative (give them what they need) role? Such issues intertwine with the questions of who read what, when and where, how and why that historian Robert Darnton has identified as central to the history of readers and reading, a fast-growing area that overlaps the history of the book and of print culture and draws on the theories and methods of history, literary criticism, rhetoric and composition, cultural studies, and sociology.[9]

Methods for researching reading practices tend to fall into two broad categories—history and literary criticism. On the one hand, those trained in historical methods have used institutional records such as census reports, library catalogs, bookstore records, and estate inventories to identify readers of the past, along with the titles of the books and journals that they read. On the other hand, literary scholars have focused on the printed texts themselves to answer questions about how and why people read.[10] Over time, the overlap between the ethnographic/historical and literary approaches has expanded, with respect to both their orientation to texts and the types of primary sources they commonly employ. Both groups rely on readers' own writings—published and unpublished letters (including fan mail), essays, commonplace books, diaries, autograph books, journals, autobiographies, memoirs and reminiscences, and marginal annotations—to link real people to the texts that they read. An early example of research that bridged the gap between readers and texts was Janice A. Radway's *Reading the Romance: Women, Patriarchy, and Popular Literature*. First published in 1984, this project not only focused on a publication genre that scholars had previously neglected—romance novels—but also sought out real readers in an ethnographic effort to uncover their motivations and interpretations.[11] In this volume, Wayne A. Wiegand's essay (appearing first) veers more toward the standard historian's approach, while Janice A. Radway's (appearing at the end) is that of the literary scholar. Although the theories that each promotes are not the same, both give weight to libraries and librarians as institutional actors in a shifting, multiply constituted system of print culture in the long twentieth century.[12]

Recognizing the role of organizations in providing opportunities for reading helps us discern the activities of those millions of ordinary readers and writers for whom the technologies and practices of literacy were (and are) an indispensable part of everyday life.[13] An explicitly institutional view gives researchers a window onto the acts of reading and writing by non-elite groups for whom few individual records survive. Collections of institutional records, including minutes, memos, correspondence, work diaries, publication lists, and accessions and circulation records are rich repositories of primary source materials on print culture that require close scrutiny.[14] Such a focus also lets us build thick description by bringing to the fore primary sources that individual analysis might overlook. Institutional sites of print such as libraries can be imagined as a "middle layer" that bridges the gap between social structure and individual agency and between macro (societal) and micro (individual) views. Libraries are both sites and sources of regulating processes. The interactions of multitudes of authors and readers are shaped in part by the metatexts of the library's operations: its classification and cataloging practices, its shelving system and the principles on which it bases reader access to those shelves; its circulation rules, its spatial and temporal arrangements for in-house reading; its provision of printed signs and guides to the collection, its use of Web pages and personnel to steer readers along predefined and recognizable paths. Yet, just as individual readers engage in ruses that allow them to appropriate individual texts, so those who read *in* the library read the library itself—becoming, in the process, potentially resistant readers *of* the library.

Libraries are social institutions; although by their standardized bureaucratic characteristics they may seem to transcend the particulars of time and space and take on universal qualities, beneath the administrative jargon local variations emerge. A voluminous nineteenth- and twentieth-century professional literature reveals ideologies of reading that both reflected and influenced prevailing concepts of cultural capital and authority in different regions and at different times. Scrutinizing the public library's history reveals that while library leaders demonstrated how they construed the ideal reader through their professional rhetoric, organizational structures, buildings, and collecting policies, these were not simply imposed on a passive reading public. As some of the essays in this volume demonstrate, research into historical readers in specific localities can provide an important corrective to top-down analysis that overprivileges a monolithic interpretation of cultural authority. Such studies foreground readers' own choices and influences on local library practice—influences that sometimes reinforced and at other times subverted official policies and goals. Local librarians, too, might diverge widely from authoritative recommendations; articles published in professional journals may not necessarily be interpreted as accurate guides to actual practice. And official policy itself is never unified or uniform. Even in the nineteenth century, the rhetoric on reading in public libraries was divided as library leaders attempted to balance competing ideologies while promoting the health of this always financially challenged institution.

The Structure of *Libraries and the Reading Public*

Contributors to *Libraries and the Reading Public* took part in a three-day conference at the University of Wisconsin–Madison in September 2010, titled "Library History Seminar XII: Libraries in the History of Print Culture," jointly sponsored by the Center for the History of Print Culture in Modern America (now the Center for the History of Print and Digital Culture) and the Library History Round Table of the American Library Association. The editors selected these thirteen essays from the fifty or so presented at the conference because they help build a picture of the place of public libraries in the life of American readers during the long twentieth century.

We have divided this volume into four sections. The essays in part 1, "Methods and Evidence," explore theoretical and practical approaches to using library records to uncover reading practices. The first two contributions report on large-scale, ambitious projects from which a number of publications will eventually emerge. Wayne A. Wiegand sets out the theoretical assumptions that guide his recent book, *Main Street Public Library: Community Places and Reading Spaces in the Rural Heartland, 1876–1956*, a study of four midwestern public libraries.[15] Taking issue with a common interpretation by librarians that during this period American public libraries played a vital role in fostering an informed citizenry and that librarians exercised a powerful role in determining what constituted "good reading," Wiegand argues that these standard views ignore local forces—the local community leaders and library patrons who strongly influenced what public libraries actually collected (as opposed to what national leaders recommended). Wiegand's research rests on an extensive database built primarily from the acquisitions records of the five libraries in his study as well as on other library archival material and published primary sources that include library annual reports and local newspapers. In addition to the book described in this essay and an additional article by Wiegand, several other authors contributed papers that made use of the Main Street database to the 2010 print culture conference. These papers appeared in a special issue of *Library Trends* in 2012.[16]

The second collaborative project represents the work of several scholars at Ball State University: the What Middletown Read database. As Frank Felsenstein, John Straw, Katharine Leigh, and James J. Connolly explain in their essay, during 2003, renovations to the Carnegie Library of Muncie, Indiana (the city Robert and Helen Lynd's 1929 Middletown study made famous), brought to light a treasure trove of circulation and accessions records from the pre-Carnegie Muncie Public Library. Particularly useful library documents are those that record circulation—lists of borrowers' names and the titles of the books they checked out—because they allow researchers to link specific texts with real readers. This is especially valuable for ordinary readers, who may have left no other records of their reading experiences. By linking the library records with manuscripts of federal and state census population schedules, researchers of earlier periods can go an important step further by linking the reading of specific texts to demographic variables such as age, sex, marital status, occupation, race, and sometimes even religion.[17]

Given their scholarly potential, one might expect circulation records to be carefully preserved in libraries, and readily available for inspection by researchers. Some thoughtful librarians and archivists have indeed seen the value of such records and provide researchers with access to them. More commonly, however, circulation records have been discarded; public libraries are notoriously short of space, and librarians often lack training in the history of their own institution. In recent times, two interconnected trends have accelerated this process. Automated library record-keeping techniques need leave no paper trail, and an increased value for patrons' privacy (combined with fear of government snooping) has encouraged librarians to deliberately ensure that circulation records do not survive beyond the very short period required to ensure that books are properly returned.[18] For these various reasons, circulation records have unfortunately rarely survived, and even more rarely have archivists processed them for ready retrieval. The discovery in Muncie of approximately 180,000 such records is therefore an extraordinary find. With support from various bodies, including the National Endowment for the Humanities, the Ball State team has built a database of these records and contemporary census data. In their essay, Felsenstein, Straw, Leigh, and Connolly discuss the practical issues associated with constructing this major resource and illustrate its use by tracking the borrowings of one library patron, Norene Hawk, between 1891 and 1902.[19]

The remaining two essays in this section present contrasting examples of library records that illustrate the range of possibilities as primary sources in the history of readers and reading. Ross Harvey's chapter, "'Story Develops Badly, Could Not Finish': Member Book Reviews at the Boston Athenæum in the 1920s," shows how this celebrated social library ("public" in the antebellum sense of "not private") sought and received feedback from readers on popular fiction borrowed during the 1920s. Readers leave few physical traces of their experiences; adding marginal comments and annotations in library books is not encouraged. The Athenæum collection of reader responses, therefore, represents a rare opportunity for researchers. In the early twenty-first century, reader reviews are routinely available at the websites of online booksellers such as Amazon, but unlike the slips of paper the Athenæum made available to readers, carefully retained and archived for future use by researchers, the future accessibility of such modern evaluations is less assured. As Harvey points out, the Athenæum's review system is also significant in that it signals a change in the relationship of the library to its readers; the library's role as "center of authority" is modified, and readers are encouraged to share their knowledge and opinions with other readers.

The Library of Congress counts as another kind of "public" library. Jane Aikin's work draws on the annual reports of the Superintendent of the Reading Room to show how the Library of Congress served the general public extensively during the 1920s and 1930s. Analysis of the classes of books requested reveals that fiction was much in demand there as it was at other libraries but that other much-requested material included genealogy, business, and history. The annual reports also provided some details about the readers themselves: American and international academics, students, clerics, as well as researchers from government agencies, and members of the general public that included the unemployed as well as business people. Of all the types of library records that researchers might want to use as primary sources, annual reports are among the most readily available. Larger libraries often published their annual reports and distributed them quite widely, and even the manuscript or typescript reports of smaller libraries were valued by local record-keepers and therefore more likely to survive than ephemeral circulation records.[20]

The three chapters in part 2, "Public Libraries, Readers, and Localities," show how libraries might shape their programs and activities to the needs of particular communities. During the twentieth century, tax-supported public libraries were the only secular community institution in principle open to all. In practice, this liberality could be severely restricted. Working-class Americans (especially men) were less likely to take advantage of the services the public library offered, perhaps believing themselves out of place in the genteel middle-class atmosphere that undoubtedly prevailed in many libraries, despite librarians' best-intentioned efforts to create a space welcoming to all.[21] In many areas, as late as the 1970s—in the North as well as the South—African Americans were outright denied entry, or admitted only on restricted terms. However, millions of Americans did find in the library a community space where what Wayne Wiegand terms "dependable pleasures" as well as useful information were accessible. From the Great Books projects of the mid-twentieth century to present-day One Book, One City projects that consciously promote reading within geographic communities, many policy initiatives have tried to build on the interconnectedness of reading and locality.[22]

In "Going to 'America': Italian Neighborhoods and the Newark Free Public Library, 1900–1920," Ellen Pozzi argues that in the early 1900s public libraries were an "information node" in Italian neighborhoods in Trenton, New Jersey, along with bookstores, newspapers, churches, and social support services as well as more informal networks of friends or community leaders. In the Italian neighborhood, children were enthusiastic patrons of the public library, acting as a bridge, Pozzi says, "connecting their parents in the privatized public space of the ethnic enclave with the public sphere of the library."[23] In an effort to assimilate adult immigrants to the "American way of life," public libraries commonly held Americanization programs at the turn of the century. Pozzi reports that the Newark Free Public Library designated one of its seven branches as "the Foreign Branch." This catered to a variety of ethnic groups—including Jews, Poles, and Russians, by providing materials in their native languages—though not, apparently, to Italians.

In an effort to attract immigrants, large urban libraries routinely collected books in foreign languages. By 1913, 10 percent of the New York Public Library's holdings were printed in twenty-five foreign languages.[24] In some rural areas, traveling libraries carried foreign-language materials.[25] Some public libraries also offered classes and carried books in simple English on topics related to citizenship and American culture in an effort to wean immigrants away from their native literatures. By the 1920s, however, Americanization programs were giving way to more general adult education programs. An advantage of such programs, some library leaders believed, was that they might entice more men to use the public library and might at the same time divert the many women who already used the library away from reading fiction. After Carnegie's death in 1919, the Carnegie Corporation continued to support library development but changed course from an exclusive focus on building and instead partnered with the American Library Association to support adult education programs.

The theme of immigration continues in Joyce Latham's "'A Liberal and Dignified Approach': The John Toman Branch of the Chicago Public Library and the Making of Americans, 1927–1940." The Chicago Public Library had long debated how to serve the city's immigrants and working poor. In 1904 the Chicago Public Library (CPL) introduced what turned out to be its most durable form of extension—the branch library. However, Chicago lagged behind other cities of its size. Boston, for instance, had opened its first branch in 1871 and already by 1875 had six branches.[26] Despite repeated assertions of the need to serve immigrants through foreign-language collections, the CPL consistently fell short, however. In the 1880s, foreign-language materials constituted nearly a quarter of the whole collection, but as purchases of new foreign-language materials failed to keep pace with English acquisitions, this proportion fell steadily, despite the rise during this period of Chicago's non-English-speaking population. By 1927, the proportion of the total collection in languages other than English had dropped to 8 percent.[27] In the 1930s, the issue remained alive, as Latham's chapter demonstrates. At the CPL's John Toman branch, community members worked with librarians to create an enduring local space where those of Czech descent could learn about their culture and nurture it rather than try (as in older Americanization programs) to suppress it.

The final essay in this section is Jean Preer's "Counter Culture: The World as Viewed from Inside the Indianapolis Public Library, 1944–1956." The chapter's central figure, Marian McFadden, embodied the ideal characteristics of the midcentury librarian. Educated at Smith College, a premier women's institution, and then at Columbia University's School of Library Service, one of the nation's most prestigious library schools, McFadden could even claim a slight personal connection to Andrew Carnegie. Her education and personal characteristics set her well above her more run-of-the-mill colleagues, and it probably came as no surprise to anyone when she eventually became director of the Indianapolis Public Library. Although women predominated in the profession as a whole, for most of the twentieth century, most leaders of major libraries (both public and academic) were men, and for McFadden to rise to this position was an extraordinary achievement. Preer sets her analysis of McFadden's career firmly in the context of Indiana, a state characterized by cultural contradictions. On the one hand, home of prominent critical authors such as Theodore Dreiser and Kurt Vonnegut, on the other, Indiana was nevertheless a center for the resurgence of the Ku Klux Klan and known for its conservative political order. When the federal government first provided support for public libraries through the Library Services Act (LSA) of 1956, Indiana was the only state to refuse LSA funds.[28] McFadden's career demonstrated some of the same cultural contradictions as her home state. A lifelong Republican, McFadden strongly supported the adult educational role of the public library and instituted programs to inform community members about the United Nations and other topics that were controversial at the time, including race relations and communism.

Preer's essay shows how Marian McFadden confronted issues of intellectual freedom that had real consequences for librarians, especially during the early years of the Cold War, a theme that continues in the four chapters of part 3, "Intellectual Freedom."[29] In the early years of the twentieth century, librarians had taken for granted that guiding readers toward better books was part of their professional responsibility. From the eighteenth century on, anxieties had centered on the effects of new kinds of publication—such as the novel—on the reader's moral development. Since the exercise of responsible, virtuous citizenship was considered to depend on informed moral character, what individuals and groups selected to read in a world of increasing choice was a matter of vital social concern. In the nineteenth century, a greatly expanded market for publications resulted in fears that some of these printed publications could have a corrupting influence on impressionable minds.[30]

At a time when character and virtue were held vital to the exercise of citizenship, the link between morality and democracy was clear. That libraries should provide access only to morally acceptable books was indisputable. Popular novels stood on the margins of what counted as morally acceptable, and some argued that public libraries should refuse to include them, just as public schools did.[31] In the late nineteenth century, librarians began to publish guides to help select "the best reading," a move that both encouraged the professionalization of collection development and raised questions about selection principles. The early years of the twentieth century saw heightened activity by those who, like the vice societies, sought to restrict what books the public might read. Wealthy and well-connected contributors to vice organizations who also contributed to libraries and other cultural organizations included Andrew Carnegie himself.[32] As libraries increasingly opened their doors to children, concerns intensified about how to regulate what young people might find on their shelves (now more likely to be directly accessible to the public). Imbued with a civilizationist ethic, librarians did not hesitate to censor on the basis of moral judgment.

During World War I, librarians took on an ever more active censorship role, as anti-German sentiment resulted in the outright suppression of German-language reading materials.[33] Julia Skinner's essay, "Censorship in the Heartland: Eastern Iowa Libraries during World War I," describes how some Iowa librarians responded to calls to remove German materials from library shelves. Based on annual reports and minutes of board meetings from six eastern Iowa libraries, Skinner's essay shows that although in all six libraries the librarians quickly complied with requests to censor materials that outside bodies identified as war-sensitive, in the period before the United States entered the war, they continued to collect foreign-language materials and focus on the needs of immigrant (including German) populations. After the war, peace brought little sense of tranquility, as fear of Russian Communism quickly replaced fear of German militarism. Racial unrest mounted, too, as all over the country millions of white Americans joined the Ku Klux Klan, and in the South, Klansmen and other white supremacist groups stepped up their campaign of terror against African Americans. Censorship became more blatant, as in Boston a period ended in which booksellers, the Watch and Ward Society, the Catholic Church, and Brahmins (Boston's leading families) had collaborated to quietly suppress controversial literature. What followed were much more active attempts to ban major works by notable writers such as Sinclair Lewis, Theodore Dreiser, and Warwick Deeping and even works like Nathaniel Hawthorne's *The Scarlet Letter*, George Eliot's *Adam Bede*, and Thomas Hardy's *Tess of the d'Urbervilles*. These backfired, though, spurring the eruption of an anticensorship campaign in Massachusetts that spread to other cities and prompted librarians to revise their earlier professional commitment to censorship.[34]

This revision process continued in the 1930s. The proposed 1929–30 code of ethics for librarianship advised librarians that books "should represent all phases of opinion and interest rather than the personal tastes of librarian or board members." Moreover, the code stated, "In an official capacity, the librarian and members of the staff should not express personal opinions on controversial questions, as political, religious, economic issues, especially those of a local nature."[35] The rise of fascism in Europe, accompanied by well-publicized book burnings, helped propel librarians slowly toward a stance of not simply rejecting censorship but actively embracing intellectual freedom. The success of Nazi campaigns in manipulating German public opinion underlined in librarians' minds the need for vigilance against the effects of propaganda. An awareness of similarities between racial injustice at home and the rise of fascism abroad prompted librarians to take explicit stands against censorship. By 1935, many librarians were rejecting their previous accommodationist stances of avoiding controversy and instead promoting active support of freedom of access to all kinds of information.

In June 1939 the American Library Association's (ALA) Council adopted a document titled the Library's Bill of Rights that set out principles that, when strengthened in 1948 with active opposition to censorship, would remain the core statement of the profession's commitment to intellectual freedom for the rest of the century.[36] ALA's adoption of the Library's Bill of Rights hardly translated into an instant transformation of library practice, however. Librarians were often unwilling to confront their boards of trustees or other prominent community members, and when calls to ban John Steinbeck's *Grapes of Wrath* multiplied in 1939, many librarians complied.[37] Librarians had to work out what the revised 1948 Library Bill of Rights meant through the process of dealing with challenges to library materials.

Joan Bessman Taylor's essay, "Locating the Library in the Nonlibrary Censorship of the 1950s: Ideological Negotiations in the Professional Record," moves the analysis into the fraught period of the Cold War. Library leaders complained in their professional literature about "book-banning and Witchhunts" and protested efforts "to purge all libraries, schools, and book stores of 'subversive' books."[38] However, ALA's anticensorship policy put librarians at odds with what seemed the opinion of the majority of Americans, many of whom saw communism as a peril and censorship of left-leaning materials as justifiable. By 1950 and 1951 groups like the American Legion and the Sons of the American Revolution had escalated their attacks on books and films that they considered dangerous.[39] Yet little practical support in terms of suggestions for institutional procedures and educational initiatives was forthcoming from ALA, despite its brave policy statement. Much as librarians might have preferred to keep their professional decisions decently screened from outside view, the events of the 1950s forced them to interact with forces outside the library and well beyond their control. In Dubuque and Ottumwa, city librarians found themselves embroiled in complex rhetorical battles being waged outside the library's walls. Drawing on the records of the Iowa Library Association's Intellectual Freedom Committee, administrative correspondence, and published professional articles of the day, Taylor teases out the details of these local controversies and shows how librarians navigated the confused and dangerous riptide where their professional commitment to intellectual freedom ran into demands by organized community groups for local control over reading materials.

During the years 1952 to 1960, ALA members gradually began to evolve a set of effective strategies for promoting intellectual freedom, but it was not until the mid-1960s that the organization opened its Office of Intellectual Freedom, devoted to helping librarians and others withstand censorship, while educating the public about the right to read.[40] However, the issues of intellectual freedom continued to present librarians with professional moral dilemmas. The last two essays in this section describe contemporary instances of censorship and public libraries in the late twentieth and early twenty-first centuries. Loretta Gaffney's chapter, "'Is Your Public Library Family Friendly?' Libraries as a Site of Conservative Activism, 1992–2002," shows that despite a half century of outreach efforts at educating the public, librarians continue to face organized opposition from national and community groups intent on controlling library collecting and access policies. The end of the Cold War did little to mitigate these clashes, as the rise of a powerful Christian right wing during the 1990s shifted the focus of complaint away from communism and toward sexual orientation and abortion. Gaffney traces the history of Family Friendly Libraries (FFL), an organization with national reach, devoted to combating ALA's intellectual freedom policies. However, FFL's most effective argument rests on the claim that local libraries should be answerable to local demands and that control of library collections and services is vested in the tax-paying communities that provide financial support for them, not in a professional body such as the ALA. In "The Challengers of West Bend: The Library as a Community Institution," Emily Knox analyzes the rhetoric used in a particular case of a challenge to library materials in 2009. As in the case of FFL, the West Bend, Wisconsin, challengers appealed to a need for community control over library materials and services and argued for the use of library practices (such as labeling materials and placing controversial materials in a restricted space) that ALA's Library Bill of Rights specifically condemns.

Part 4, "Librarians and the Alternative Press," continues the theme of censorship by focusing on librarians' involvement with publications that fall outside the mainstream. As Alycia Sellie's essay, "Meta-Radicalism: The Alternative Press by and for Activist Librarians," explains, since the 1960s librarians have advocated for the inclusion of materials that appear in nonstandard formats or reflect controversial or minority viewpoints. One of the best-known and extensive collections of alternative press materials is that of the Wisconsin Historical Society (WHS), thanks to the untiring efforts of former newspaper and periodicals librarian James P. Danky, who, over the course of his thirty-year career at the WHS, added to the library's collection more than thirty thousand titles, many of which are available in no other libraries.[41] Rather than being challenged by external groups, such materials are often subject to self-censorship by librarians. As Sellie points out, historians need to look beyond the pages of the mainstream professional library literature to seek out these less widely distributed publications in which they can find the expression of alternative viewpoints by librarians.

Janice A. Radway's "From the Underground to the Stacks and Beyond: Girl Zines, Zine Librarians, and the Importance of Itineraries through Print

Culture" (the final essay in this section and in the book) focuses on girl zines, a phenomenon not of the radical 1960s but of the 1990s. For Radway, uncovering the details of girl zine production is a vehicle for discussing power, domination, and dissent, and for focusing on the mobility and circulation at the heart of U.S. print culture in terms that avoid the limitations of spatial metaphors (culture from "below") or the binary (elite versus dispossessed). Radway calls for a way of understanding power, domination, and dissent that brings to the fore actors like librarians, publishers, editors, journalists, and teachers—rather than sidelining them as mere mediators between texts and their readers, as has often been the practice in the history of the book. An integral part of the story of girl zines, then, is the story of the librarians who make decisions about "what gets counted as the cultural tradition" and "that which is subsequently made available to others to be selected from, read, and mined for potentially new purposes." Pointing to the performative character of girl zine production, Radway shows how the zine activities of the 1990s persisted through time, in the enduring networks that girl zinesters created and in the activities of zine librarians campaigning to establish zine collections in their libraries. To the extent that they are successful in achieving this aim, they are also, Radway argues, helping redefine the literary field by "insisting that any understanding of that field take into account not simply books or even the larger universe of print but also zines and all of the one-off, handmade, self-circulated publications generated by the alternative press." Radway calls for print culture historians to study the labor of the so-called mediators in their efforts to trace "itineraries of circulation" in which not just readers and texts but librarians, booksellers, and the like are fellow travelers.

NOTES

1. Wayne A. Wiegand, "Community Places and Reading Spaces: Main Street Public Library in the Rural Heartland, 1876–1956," this volume, 23.

2. Department of the Interior, Bureau of Education, *Public Libraries in the United States of America: Their History, Condition and Management; A Special Report* (Washington, DC: Government Printing Office, 1876), xi, xvi, 773. These libraries were not freely open to the community, however, but like college or subscription libraries were institutionally rather than individually owned.

3. Sidney Ditzion, *Arsenals of a Democratic Culture: A Social History of the Public Library Movement in New England and the Middle States from 1850 to 1900* (Chicago: American Library Association, 1947), 30. The motives of Boston Public Library's founders, particularly George Ticknor, have been a subject of controversy among historians. Ditzion believed Ticknor was driven by "a deep concern for the preservation

of our republican institutions on the foundation of an intelligent population" and that he "loved and trusted the great majority of his fellow citizens as much as he feared and hated what he termed illiterate mobs" (16–17). However, revisionist scholars such as Michael H. Harris have argued for an alternative view. See Michael H. Harris, *The Role of the Public Library in American Life: A Speculative Essay*, University of Illinois Graduate School of Library Science Occasional Papers 117 (Champaign: Illinois Graduate School of Library Science, 1975). Harris presents Ticknor as "an arrogant patrician" and "narrow-minded bigot" whose principal goals for the new public library were, first, to educate the masses so that they would follow the "best men" and, second, to provide the elite minority who would someday become leaders of the political, intellectual and moral affairs of the nation with access to "the best books" (7).

4. Daniel Goldstein, "The Spirit of an Age: Iowa Public Libraries and Professional Librarians as Solutions to Society's Problems, 1890–1940," *Libraries and Culture* 38, no. 3 (Summer 2003): 215–16.

5. Eric C. Schneider, *In the Web of Class: Delinquents and Reformers in Boston, 1810s–1930s* (New York: New York University Press, 1992), 146.

6. Theodore Jones, *Carnegie Libraries across America: A Public Legacy* (New York: John Wiley & Sons, 1997), 128–30.

7. For an account of the public library's role in one community, see Christine Pawley, *Reading on the Middle Border: The Culture of Print in Late-Nineteenth-Century Osage, Iowa* (Amherst: University of Massachusetts Press, 2001), esp. 61–116.

8. According to Daniel Goldstein, it was the interaction between three institutions—women's clubs, the state library commission, and the state library association—that contributed to the flourishing state of Iowa's public libraries during the period 1890 to 1940 (Goldstein, "Spirit of an Age," 214).

9. Scholars with research and teaching interests in the study of reading practices can be found in American studies, education, journalism and communication studies, and library and information studies. For useful introductions to the history of reading, see *Literacy in the United States: Readers and Reading Since 1880*, ed. Carl F. Kaestle et al. (New Haven, CT: Yale University Press, 1991), 33–72; Robert Darnton, "History of Reading," in *New Perspectives on Historical Writing*, ed. Peter Burke (University Park: Pennsylvania State University Press, 1992), 140–67; Joan Shelley Rubin, "What Is the History of the History of Books," *Journal of American History* 90, no. 2 (September 2003): 555–75; Leah Price, "Reading: The State of the Discipline," *Book History* 7 (2004): 303–20. See also the excellent introductory essays in the five volumes of *A History of the Book in America*, ed. David D. Hall (Chapel Hill: University of North Carolina Press, 2010).

10. For a summary of theoretical and methodological issues involved in these approaches to the history of reading, see Leon Jackson, "The Reader Retailored: Thomas Carlyle, His American Audiences, and the Politics of Evidence," in *Reading Acts: U.S. Readers' Interactions with Literature, 1800–1950*, ed. Barbara Ryan and Amy M. Thomas (Knoxville: University of Tennessee Press, 2002), 79–106, esp. 80–82.

11. Janice A. Radway, *Reading the Romance: Women, Patriarchy, and Popular Literature* (Chapel Hill: University of North Carolina Press, 1991).

12. For the purposes of this book, we conceive of the long twentieth century as running from 1890 to 2010.

13. Christine Pawley, "Seeking Significance: Actual Readers, Specific Reading Communities," *Book History* 5 (2002): 146.

14. For an extended version of this argument, see Christine Pawley, "Beyond Market Models and Resistance: Organizations as a Middle Layer in the History of Reading," *Library Quarterly* 79, no. 1 (January 2009): 73–93.

15. Wayne A. Wiegand, *Main Street Public Library: Community Places and Reading Spaces in the Rural Heartland, 1876–1956* (Iowa City: University of Iowa Press, 2011). Wiegand analyzes a fifth library in a separate publication: Wayne A. Wiegand, "'An Established Institution': The Morris Public Library of Morris, Illinois, 1913–1953," *Journal of Illinois History* 13 (Winter 2010): 263–88.

16. See Wayne A. Wiegand, ed., "Windows on the World: Analyzing Main Street Public Library Collections," special issue, *Library Trends* 60, no. 4 (Spring 2012).

17. This method is sometimes known as "nominal record linkage." See Cheryl Knott Malone, "Reconstituting the Public Library Users of the Past: An Exploration of Nominal Record Linkage Methodology," *Journal of Education for Library and Information Science* 39, no. 4 (Fall 1998): 282–90. See the following for examples of analyses of library circulation records: William Gilmore, *Reading Becomes a Necessity of Life: Material and Cultural Life in Rural New England, 1780–1835* (Knoxville: University of Tennessee Press, 1989); Pawley, *Reading on the Middle Border*; Emily B. Todd, "Walter Scott and the Nineteenth-Century American Literary Marketplace: Antebellum Richmond Readers and the Collected Editions of the Waverley Novels," *Papers of the Bibliographical Society of America* 93, no. 4 (1999): 495–517; Ronald Zboray, *A Fictive People: Antebellum Economic Development and the American Reading Public* (New York: Oxford University Press, 1993).

18. Leigh S. Estabrook, "Sacred Trust or Competitive Opportunity: Using Patron Records," *Library Journal* 121, no. 2 (February 1, 1996): 48–49.

19. The What Middletown Read database is publicly available at http://www.bsu.edu/libraries/wmr/.

20. For a discussion of the history of public library annual reports see Bernadette Lear, "'Tis Better to Be Brief than Tedious'? The Evolution of the American Public Library Annual Report," *Libraries and the Cultural Record* 41, no. 4 (2006): 462–86.

21. Dee Garrison attributes the gentility of public libraries to the recruitment as librarians of middle-class women during the latter half of the nineteenth century, a view contested by other historians. See Dee Garrison, *Apostles of Culture: The Public Librarian and American Culture, 1876–1920* (Madison: University of Wisconsin Press, 2003), 173–85.

22. Print culture historians recognize the social nature of reading that renders place significant. Elizabeth Long refers to the social infrastructure of reading (Elizabeth Long, "Textual Interpretation as Collective Action," in *The Ethnography of Reading*, ed.

Jonathan Boyarin [Berkeley: University of California Press, 1993], 190–92). Roger Chartier and Guglielmo Cavallo remind us that the practice of reading takes place as a "specific act and habit, and in specific places." One of our tasks as historians, they say, is to "identify the . . . distinctive traits of communities of readers, reading traditions and ways of reading" (Guglielmo Cavallo and Roger Chartier, introduction to *A History of Reading in the West,* ed. Guglielmo Cavallo and Roger Chartier [Amherst: University of Massachusetts Press, 1999], 2).

23. Ellen Pozzi, "Going to 'America,'" this volume, 106.

24. Garrison, *Apostles of Culture,* 217.

25. Christine Pawley, "Advocate for Access: Lutie Stearns and the Traveling Libraries of the Wisconsin Free Library Commission, 1895–1914," *Libraries and Culture* 35 (2000): 434–58.

26. Carleton Bruns Joeckel and Leon Carnovsky, *A Metropolitan Library in Action: A Survey of the Chicago Public Library* (Chicago: University of Chicago Press, 1940), 34–35.

27. Eric Novotny, "Library Services to Immigrants: The Debate in the Library Literature, 1900–1920, and a Chicago Case Study," *Reference and User Services Quarterly* 42, no. 4 (2003): 348–49.

28. Indiana's Republican governor, Harold Handley, was reported as fearing that Hoosiers would be "brainwashed with books handpicked by Washington bureaucrats," and turned down $700,000 of funding in the first four years after the Library Services Act passed. James W. Fry, "LSA and LCSA, 1956–1973: A Legislative History," *Library Trends* 24, no. 1 (1975): 11, 12. The LSA was renewed in 1962 as the Library Services and Construction Act (LSCA) and in 1996 as the Library Services and Technology Act (LSTA).

29. For example, in *The Dismissal of Miss Ruth Brown: Civil Rights, Censorship, and the American Library* (Norman: University of Oklahoma Press, 2000), Louise S. Robbins describes how in 1950 Ruth Brown, the director of the Bartlesville, Oklahoma, Public Library, was dismissed for refusing to remove materials (including the *Nation*) deemed "subversive" from the library's collection. Brown was also a civil rights activist, which earned her the enmity of some of the town's prominent leaders.

30. Isabelle Lehuu, *Carnival on the Page: Popular Print Media in Antebellum America* (Chapel Hill: University of North Carolina Press, 2000), 16–17.

31. Evelyn Geller, *Forbidden Books in American Public Libraries, 1876–1939: A Study in Cultural Change* (Westport, CT: Greenwood, 1984), 11, 13, 12.

32. Paul S. Boyer, *Purity in Print: Book Censorship in America from the Gilded Age to the Computer Age* (Madison: University of Wisconsin Press, 2002), 25.

33. Wayne A. Wiegand, *An Active Instrument for Propaganda: The American Public Library during World War I* (New York: Greenwood, 1989).

34. Geller, *Forbidden Books,* 134–35.

35. Ibid., 141, 143, 147–48; "Suggested Code of Library Ethics," *Library Journal* 55, no. 4 (1930): 165.

36. *ALA Bulletin* 33, no. 11 (1939): 60.

37. Louise S. Robbins, *Censorship and the American Library: The American Library Association's Response to Threats to Intellectual Freedom, 1939–1969* (Westport, CT: Greenwood, 1997), 14. The name "Library's Bill of Rights" was subsequently changed to "Library Bill of Rights."

38. David K. Berninghausen, "Book-Banning and Witch-Hunts," *American Library Association Bulletin* 42, no. 5 (1948): 204; David K. Berninghausen, "Current Attacks on Books," *American Library Association Bulletin* 42, no. 5 (1948): 58.

39. Robbins, *Censorship and the American Library*, 50.

40. Ibid., esp. chapters 3 and 4.

41. For a comprehensive discussion of alternative publications, see James P. Danky in *A History of the Book in America*, vols. 4 and 5, *Print in Motion: The Expansion of Publishing and Reading in the United States, 1880–1940*, ed. Carl F. Kaestle and Janice A. Radway (Chapel Hill: University of North Carolina Press, 2009), 339–58, and *The Enduring Book: Print Culture in Postwar America*, ed. David Paul Nord, Joan Shelley Rubin, and Michael Schudson (Chapel Hill: University of North Carolina Press, 2009), 269–85. Danky's article in volume 5 has subsections devoted to the left- and right-wing press, feminist publishing, and GLBTQ literature. See also Juris Dilevko, "An Alternative Vision of Librarianship: James Danky and the Sociocultural Politics of Collection Development," *Library Trends* 56, no. 3 (2008): 678–704.

PART I

METHODS AND EVIDENCE

Community Places and Reading Spaces

Main Street Public Library in the Rural Heartland, 1876–1956

WAYNE A. WIEGAND

In 2012 the United States has more public libraries than McDonald's restaurants. In the twenty-first century's first decade, two-thirds of the population visited a public library at least once annually, and two of three were registered borrowers. These statistics state the obvious. The American public library is a heavily used and ubiquitous institution, and because 80 percent of public library systems serve towns with populations of less than twenty-five thousand, this is especially true in small-town America. Rare is the small town without a public library, an institution that since the late nineteenth century has become the model other countries have sought to emulate. In the twentieth century alone, thousands of small public libraries served as particular destination places, and have circulated billions of books to citizens of all ages, economic classes, and ethnicities. With few exceptions, however, we know very little about the histories of small-town public libraries.[1]

Main Street Public Library (2011) attempts to address this deficiency.[2] To contain the study, it begins coverage in 1876, when the federal government issued its first published report on U.S. public libraries, and ends with the Library Services Act in 1956, which for the first time provided federal funds for public library services through state library agencies. To contain the study geographically, it focuses on "typical" public libraries in five rural Midwest communities: the Bryant Library in Sauk Centre, Minnesota; the Sage Library in Osage, Iowa; the Morris Public Library in Morris, Illinois; the Moore Library in Lexington, Michigan; and the Rhinelander Public Library in Rhinelander, Wisconsin. Readers may recognize the first site; Sinclair Lewis was born there, and many have argued that Sauk Centre is the fictionalized Gopher Prairie he describes in his best-selling 1920 novel *Main Street*.

Three of the five libraries reside on Main Street (the other two just off Main Street); four are housed in buildings erected with funds provided by Andrew Carnegie. All also had archives; all were located in towns with newspapers easily accessed on microfilm; and, most important, all saved their accessions books—developed in the 1880s by a library supplies company as a common form to systematically record every book acquired by a library. In 1992 research assistants began to key this information into a relational database that allowed searching the collections of the libraries collectively or individually over the decades.[3] Besides *Main Street Public Library*, this database also grounds the research of seven essays in *Library Trends*.[4]

I approach my research from a different perspective than most library historians. First, I do not automatically assume that the public library has been an essential good or that it has functioned in the same ways for all people. In the professional rhetoric, these ubiquitous institutions are seen as neutral agencies whose primary responsibility is to make accessible the kinds of information thought essential to democracy—itself a legacy of the Enlightenment's faith in the power of knowledge. But is that perception justified? Merely asking these kinds of questions runs contrary to the library faith—a conviction in the library profession that assumes with Thomas Jefferson that without an informed and educated citizenry democracy cannot exist and then extends this principle by arguing that without libraries available to all citizens Americans cannot be fully educated or informed.[5]

Second, in its history I see a particular moment in the late nineteenth century when the library profession defined a jurisdiction creating a set of professional boundaries that have governed its options ever since. When in 1879 the American Library Association (ALA) adopted the motto "The best reading for the greatest number at the least cost," it identified a set of goals that library leaders used to distinguish librarianship from other emerging professions. On the one hand, it was built on an ideology of learned reading shared with fellow middle-class professionals who believed that good reading led to good social behavior, bad reading to bad social behavior. On the other hand, it relinquished to other professionals—especially those in the academic and literary establishments—the authority to identify what was "best reading." The only exception was children's literature, which children's librarians seized as their arena of responsibility at the beginning of the twentieth century.[6] In part, librarians chose not to compete for this authority to streamline efficiency among professional responsibilities and avoid confrontation, and in part, their connections made it easier to abdicate responsibility for defining canonical

literatures. By the turn of the twentieth century, the library profession had settled into a familiar if sometimes uncomfortable niche in a growing fraternity
of professions it has occupied ever since.[7]

Finally, because civic institutions established in Western cultures have been
shaped by a mix of forces, I argue that within public libraries, people who ran
them (trustees and managers) and people who used them (patrons) were two
major forces in this mix. Unlike most other civic institutions (courts, hospitals,
schools), however, use of the American public library is not compulsory—
people patronize it because they want to, not because they have to. Because of
this fundamental difference, I suspected that over the years library users significantly influenced library institutions in multiple ways. But how?

In searching for answers to that question, I was automatically led to two
new areas of scholarship with theoretical principles that opened up new ways
of thinking about the "library in the life of the user" (which gives the latter
agency and power) rather than the "user in the life of the library" (which
encourages top-down thinking and mimes the current management-oriented
discourse in professional librarianship).[8] The first area is the history of reading. Part of that literature follows the very influential "communications circuit" theory of Robert Darnton, who envisioned a relatively passive group of
readers as the final link in a chain of production that began with the producers
of print (writers and publishers). Another part follows Michel de Certeau,
who focuses on the "resistance" readers evidence when they "poach" texts
for purposes unique to their reading experiences. For my study, Darnton's
theory gave too much authority to structure, and de Certeau's was too focused
on oppositions individual readers built into their reading practices. What I
needed instead was what Christine Pawley calls a "middle layer"—one in
which theoretical principles would help me understand the complexities of
how spatially bound gendered, race, class, and creed-based information cultures interacted with the services and traditions of the local cultural institutions they created—specifically their local public libraries.[9] Several texts were
particularly helpful.

Janice Radway's *Reading the Romance: Women, Patriarchy, and Popular Literature* (1991) is an ethnographic case study that describes the multiple ways
romance novels functioned as agents in the everyday lives of women who
patronized a particular suburban mall bookstore in the 1970s. Radway demonstrates the multiple ways these women used reading to claim their own mental
space and to escape—if only temporarily—the practical demands of being wife
and mother.[10] Benedict Anderson's *Imagined Communities: Reflections on the*

Origin and Spread of Nationalism (1983) has been equally influential. People organize themselves into large and small "imagined communities," he argues, to orient and affiliate with each other. Cultural texts of all kinds function as agents to help construct these imagined communities by providing common sets of experiences, including the reading of shared printed texts. Anderson adds another dimension to the social nature of reading, however; he notes that sometimes this reading takes place in groups, on public property, and in cultural spaces.[11]

In *Book Clubs: Women and the Uses of Reading in Everyday Life* (2003), Elizabeth Long analyzes reading's capacity to stimulate imagination and construct community through shared meaning. As a cultural practice, reading is socially framed. Groups of authorities (like literary critics and teachers) and cultural institutions (like schools and universities) "shape reading practices by authoritatively defining what is worth reading and how to read it." Yet because readers can control it, the act of voluntary reading can become dependably pleasurable, empowering, intellectually stimulating, and socially bonding. Laced throughout the act of reading, she notes, are issues of power, privilege, exclusions, and social distinctions, all combining in multiple ways so that reading is never "disembodied," never "unsituated."[12] And it is here that social and cultural acts of defiance—sometimes overt, sometimes covert, sometimes conscious, sometimes subconscious—take place. If authorities at whatever level lack the power to check the voluntary reading of common people for an interpretation made legitimate by dominant cultures, ordinary readers can and do construct their own meanings, sometimes as groups, sometimes as individuals. Stephen Greenblatt calls this process "self-fashioning," Barbara Sicherman "self-authorization." Gordon Hutner notes "how the talk about books becomes the sound of culture conversing with itself."[13]

"Imagined communities," "civic texts," "appropriate," "self-fashion," "self-authorize." These words and phrases now function as part of a new vocabulary to explain how reading constructs community, even if the reading is done in solitude. Where some see reading primarily as a solitary behavior, Long and a growing number of scholars examining the act of reading see it primarily as an associational behavior. More recently, their findings have even found support among neuroscientists analyzing human interactions with fiction. Brain networks used to understand stories in which readers experience the thoughts and feelings of fictional characters, research suggests, overlap with networks used to foster social interactions. As a result, the reading of fiction sharpens social skills, expands perspective, and augments the ability to empathize.[14]

The second body of scholarship that helps illuminate "the library in the life of the user" focuses on "place" and specifically on the use people make of public spaces. In *The Structural Transformation of the Public Sphere: An Inquiry into a Category of Bourgeois Society* (1992), Jürgen Habermas argues that during the eighteenth century the growing middle classes sought to influence government actions by assuming control of an emerging "public sphere" of deliberation that eventually found an influential niche between governments and marketplaces. Within this public sphere, members of the middle classes developed their own brands of reason, and over time they created their own networks of institutions and sites (e.g., newspapers and periodicals, political parties, and academic societies). In and through these institutions they refined a middle-class-based discourse into an expression of the "public interest" that governments and markets dared not ignore.[15]

Once Habermas's theory established a foundation for understanding how social and cultural preconditions shaped the public sphere, other scholars began to analyze the institutions and sites where this rationalized discourse has been practiced. And it is out of analyses of these institutions and sites that a refined concept of the role of "place" as cultural space has emerged. Over the generations, millions of patrons have demonstrated their support of the public library as a place by repeatedly visiting, in part to exchange social capital—one manifestation of public-sphere thinking and yet another dimension to the social nature of reading. Only recently have researchers begun to explore the role libraries play as a public-sphere place in their communities.[16]

Jeffrey Alexander provides a bridge between place and the social nature of reading. In *The Civil Sphere* (2006), he argues that a set of "communicative institutions" in civil society functions to "regulate" public discourse. Communicative institutions can exert influence on political questions by what information they make available. They can also function as sites where political and social dissent is articulated or where the dominant cultures reinforce themselves. These communicative institutions function through several agencies, including "factual media" and "fictional media." The latter "weave the binary codes of civil society into broad narratives and popular genres" and create "long-lasting frames for democratizing and anticivil processes alike. They constrain action by constituting a teleology for future events, even as they seem merely to be telling stories about people and life in an ahistorical and fictional way." The folklore and folk dramas contained in popular fiction "have always performed similar kinds of sentimental education," Alexander says, and provided representations that allow Americans "to express their civil judgments in figurative rather than intellectual language, which made it easier, in turn, to identify with one or another solidary group."[17] For any analysis of the public library, Alexander's conclusions create a platform from which one can observe a marriage of place and reading—especially popular fiction—that still allows both a multiplicity of roles, all the while retaining agency for library users.

Armed with these perspectives on reading and on the roles public spaces play in constructing community, I look at the public library in the life of its users, and particularly users in Midwest small towns—often symbolically referred to as "Main Street."[18] By focusing on "Main Street," which has been heavily invested with civic meaning and perceived as a community melting pot and reflection of the democratic ideal, I deliberately avoid using a national story of library development as a point of departure and instead allow the local libraries, their managers, and, as much as possible, their users to identify their particularities and speak memory to history. A word of warning, however: readers who cannot accept that fictional media can inform, inspire, educate, socialize, authorize, validate, empower, and entertain will find my arguments unconvincing. Conclusions I reach will make no sense unless one is prepared to accept that patrons used the fictional media made available to them at their public libraries to deepen understanding of the world around them, minimize confusion in their everyday lives, and reinforce existing value systems.

Although these libraries were in the Midwest, one is hard-pressed to identify particular characteristics that would specifically mark them as regional. Each town had a Main Street, which in small-town America constituted what Richard Lingeman calls the "main artery through which the lifeblood of the town flowed" and Richard Francaviglia calls "primarily a social environment."[19] Admittedly, the communities into which library trustees imagined themselves were largely local. As local people, these trustees identified mostly with local problems, values, rules, and patterns of behavior. And because of that identification, they generally held the community's trust, for good and ill, as they built their civic institutions.

Although Main Street reflected regional cultures, its public library was more an occupant of Main Street than a contributor to regional culture. Local public libraries did generally carry their local newspapers and one major state one and often the works of local authors and famous native sons and daughters who moved away. But their communities did not ask libraries to be regionally distinctive; rather, within limits libraries were expected to homogenize local culture and accommodate and reinforce local, state, and national values. By refusing to stock foreign-language titles, for example, they did little to assimilate immigrants unless the latter first learned English. And for all five communities, race was not an issue: people citizens saw on Main Street and the world they constructed around them were almost entirely white.

Through their books and national periodicals, these libraries connected local populations to outside worlds and facilitated the imagined communities that reading common texts provided. These Main Street public libraries certainly were repositories for the literary establishment that dominated the intellectual world, but they were also active agents in a reading culture that looked to middle-brow popular fiction for imagination and information to help minimize confusion in their everyday life. The books and periodicals these public libraries processed into their collections largely reinforced dominant myths of American exceptionalism, egalitarianism, and consensus.[20]

In all cases these public libraries grew out of institutions their Yankee founders replicated from New England social libraries. All were established by Protestants (especially Congregationalists) who had a tradition of using print. Boards of trustees included Roman Catholics and Lutherans only over time, and never Jews or open atheists. Eventually, the influence of specific lodges, church groups, and women's clubs to which these trustees belonged waxed and waned, but one constant remained. Before 1956 these five small public libraries were among the few civic institutions where women led. That more women than men used the library may explain this; that the former functioned as caregivers for children much more than the latter probably also helps us understand why story hours and summer reading programs were so important to these libraries.

In the five Main Street public libraries, community leaders (a small-town bourgeoisie of middle-class local professionals like lawyers, teachers, and clergy who functioned as mediators to the outside world and local carriers of culture) and a substantial but ever-changing fraction of the local citizenry (whose own perceptions of class were often muted by a comfortable sense of unity and stability their small towns embodied) combined to create local practices they left to subsequent generations. A part of these practices were carried in public library services they crafted into a set of expectations subsequent generations not only embraced but also supported. And as these expectations sedimented into traditions, the traditions automatically imposed limits on what public libraries were willing to assume or not to assume as community priorities and responsibilities. Certainly the provision of stories contained in printed texts was one tradition, but in the early twentieth century, preserving these printed stories received a higher priority than providing public space for community meetings, and as these stories cumulated into larger collections, the libraries sacrificed the meeting space to preserve the texts. And for the most part, their patrons seemed to agree with this priority. Between 1876 and 1956, local newspapers reported no resistance.

At the same time, however, the leadership and local patrons of these Main Street public libraries decidedly flattened a hierarchy of reading defined by a national literary establishment. In part, this exercise of local power looks like cultural democracy at work, perhaps even an act of defiance against outside influences. But it nonetheless had carefully defined limits. Although these library collections provided some opportunities to challenge the race, class, and gender biases manifest in the everyday lives of local citizens who used them, patrons generally preferred reading materials that offered dependable pleasures, and from these texts they appropriated in ways that tended to reinforce values and reaffirm the convictions about life they had inherited from previous generations.

But not always, and not without exception. These libraries reached substantial fractions of the citizens in their communities in profound ways difficult to discern because they generally worked quietly and enabled their users to appropriate freely without interference except for the general parameters the traditions of services and collections have imposed. By 1956, public library use in these communities had been in many ways habitualized and ritualized, and for different people of different ages and both genders in different ways. To some extent, experience had trained public library users to employ their public libraries in different ways at different times in their lives, sometimes as places, sometimes as sources of information, most often as sources of reading materials. Sometimes, however, they were all three. On occasion they fed the dreams of young people like Sinclair Lewis by expanding on the official knowledge local compulsory educational institutions controlled so tightly.[21] At the same time, however, the historical record does not demonstrate these Main Street public libraries functioned as important information institutions to address local economic problems.

Physically, most looked alike. Even today, Americans can recognize a "Carnegie" public library, upon whose steps thousands of children strapped their skates in the 1930s and on whose lawns they twirled hula hoops in the 1950s. As places, these five public libraries functioned as destination sites local citizens used to model appropriate social behaviors, manifest civic participation, and celebrate citizenship. Figuratively, through the materials they supplied, and literally, through the public space they provided, these public libraries brought together close friends, family, and acquaintances and provided a safe place to assimilate strangers and newcomers into the community. To an extent, public libraries were places to see and be seen and primarily sites of self-presentation rather than confrontation. Mostly, they were benign agents in local socialization activities, primarily reinforcing local definitions of normalcy rather than challenging age, ethnicity, gender, and class patterns. In these five communities, the public library was one site where people became aware of their interconnections and formed interdependencies. The ritual of public library use helped habituate local citizens into the local culture and at the same time celebrate reading and literacy. To some extent, in the minds of community citizens the local public library was fact, symbol, and myth.

On Main Street, public libraries were less ambiguous space, not as affected by ethnicity, race, class, gender, and age as the street itself. On occasion, where to locate them became negotiation points for arranging Main Street, but always they were a positive element to be featured, not to be hidden. Admittedly, some space within the library building was segregated (e.g., children's departments), but for the most part, patrons of all classes and either gender were free to wander about inside. And although over time these buildings provided community space for thousands of meetings and encounters of all kinds, the vast majority of these activities were firmly grounded in approved middle-class tastes and values. While professionalism improved library administration, service, and efficiency over the decades, librarianship's researchers largely ignored two of the most important services Main Street public libraries provided for most of the twentieth century. First, analysis of "library as place" was largely absent from their research agendas, even though—as *Main Street Public Library* demonstrates—libraries regularly served as important public spaces for the kinds of meetings and informal gatherings that knit communities together.

Second, an even greater failing was lack of attention to the multiple roles reading plays in everyday life, especially the popular fiction that drove circulation rates in public libraries across the country. When Louise Rosenblatt argued in *Literature as Exploration* (1938) that fiction of any kind has the potential to spark imagination and inform in many ways, the professional library community largely ignored her conclusions.[22] Instead, researchers assumed nonfiction works had the primary power to facilitate "reading for information." After World War I, the purpose of most reading research in librarianship was aimed at reducing fiction reading and increasing nonfiction reading. When Douglas Waples and Ralph Tyler stated in *What People Want to Read About* (1931) that "for women of limited schooling to overcome their indifference to political and economic problems would do more to improve the condition of American society at large than for men to take more interest in art," and when Pierce Butler argued in *An Introduction to Library Science* (1933) that "the complacent American toleration of the feminization of its culture" was evident in women's novel reading, they overlooked the possibility that library patrons (most of whom were women) were not indifferent to "political and economic problems" simply because they read fiction. Because positivist researchers like Waples and Tyler assumed printed books had single meanings that led to predictable "satisfactions," they could not discern that the political and economic circumstances in which "women of limited schooling," members of different social classes, and people of different races, ages, and ethnicities found themselves were being addressed in many ways in the popular fiction they were reading.[23]

Similarly, efforts to identify a library philosophy and articulate a library purpose and mission have been limited largely because they take a "user in the life of the library" rather than a "library in the life of the user" approach. The former mostly ignores patron influence on public library practices, but the latter allocates a degree of power to patrons who by their own volition use the public library and thus makes that influence essential to understanding the public library's multiple community roles. For example, Jesse Shera says the library's basic mission "is to maximize the social utility of graphic records," clearly a top-down perspective. Similarly, Charles B. Osburn argues the "function" of the library "is the stewardship of the social transcript," which, as "culture in transit," he perceives to be ever shifting. Patrick Williams's *The American Public Library and the Problem of Purpose* (1988) calls for a return to "purpose" built on a narrow definition of "education." Because of this top-down thinking, he does not consider that people engage different kinds of texts (including fictional media) for different reasons in different ways at different times in their lives.[24]

While I do not suggest traditional top-down observations are entirely wrong, because they take a "user in the life of the library" approach they fail to evaluate the purposes, functions, and missions the public library serves as public space. In addition, because that approach generally leads them to overlook fictional media, they fail to adequately account for the power its stories have to foster ideas, construct community, develop a sense of discovery, inspire, and offer encouragement. Over the years these well-organized Main Street public libraries certainly provided reference services and defined what graphic records and what parts of the social transcript they wanted to pass on to subsequent generations. At the same time, however, they did so much more for their communities.

But there are clear differences between these typical small-town libraries that help identify each community's unique acceptable cultural center. The cultural politics of a library are writ in its collections. What gets placed there are the end results of a mediated process—sometimes open, sometimes muted—that involves a number of influences, including an understanding of the library's history and a perception of its future. What David Welky finds for the culture of print in the Great Depression applies equally to these five libraries between 1876 and 1956. Mainstream print culture's "ability to preserve the comfortable messages of yesteryear while absorbing the lessons of the present was vital," he says, and "made the cultural center a continual work in progress."[25] These Main Street public libraries helped to shift that center over the decades. By helping define and determine the cultural centers of their local communities, they constituted themselves as reading spaces and meeting places essential to preserving the social order and minimized a sense of threat, fear, and separation. Sometimes that meant not buying materials on controversial topics—like socialism and women's right to vote in the early twentieth century.

Before 1956, whenever the library profession tried to force limitations on popular fiction, Main Street public libraries consistently and successfully resisted, albeit not uniformly. Something in the local culture explains the differences. Some "good" books took a long time for these public libraries to acquire; others never made it into collections. Perhaps because of belated approval of Theodore Dreiser's *Sister Carrie* (1900) in library collection guides, the Bryant Library did not obtain a copy until 1927, Morris until 1943, Rhinelander until 1963, and Sage and Moore not before 1970. And while all five libraries purchased copies of John Steinbeck's controversial *Grapes of Wrath* within a year of publication, only the Bryant had a copy of Marx's *Das Kapital* before 1970; it was accessioned in 1899.

In 1905, the four public libraries in this study that existed all owned copies of George Eliot's *Daniel Deronda*, Lew Wallace's *Ben Hur*, and Frances Hodgson Burnett's *Little Lord Fauntleroy*, but Harriet Beecher Stowe—eighth most popular author at the Sage Library in 1895 and represented on the Bryant shelves with sixteen titles—had only three titles on the Moore shelves, none on the Rhinelander. In 1929, the Moore had twenty-one titles by Horatio Alger, twenty-six by Oliver Optic, and forty *Bobbsey Twins* titles; the Sage had similar numbers. The Bryant, however, had plenty of Algers and Optics, but no *Bobbsey Twins*. The Rhinelander Public Library had only two Algers, four Optics, and six *Bobbsey Twins*. The Morris Public Library had no Algers or Optics and only three *Bobbsey Twins*. Similarly, scores of *Nancy Drew* mysteries found their way onto the Sage and Moore library shelves by 1956, but none appeared on the shelves of the Rhinelander, Morris, or Bryant libraries. The Rhinelander and Morris also refused to stock *Hardy Boys* mysteries; by 1970 the Bryant had eight, the Moore eighty-five, and the Sage ninety-eight. Yet in the politically charged McCarthy era of the 1950s, none of the libraries appear to have pulled any titles on U.S. Department of State banned-books lists.

Analyzing the seventy-nine titles Alice Hackett identifies in *Sixty Years of Best Sellers, 1895–1945* against the collections of these libraries reveals striking consistencies.[26] Holdings for all libraries range from a low of 72 percent for the Moore to a high of 90 percent for the Bryant. Of the best-selling titles missing for all libraries, however, the majority were nonfiction. Seventeen of the twenty-two titles on Hackett's list not in the Moore collections were nonfiction; five of eight in the Bryant were nonfiction. Although all these libraries quickly acquired copies of Emily Post's *Etiquette* (1924) and Dale Carnegie's *How to Win Friends and Influence People* (1937), none owned a copy of Henry Adams's bestselling *The Education of Henry Adams* (1919) or Lin Yutang's *The Importance of Living* (1938). Only the Sage owned a copy of Lulu Hunt Peters's *Diet and Health* (1925). This suggests each of the libraries privileged fiction in acquisitions practices. This impression is strengthened by the fact that almost all best-selling titles purchased in multiple copies were fiction.

Little in the primary-source data screened for this study indicates any of these communities established and supported their public libraries primarily to keep their local citizens informed so that political democracy could function. Admittedly, some of this occurred in reading rooms frequented by retired men, story hours visited by grade-schoolers, term papers researched by high-schoolers on weekday evenings and Saturdays, and reports constructed by women's club members. But seldom in the history of these libraries did anything "learned" in these information-seeking practices show up later in public discourse on controversial political issues. Because local controversies covered in newspapers seldom cited library resources or programs, one would also have to conclude that these Main Street public libraries did not make many contributions to the critical debates about sewer systems and street paving in the local public sphere. All established libraries functioned primarily as reading institutions for the dissemination of "good" books, as defined by those who selected them. And statistics show that the introduction of new communications technologies (movies, radio, television) had little impact on this connection before 1956. Comparing mid-twentieth-century statistics with early-twenty-first-century statistics demonstrates that, like the patrons they served, these five public libraries over the years broadened the realm of fictional media they acquired and circulated to include a variety of new textual forms, like DVDs.

If the library faith was fact, this study should have shown the small-town public library was a locally supported civic institution that over the years (and especially after ALA passed the Library Bill of Rights in 1939) resisted attempts to censor while at the same time provided (sometimes controversial) information essential for an informed citizenry. "Books and reading matter selected for purchase from the public funds should be chosen because of the value and interest to the people of the community," declared the 1939 version of the Bill of Rights's principle 1, "and in no case should the selection be influenced by race or nationality or the political or religious views of the writers." Principle 2 read: "As far as available materials permit, all sides of questions on which differences of opinion exist should be represented fairly and adequately in the books and other reading matter purchased for public use."

But *Main Street Public Library* shows that is not how these five communities developed and used their collections. Rather, the Main Street public libraries studied from a "library in the life of the user" perspective became local agents, physical and figurative, through which their community's citizens, elite and common, accomplished two tasks essential for local harmony. First, they provided public space to demonstrate and teach social behaviors and responsibilities acceptable to the community. Second, they provided literary space through collections and services that offered models for successful living, solving problems, and an orderly life at the same time as they mediated in peaceful ways a set of ever-shifting cultural values constantly influenced by inside and outside forces. Sinclair Lewis disliked the social harmony and behavioral conformity he saw in his hometown, and he could only appreciate the public library he wrote into *Main Street* for the potential its collections had to transport him to other places. "To the Bryant Library," he inscribed on a gift copy sent back home in 1937, "with love and lively memories of the days when its books were my greatest treasure."

As civic institutions, the Main Street public libraries studied here had as their purpose and mission not primarily to supplement formal education, fight censorship, or provide information considered essential for the marketplace or the politics of democracy. Those were secondary, and because of the public library's position as a civic institution that local citizens did not have to patronize, these goals were regularly and necessarily compromised, despite professional rhetoric. Rather, their primary purpose and mission—as designed over the generations by local leaders and users—was to foster the kinds of social harmony that community spaces and stories, shared and experienced, provide.

NOTES

1. Deanna Marcum, *Good Books in a County Home: The Public Library as a Cultural Force in Hagerstown, Maryland, 1878–1920* (Westport, CT: Greenwood, 1994); Ronald E. Berquist, "'It Could Have Been Bigger, but Its Residents Like It As It Is': Small Town Libraries in Moore County, North Carolina" (PhD diss., University of North Carolina at Chapel Hill, 2006).

2. Wayne A. Wiegand, *Main Street Public Library: Community Places and Reading Spaces in the Rural Heartland, 1876–1956* (Iowa City: University of Iowa Press, 2011). The original study included five libraries, but this book pares coverage to four. The fifth library is covered in Wayne A. Wiegand, "'An Established Institution': The Morris Public Library of Morris, Illinois, 1913–1953," *Journal of Illinois History* 13 (Winter 2010): 263–88.

3. One library had saved its circulation records for 1890–95. For a superb analysis of what these records show us about the culture of print in a particular late-nineteenth-century Midwest small-town community, see Christine Pawley, *Reading on the Middle Border: The Culture of Print in Late-Nineteenth-Century Osage, Iowa* (Amherst: University of Massachusetts Press, 2001).

4. Wayne A. Wiegand, ed., "Windows on the World: Analyzing Main Street Public Library Collections," special issue, *Library Trends* 60, no. 4 (Spring 2012).

5. About the library faith, see also Oliver Garceau, *The Public Library in the Political Process: A Report of the Public Library Inquiry* (New York: Columbia University Press, 1949), 50–51. For the work that cemented this concept into American library history, see Sydney Ditzion, *Arsenals of a Democratic Culture: A Social History of the American Public Library Movement in New England and the Middle States from 1850 to 1900* (Chicago: American Library Association, 1947). For other library professionals who question this article of faith, see Alison Lewis, ed., *Questioning Library Neutrality: Essays from Progressive Librarian* (Duluth, MN: Library Juice Press, 2008).

6. See Leonard S. Marcus, *Minders of Make-Believe: Idealists, Entrepreneurs, and the Shaping of American Children's Literature* (Boston: Houghton Mifflin, 2008), 32–70; and Jacalyn Eddy, *Bookwomen: Creating an Empire in Children's Book Publishing, 1919–1939* (Madison: University of Wisconsin Press, 2006), 30–48.

7. See Wayne A. Wiegand, "The American Public Library: Construction of a Community Reading institution," in *A History of the Book in America*, vol. 4, *Print in Motion: The Expansion of Publishing and Reading in the United States, 1880–1940*, ed. Carl F. Kaestle and Janice A. Radway (Chapel Hill: University of North Carolina

Press, 2009), 431–51. See also Wayne A. Wiegand, "The Structure of Librarianship: Essay on an Information Profession," *Canadian Journal of Library and Information Studies* 24 (April 1999): 17–37.

8. The phrases "user in the life of the library" and "library in the life of the user" are not my creations. I am indebted to my former University of Wisconsin colleague Doug Zweizig, who used them in his 1973 dissertation. See Douglas L. Zweizig, "Predicting Amount of Library Use: An Empirical Study of the Public Library in the Life of the Adult Public" (PhD diss., Syracuse University, 1973).

9. See Robert Darnton, "What Is the History of Books?," in *Reading in America: Literature and Social History*, ed. Cathy N. Davidson (Baltimore: Johns Hopkins University Press, 1989), 27–52; and Michel de Certeau, *The Practice of Everyday Life*, trans. Steven F. Rendall (Berkeley: University of California Press, 1984). Like "library in the life of the user," the idea of finding middle ground between "market" and "resistance" models in the social history of reading is not original with me. See Christine Pawley, "Beyond Market Models and Resistance: Organizations as a Middle Layer in the History of Reading," *Library Quarterly* 79, no. 1 (January 2009): 73–93.

10. Janice Radway, *Reading the Romance: Women, Patriarchy, and Popular Literature* (Chapel Hill: University of North Carolina Press, 1991).

11. Benedict Anderson, *Imagined Communities: Reflections on the Origin and Spread of Nationalism* (New York: Verso, 1983). More recently, François Furstenberg refers to printed works read in common by people not geographically connected as "civic texts." See François Furstenberg, *In the Name of the Father: Washington's Legacy, Slavery, and the Making of a Nation* (New York: Penguin, 2006), 20–21.

12. Elizabeth Long, *Book Clubs: Women and the Uses of Reading in Everyday Life* (Chicago: University of Chicago Press, 2003), 9.

13. Stephen Greenblatt, *Self-Fashioning: From More to Shakespeare* (Chicago: University of Chicago Press, 1980); Barbara Sicherman, "Sense and Sensibility: A Case Study of Women's Reading in Late-Victorian America," in Davidson, *Reading in America*, 201–25; Gordon Hutner, *What America Read: Taste, Class, and the Novel, 1920–1960* (Chapel Hill: University of North Carolina Press, 2009). For examples of cultural studies research in popular fiction genres, see Erin A. Smith, *Hard-Boiled: Working-Class Readers and Pulp Magazines* (Philadelphia: Temple University Press, 2000); Sally R. Munt, *Murder by the Book? Feminism and the Crime Novel* (New York: Routledge, 1994); Matthew J. Pustz, *Comic Book Culture: Fanboys and True Believers* (Jackson: University Press of Mississippi, 1999); Camille Bacon-Smith, *Science Fiction Culture* (Philadelphia: University of Pennsylvania Press, 2000); and Jane Tompkins, *West of Everything: The Inner Life of Westerns* (New York: Oxford University Press, 1992).

14. Raymond A. Mar, "The Neural Bases of Social Cognition and Story Comprehension," *Annual Review of Psychology* 62 (2011): 103–34; Raymond A. Mar, Keith Oatley, and Justin Mullen, "Emotion and Narrative Fiction: Interactive Influences before, during, and after Reading," *Cognition and Emotion* 25, no. 5 (August 2011): 818–33. See also Annie Murphy Paul, "Your Brain on Fiction," *New York Times*, March 18, 2012, SR 6.

15. Jürgen Habermas, *The Structural Transformation of the Public Sphere: An Inquiry into a Category of Bourgeois Society* (Cambridge, MA: MIT Press, 1992).

16. Linda Most, "The Rural Public Library as Place in North Florida: A Case Study of the Gadsden County Public Library System" (PhD diss., Florida State University, 2009); John E. Buschman and Gloria J. Leckie, *The Library as Place: History, Community, and Culture* (Westport, CT: Libraries Unlimited, 2007). In the latter, see especially Julia A. Hersberger, Lou Sua, and Adam L. Murray, "The Fruit and Root of the Community: The Greensboro Carnegie Negro Library, 1904–1964," 79–99. For other examples of works that explore the role of place in American history, see James A. Secord, *Victorian Sensation: The Extraordinary Publication, Reception, and Secret Authorship of "Vestiges of the Natural History of Creation"* (Chicago: University of Chicago Press, 2001), and David Henkin, *The Postal Age: The Emergence of Modern Communications in Nineteenth-Century America* (Chicago: University of Chicago Press, 2006). Surprisingly, Robert V. Putnam's very influential *Bowling Alone: The Collapse and Revival of American Community* (New York: Simon & Schuster, 2000) fails to analyze the role of library as place. D. W. Davies's *Public Libraries as Culture and Social Centers: The Origin of the Concept* (Metuchen, NJ: Scarecrow, 1974) is useful but largely manifests a "user in the life of the library" perspective.

17. Jeffrey Alexander, *The Civil Sphere* (New York: Oxford University Press, 2006), 54, 75–76, 78–79. Other historians have made similar points. "Socioliterary experience," argue Ronald J. and Mary Saracino Zboray, often occurs in "dense networks of kin, friends, and neighbors, deeply imbuing it with social relations and implicating it in them." See Ronald J. Zboray and Mary Saracino Zboray, *Everyday Ideas: Socioliterary Experience among Antebellum New Englanders* (Knoxville: University of Tennessee Press, 2006), xviii.

18. "Main Street" has a rich historical literature. See, for example, Lewis E. Atherton, *Main Street on the Middle Border* (Bloomington: Indiana University Press, 1954); Richard V. Francaviglia, *Main Street Revisited: Time, Space, and Image Building in Small-Town America* (Iowa City: University of Iowa Press, 1996); and Richard O. Davies, *Main Street Blues: The Decline of Small-Town America* (Columbus: Ohio State University Press, 1998). For good summary pieces on Midwest history, see James H. Madison, ed., *Heartland: Comparative Histories of the Midwestern States* (Bloomington: Indiana University Press, 1988), and Andrew R. L. Cayton and Susan E. Gray, eds., *The Identity of the American Midwest: Essays on Regional History* (Bloomington: Indiana University Press, 2001), especially Andrew Cayton's essay, "The Anti-Region: Place and Identity in the History of the American Midwest," 140–59.

19. Richard Lingeman, *Sinclair Lewis: Rebel from Main Street* (New York: Random House, 2002), 295; Francaviglia, *Main Street Revisited*, 167.

20. The richness and reach of the essays in Kaestle and Radway's *Print in Motion* bear witness to the narrowed contours these Main Street public libraries crafted for their collections in a much larger culture of American print.

21. Late in life, Sinclair Lewis noted in his "Chronology" that he had a "totally normal boyhood—dull school routine, skating, sliding, skiing, swimming, duck-hunting—

except for inordinate (and discoordinated) [*sic*] reading." Most of that reading came from the collections of the Bryant Library. See folder 834, "Chronology—Sinclair Lewis," box 58, Sinclair Lewis Papers, Beinecke Library, Yale University, New Haven, CT.

22. Louise Rosenblatt, *Literature as Exploration* (New York: Appleton-Century, 1938). Although this book merited four more editions in the twentieth century, *Library Quarterly* never reviewed it.

23. See Pierce Butler, *An Introduction to Library Science* (Chicago: University of Chicago Press, 1933), 82; and Waples and Tyler, *What People Want to Read About: A Study of Group Interests and a Survey of Problems in Adult Reading* (Chicago: American Library Association, 1931), 82. Joan Shelley Rubin explains this research in "Making Meaning: Analysis and Affect in the Study and Practiced of Reading," in Kaestle and Radway, *Print in Motion*, 511–27. See also Helen Damon-Moore and Carl F. Kaestle, "Surveying American Readers," in *Literacy in the United States: Readers and Reading since 1880*, ed. Carl Kaestle (New Haven, CT: Yale University Press, 1991), 180–203.

24. Jesse Hauk Shera, *Knowing Books and Men: Knowing Computers, Too* (Littleton, CO: Libraries Unlimited, 1973), 94; Patrick Williams, *The Public Library and the Problem of Purpose* (Westport, CT: Greenwood, 1988); and Charles B. Osburn, *The Social Transcript: Uncovering Library Philosophy* (Westport, CT: Libraries Unlimited, 2009), 135, 208.

25. David Welky, *Everything Was Better in America: Print Culture in the Great Depression* (Urbana: University of Illinois Press, 2008), 218.

26. Alice Payne Hackett, *Sixty Years of Best Sellers, 1895–1955* (New York: R. R. Bowker, 1956).

Reading Library Records

Constructing and Using the
What Middletown Read Database

FRANK FELSENSTEIN, JOHN STRAW,
KATHARINE LEIGH, AND JAMES J. CONNOLLY

Am pretty lonesome and have nothing to read.

—NORENE HAWK, July 8, 1899

This plaintive cri de coeur appears in the diary of Norene Hawk, a young woman of twenty-one, living in Muncie, Indiana. Who was she? And why is her diary a significant artifact for research on that most elusive of subjects, popular reading?

Norene Hawk (1878–1966) was the daughter of George Hawk (1852–1941) and Mary Jennie Walburn Hawk (1855–1943). George was a carriage maker, a skilled blue-collar profession that, until the advent of the motor car in the decade that followed, provided a thoroughly dependable income. Norene had an older brother, Winton (1877–1908). Both she and Winton were pupils at Muncie High School, and, despite that he was a year older than she, they were both members of the graduating class of 1896. Three years before graduating, on Friday, March 3, 1893, Norene joined the Muncie Public Library (MPL) as Patron No. 4192, where she was registered as "Nora Hawk." Four years earlier, on April 2, 1889, Winton, then aged twelve or thirteen, had applied separately for a library card in his own name, becoming Patron No. 2526. Winton's engagement with the institution is also inscribed in the minutes of the library board, where he is thanked for the donation of a book.[1] Among Norene Hawk's own borrowings as a schoolgirl were Oliver Optic's *Up and Down the Nile* (1894) and issues of *St. Nicholas Magazine* and the *Atlantic Monthly*. Evidence of her precociousness as a reader is that she also borrowed Tennyson's long narrative poem, *Enoch Arden*, quite a mature choice for a seventeen-year-old. However, her penchant for reading was shared by many of her peers. Of the thirty members of her graduating class, at least eighteen were patrons of the Muncie Public Library (MPL) under their own names, and five others had members of their immediate family as library patrons and so may have borrowed books through them.[2]

We know something about the reading habits of Norene Hawk, her family, and her peers as a consequence of the chance discovery in 2003 of the virtually intact circulation records of the Muncie, Indiana, public library dating from 1891 through 1902. These records have survived in three parts: the manuscript register of the library's borrowers, numbered sequentially, encompassing approximately sixty-three hundred patrons, going back to its establishment in 1875; the corresponding and very detailed handwritten register of approximately thirteen thousand books, also with sequential numeration, acquired and held during the same period; and, most remarkably, twenty-five (out of a possible twenty-eight) totally unpropitious-looking ledgers that record, mainly in pencil, each single circulation transaction for the eleven-year period that encompasses most of the 1890s and almost the whole of the first two years of the twentieth century. Taking account of the absence of three ledgers that were probably destroyed as a precautionary measure following a smallpox epidemic in the city in 1893, the total number of recorded transactions during this period is in the order of 175,000. These fragile ledgers provide the glue that links the borrowers' and books' registers. Together these records form the basis of the What Middletown Read database (WMRD), a freely available online resource (www.bsu.edu/libraries/wmr).[3]

The archives were recovered intact from the out-of-bounds attic of the Carnegie Library, which was opened in 1904, during its centennial renovation in 2003. Their survival is all the more remarkable given that there were intermittent leaks through the roof of the library and that the crawl space had become home to nesting pigeons as well as vermin. The physical material recovered from its attic all precedes the Carnegie Library; it is the serendipitously preserved remnant of the old Muncie Public Library, which, in its original incarnation, was housed in the long-since-demolished City Building that also provided the home for the local firehouse. Librarians are loath to destroy anything of value; we assume that, with the inauguration of the new library, they arranged for papers from the old one to be carted, along with the books, to the new building. Upon their arrival, the books were shelved, and the archives were, if we can borrow an appropriate theatrical term, "sent to the gods."[4]

The chance recovery of these materials provides us with a unique historical resource. The only other equivalent records—about a tenth of the size—are

Carnegie Public Library, Muncie, Indiana. Drawing from Charles Emerson, *Emerson's Delaware County Rural Route Directory, 1907–1908* (Muncie, IN: Central Printing Company, 1907), 61.
(Courtesy of Archives and Special Collections, Ball State University Libraries)

those of Osage, Iowa, which Dr. Christine Pawley so brilliantly explored and analyzed in her pioneering book *Reading on the Middle Border* (2001).[5] Above all, what makes the records from Muncie unique is that it was this city that was the chosen one out of many, made by the husband-and-wife team of Robert and Helen Lynd, as the anonymous site of their sociological study *Middletown: A Study in American Culture* (1929), and of so much subsequent work.[6] Without exaggeration, Muncie, Indiana, is the most closely studied small city in the United States of America, so our work on its cultural life slots in perfectly with the extensive research into so many different aspects of this arguably "typical" midwestern community that has been the focus of intense academic inquiry for over eighty years. Recently, the locus for this research has been Ball State University's Center for Middletown Studies. However, the construction of an extensive digital database of library records would not be possible without the direct involvement of a team of highly trained library scientists, archivists, catalogers, and computer geeks.

City Building, Muncie, Indiana. Drawing from City Building, Local History photographs, Archives and Special Collections, Ball State University Libraries, City_Building-P.043.005.

In the following sections, we shall recount the process of building the data-base, touching on the difficulties inherent in the material from which we worked and the complexities of converting them to a digital resource; present some preliminary conclusions about the library and its users; and examine the evidence that can be extracted from a diary such as the one Norene Hawk left to us.

Building the What Middletown Read Database
Working with Our Library Ancestors

The What Middletown Read database resulted from a collaborative effort between the Center for Middletown Studies, Ball State University Libraries, and the Muncie Public Library. But creating the database was, in fundamental ways, an opportunity for contemporary librarians to interact with their ancestral colleagues. The process of doing so reminded them, and reminds us, of the importance of preserving current library records that can document the cultural experiences of our own era.

Within the University Libraries, several professional units worked on the project, including Archives and Special Collections, Library Information Technology Services, Metadata and Digital Initiatives, Cataloging and Meta-data Services. The librarians in all these areas felt as if they were interacting with library colleagues from the past as they performed their various tasks on the project. As library science students, most of them had read or studied about past practices of librarianship, but on this project current librarians encountered firsthand some of the techniques past librarians had used. Examining who the library employees were, their education and training levels, the techniques and methods they employed in their daily duties, and other library-related issues may provide opportunities for academic study in addition to the information that can be gleaned about the books, patrons, and reading habits documented in the What Middletown Read database.

The creators of the records used in this project had performed certain tasks (sometimes mundane ones, no doubt) that resulted in the raw materials upon which our current work is based. These librarians of the past, most of them untrained in any formal sense, nevertheless used the education, training, skills, and tools that they had acquired to perform those duties. In the same manner, the current generation of librarians draws upon its own preparation and re-sources to bring that original information into the twenty-first century. While past librarians had recorded information using pencils, pens, and ledgers, today's librarians reformatted, transferred, migrated, and even interpreted the data with today's technology. The tools were different, and the education and skill levels also differed vastly, but the goal was the same: to record and make available information.

In addition to capturing and interpreting data from the handwritten ledgers, the University Libraries' staff digitized the original documents and created a collection available online through the Ball State Digital Media Repository (http://libx.bsu.edu). The digital images of the pages, accompanied by metadata to enhance searching, are linked to the database records so that researchers can view the actual entries as well as the information recorded in the database. Having the digital surrogate for the original artifact available for viewing adds an extra dimension to the online resource. It also illustrates the challenges that those working on the project faced in transcribing, recording, and interpreting the original data.[7]

As the Ball State librarians and archivists migrated these handwritten records to digital form, they could not help but wonder what records the current generation of information specialists will leave behind. Will the next century's researchers be bereft of these treasure troves of potential research materials on current libraries, librarians, readers, and reading matter? Thanks to technology, librarians do not have to write data by hand in ledgers, and therefore our successors will not have to decipher poor or illegible handwriting. No doubt there will continue to be misspellings, errors of omission, and other very human mistakes. The question is this, though: even with all the wonderful advanced technology, do today's librarians have the foresight to preserve their records, no matter the format or technology, so they are available for discovery and use by future generations? Who knows what form the next What Middletown Read project might take?

In addition to all the information that can be gathered and researched about readers and reading habits in America's heartland during the later part of the nineteenth and early part of the twentieth centuries, there is also interesting and potentially fertile research material from the What Middletown Read project about libraries, librarians, and library practices from the period. As well, perhaps there is a good lesson for today's and tomorrow's librarians on the value of recording and preserving their own library history.

Obstacles to Overcome

While a century ago Muncie's librarians were perhaps prescient, they nevertheless bequeathed to us records in less than pristine form. A number of obstacles beyond physical decay faced us as we converted them into a usable database. The sheer scale of the records, the difficulties in interpreting hand-writing, and the inconsistencies of the Muncie Public Library's record-keeping and lending practices all presented difficulties. Some familiarity with these challenges is necessary for the proper and effective use of this distinctive resource.

The main challenge facing us as we converted data derived from the MPL records into usable form was the inconsistency of the original sources. Varied and at times cryptic handwriting left some entries unintelligible. In other cases, the information recorded in the library records was incomplete, inaccurate, or imprecise. A few pages of records sustained damage that left information irretrievable. The nineteenth-century library staff also recorded numbers incorrectly, assigned duplicate numbers to two or more books or patrons, and used nicknames, abbreviations, and initials. It was common as well for library users to allow others to use their identification numbers to borrow books, so the patron number listed may not signify the actual reader. The city librarian, Kate Wilson, often permitted users to sign out books under her number. Of the 464 times her number was used, only 38 of them appear to be for her own choices. Such laxity means that compilations of circulation statistics for an individual or group must be used with care.

Developing demographic profiles of patrons was a substantial but relatively straightforward task. The MPL's book borrowers register listed each patron, giving their name and address, along with those of a guarantor. We searched local city directories and the 1900 federal census manuscript for further information, recording from the census their race, sex, marital status, birthplace, year of birth, and other details.[8] Some difficulty arose in locating census entries for each patron, and we have so far collected demographic data for 3,282 people. The WMRD indicates that most of them (2,592) borrowed at least one book or periodical.

Reconstructing the original accession catalog proved a larger and more complex undertaking. It consisted of two ledgers: the first contained 250 pages, and the second had 52 completed pages. Each listed approximately forty bibliographic entries per page. The first ledger's fields included date, accession number, author and title, where published (location of publisher), when (date of publication), number of volumes, size, pages, binding, of whom procured, and cost (broken down by dollars and cents and sometimes by pounds, shillings, and pence). The second ledger had the same fields, as well as a publisher field. In the first ledger, the publisher was not always recorded. When it was, it appeared in any of several fields.

REGISTRATION OF BOOK-BORROWERS,

The undersigned hereby promise to observe the existing Regulations of the Public Library of Muncie, and such as may be hereafter prescribed by due authority.

DATE	Number	NAME OF BORROWER	RESIDENCE	NAME OF GUARANTOR	RESIDENCE
May 24	1043	Lizzie J. Stewart	714 East Jackson	Warren Stewart	714 East Jackson
" "	1044		787 West Adam	Eld. M. J. Hough	787 West Adam
May 25	1145	M. J. Hough	787 West Adams	Amos Wilson	314 Howard
" 29	1046	Ella Tilda Patton	East Charles St.	Benedict Patten	East Charles
June 11	1147	R. Crawcour	East Main	J. R. Kirkwood	Cor. Main & Plum
June 20	1048	Josie Conklin	" Third St.	Theodore Conklin	East Third St.
" 24	1049	Richard Wagner	Cor. Main & High	M. G. Wagner	3 Cor. Main & High
" 25	1050		E. Adams		Cor. High & Charles
July 1	1051	May E. Hathaway	" north Muncie	Yearly Membership	
" 4	1052	Lima E. Jackson	100 East Main		100 East Main
July 6	1053	Dode Sprague	West Main Street	H. J. C. Coffeen	West Main Street
July 6	1054	Flora Mister	South Walnut	J. A. Stephenson	South Walnut
" 8	1055	Geo. Darragott	Kirby Avenue	Wm. J. Jones	East Main St.
" "	1056	J. B. du	216 Cor. Franklin Adam		216 Cor. Franklin Adam
" 9	1057	Gracie Goddard	177 Liberty Adam	Joseph Goddard	177 Liberty Adam
" 10	1058	A. S. Crane	West Main	M. J. C. Coffeen	West Main
10	1059	H. C. Day	White N.H. of Muncie		
July 16	1060		Mulberry & Wall	W. F. Jones	Mayor Office
" 20	1061	Grace Coffeen	West Main St.	M. J. S. Coffeen	West Main St.
July 22	1062	Eva Thomas	Normal Student		Cor.
July 22	1063	Sarah Thomas	Normal Student	W. Clancy	Cor.
" 25	1064		890 East Washington	H. M. Hutton	890 East Washington
July 27	1065		310 East Adams	James Howell	310 East Adams
" 29	1066	D. S. McCaslin			
" 30	1067	Amanda Lotz	West Jackson		West Jackson
" 31	1068	Higman, Flora			
" 3	1069				
" "	1070				
Aug 5	1071				
" 6	1072				
" "	1073				
" 11	1074				
" 12	1075				
" 17	1076				
" "	1077	Ella Mitchel			
" 19	1078				

Muncie Public Library book borrowers register. From Muncie Public Library, Muncie Public Library Book-Borrowers Register, 1875-05-20 to 1904-06-13, 30, Muncie Public Library Historic Documents, Digital Media Repository, Ball State University Libraries, http://libx.bsu.edu/u?/WMRead,122.

(Courtesy of Archives and Special Collections, Ball State University Libraries)

Muncie Public Library accession catalog. From Muncie Public Library, Muncie Public Library accession catalog, 1875-01-29 to 1900-03-21, 127, Muncie Public Library Historic Documents, Digital Media Repository, Ball State University Libraries, http://libx.bsu.edu/u?/WMRead,556.

(Courtesy of Archives and Special Collections, Ball State University Libraries)

We developed a custom-made data entry tool that allowed us to re-create and expand upon these records. It included fields for all the information that was recorded in the catalog, and its design facilitated quick entry of that data. We also added a separate section that had standardized "authority" data derived from other sources, including OCLC's WorldCat database, the Library of Congress catalog, and the 1905 Muncie Public Library catalog.[9] We also recorded additional information that was useful for searching and understanding the entries, such as pen names.

The sheer volume of the work meant that our initial plans proved inadequate. At first, only three people were assigned to record the data. The original goal was for each person to devote ten hours to the project and finish four pages each week. It quickly became apparent that this was not realistic; each page took ten hours to finish. In the end, we added staff until there were eleven people working on the project, each expected to finish one page per week.

Bibliographic data entry is always a time-consuming process, and this project presented many distinctive challenges. Since the accession catalog entries were written by multiple people, reading and interpreting the varied handwriting slowed the process considerably. Also, there were myriad inconsistencies and incorrect information in the bibliographic data. The use of ditto marks, which often ran too far down a column, caused problems. (Mark Twain did not write *20,000 Leagues under the Sea*!) The field "number of volumes" was problematic, since it was recorded in different ways. Sometimes the column was recorded as the number of volumes (example: 4 volumes in a set) but other times it was recorded as the volume number (example: this is volume 4). The inconsistency was usually discovered when checking WorldCat, since those records list authoritative pagination. "Playing detective" was a huge part of this project and likely consumed more time than the transcription itself.

One especially difficult problem was how to resolve erroneous accession numbers. Many of the numbers were skipped over or reused, sometimes up to three times; these errors made it impossible to match patrons to items with duplicate numbers, since a given accession number could refer to multiple items and those are not part of the searchable database. In one frustrating example of this problem, they assigned to Albion Tourgée's *Bricks Without Straw*, a best-selling account of race in the South during Reconstruction, the same number as May Agnes Fleming's popular novel *A Mad Marriage*. Both are historically significant texts, but in considerably different ways, and we cannot reliably reconstruct the circulation history of either.

Designing a search tool for this often erratic data constituted a final major challenge. The inconsistency of the circulation ledger entries made it difficult to catch every appropriate item in a search. For instance, when patrons borrowed single issues of magazines, library staff often listed them in the circulation records by title and date instead of accession number. To make them searchable, we assigned a number when possible in such cases. We also had to accommodate switches to married names. Age is of course a moving target; we know the birthdates of many users, but the teen of 1891 is a full-grown adult in 1902, which makes age-based searching complicated. The 1900 U.S. Census helped us profile many of the library's patrons, but census takers often recorded the same occupation in different ways, so a search for attorneys must yield entries for lawyers. Digital technologies cannot accommodate all these variations and complexities; users still have to sift and tabulate the data to achieve the most robust analyses.

Muncie Public Library circulation ledger. From Muncie Public Library, Muncie Public Library circulation ledger 1896-01-14 to 1896-06-14, 4–5, Muncie Public Library Historic Documents, Digital Media Repository, Ball State University Libraries, http://libx.bsu.edu/u?/WMRead,872.

(Courtesy of Archives and Special Collections, Ball State University Libraries)

Only a portion of the people and books included in the database were involved in the transactions we have recorded. Of the 6,347 names in the library's records, 4,008 borrowed at least one book during the period covered by our circulation data. Likewise, of 11,592 titles listed, only about half (5,972) circulated. The set of patrons for whom we have demographic data is smaller still. Out of 4,008 active borrowers, we found data in the 1900 federal census manuscript for 2,592 (65 percent). WMRD users should take these figures into account.

Some Preliminary Conclusions

The Muncie Public Library Collection

Many things can be learned about how the Muncie Public Library accumulated books and magazines by reviewing the accession catalog. From the varied handwriting found in the ledgers, we can tell that the head librarian had help. Inconsistencies in the data suggest that the volunteers or employees were not trained particularly well for this task, nor was there oversight to review their entries. This is hardly a surprise, since head librarians Hattie Patterson (1875–89) and Kate Wilson (1891–1903) were not professionally trained. The mistakes were often discovered later, as the ledgers have notations such as "duplicate accession numbers," in addition to other corrections.[10] We noted as well that the original recorders usually added materials to the collection in batches, since the same date is recorded in the accession date field for several pages. The multitude of ditto marks suggests it was a tedious job.

Government documents comprised a significant amount of the MPL's collection. Their presence indicates that the MPL had been declared a federal depository library; the secretary of the interior, the local congressman, or one of the two Indiana senators designated the library as such. The program required that the library must contain more than a thousand books other than the government documents, that the government documents be made available to the general public, and that the documents could not be loaned outside of the library or disposed of without official permission. Starting in 1897, MPL would have received a cumulative list of government documents from the Government Printing Office (GPO) about six times per year. Librarians would have been required to check off the list, then sign and return the receipt to the GPO.[11]

Borrowing Patterns

The borrowing patterns evident in the What Middletown Read database suggest the importance of class and gender in shaping reading practices. Females constituted a slight majority (53 percent) of users for whom we collected demographic information, a finding consistent with other research on library use. But consideration of occupational rank provides an interesting twist to this pattern. Women and girls from white-collar families were more likely to borrow books from the library than were their husbands, sons, and brothers (57 to 43 percent). The opposite was the case among patrons from blue-collar families. By a similar ratio (56 to 44 percent), males from that group were more likely to check out books than were their female counterparts. This divergence invites further investigation of the interplay of class, gender, and reading.[12]

Socioeconomic standing itself certainly appeared to influence library use as well. Of the 2,577 patrons for whom we have occupation data (either for the patrons themselves or for the heads of their households), 1,600 (62 percent) came from white-collar families, with the remainder classified as blue collar. Such classifications have their limits: during this era there was often little difference in outlook or experience between a small shop owner and a skilled worker, and occupational classifications can serve only as a loose proxy for the more complex phenomenon of socioeconomic class. But the pattern becomes even sharper among those at the furthest ends of the occupational scale. Borrowers classified in the high white-collar category—professionals, significant public officials, and the owners or managers of substantial businesses—constituted 25 percent of these borrowers (638 patrons). At the other end of the spectrum, those engaged in unskilled or menial work (or from families headed by such a person) made up only 8 percent of borrowers (195 patrons). In a rapidly industrializing city such as Muncie, these proportions diverge sharply from those of the population as a whole. The extent of this variation suggests that social and economic standing correlated with reading behavior in meaningful ways and warrants further examination.[13]

The borrowing patterns we can discern in the What Middletown Read data conform to other research on library use in another respect. As Wayne Wiegand, Christine Pawley, and others have noted, the overwhelming preference among library users, then and now, has been for fiction. Of the books borrowed from the Muncie Public Library in the period under consideration, 77 percent were classified as fiction (according to Library of Congress subject headings). That preference held across occupational lines almost uniformly. Of loans to blue-collar patrons, 77 percent were for fiction, while white-collar borrowers chose fictional selections 76 percent of the time. High white-collar borrowers selected fiction 75 percent of the time, and users who fell into the unskilled/menial category chose fiction 77 percent of the time.

Among younger readers—those born after 1884—79 percent of loans were for fictional titles.[14]

Closer examination of the data does suggest some variation across demographic groups. For instance, high white-collar women regularly borrowed bound copies of popular magazines such as *Harper's Monthly* and *Lippincott's* during the sample year of 1895. *Harper's* for that year included serialized fiction by Thomas Hardy and Sarah Orne Jewett as well as nonfiction by Mark Twain, William Dean Howells, and Richard Harding Davis.[15] Such choices were unusual for women from the lowest rungs of the occupational ladder. They borrowed volumes of *Harper's* just five times and never selected other popular magazines such as *Lippincott's* and *Scribner's*. That variation makes sense, given the middle-class sensibility of most of the periodicals of the era. It also suggests a more extensive engagement with the literary marketplace among white-collar patrons. And too much can be made of patterns derived from so small a sample. But they at least suggest that the common preference for fiction may have masked more subtle distinctions worth investigating.

While the strong preference for fiction evident in the WMR data suggests a commonality with twenty-first-century library users, the mental world evoked by that body of literature was historically distinct. Most of the selections were of long-forgotten works. Children's books by Horatio Alger, Charles Fosdick (who wrote under the pseudonym Harry Castlemon), and Martha Finley (author of the immensely popular Elsie series), romances such as *The Second Wife* by Eugenie John, and adventure fare such as Richard Harding Davis's *Soldiers of Fortune* were among the most widely circulated titles. Taste for classics was modest: works by John Milton circulated just 72 times; and borrowers selected Shakespeare texts 268 times, 85 of them Charles Lamb's *Tales of Shakespeare*, written for children. By comparison, just one of Louisa May Alcott's children's books, *Under the Lilacs*, circulated 477 times, making it the library's most borrowed volume. Alger was by far the most popular author during this period; his books were taken out more than nine thousand times during the nine years covered by the database and by themselves account for more than 5 percent of the total circulation volume. More contemporary authors, such as Dickens and Twain, attracted some interest (the library loaned books by Dickens 672 times, and Twain volumes circulated 877 times). But demand for popular (and ephemeral) fiction, and especially popular fiction for children, overwhelmed other choices.

This brief review of the What Middletown Read data provides a glimpse of its potential. It also offers opportunities to correlate race and borrowing choices (though the local African American population was very small) or to explore such categories as place of birth, year of birth, or marital status. The data also presents the possibility of measuring the popularity of particular authors, books, publishers, or genres across demographic categories. On a more intimate level, the What Middletown Read data creates the opportunity to explore the role of the library and reading in the lives of individuals such as Norene Hawk.

THE DIARY OF NORENE HAWK

The Hawk family home overlooked the railroad tracks at 503 South Hackley Street, a row of modest working-class houses (now demolished) that stood at the edge of downtown Muncie. Norene's paternal grandmother grew up in Indiana; her paternal grandfather was born in Virginia. It is not known when Grandpa Hawk first came to Muncie, though the family was well settled in Delaware County for all of Norene's life. After she left school, Norene was to secure office work in the real estate business and as a stenographer. The 1890s were boom years for Muncie, and as it coped with the influx of new residents, there was plenty of contractual paperwork to process with the buying and selling of properties. Norene was successful at her job. By 1906, she had been appointed a notary public for the County of Delaware.[16]

The Hawks were congregants of the First Baptist Church in Muncie, which had Dr. Cassius M. Carter as its pastor for more than twelve years, beginning

Norene Hawk as a sophomore. From Muncie High School yearbook for 1894, page of photos of the class of 1896.
(Courtesy of Muncie Public Library)

in 1898. According to the church's present-day website, Carter was "three times president of the Indiana Baptist Convention [and] . . . was asked to preach, lecture, and conduct revivals across [the United States] . . . and Europe. His prominence brought to the Muncie church a recognition not enjoyed previously." During his time in Muncie, he also served as chaplain to the 2nd Infantry Regiment of the Indiana National Guard. By way of fostering attendance at his inner-city church, Carter encouraged the construction in 1900 of an institutional annex to his church that included "a gymnasium, reading room, study, social room, club room for young men, and club room for young women. The annex was kept open for long hours during the day but not twenty-four hours a day."[17]

It is apparent that even before 1900 the church contained several social clubs and a library of books. It also enjoyed a thriving Sunday school that, judging from the references to it in Norene Hawk's diary, was patronized not just by children but by young adults. As Christine Pawley so tellingly discovered in her study of the culture of print in late nineteenth-century Osage, Iowa, the Sunday school had become by that time "an 'American' institution . . . [that] inducted children into a culture of literacy and prepared them to participate in a world centered on print."[18] Even with all that was available to them through their own church, the Reverend Carter and his wife, Martha, patronized the Muncie Public Library, which they both joined in the middle of 1900, between them (according to our records) borrowing nearly eighty books—not quite a book a week—in the next two years. Several years later, Carter was elected vice president of the board of the newly built Carnegie Library.[19] It would take a separate study to gauge whether we can see patterns or trends in the nonclerical literature that was being read by Muncie's clergy during the 1890s and very early 1900s. Suffice it for the moment to emphasize that this and other Muncie churches, most of which also had flourishing Sunday schools, openly encouraged their congregants to extend their reading.

It is fortuitous that the two periods covered by the surviving parts of the diary—1898–99 and 1905—allow us insight into the place in Norene's life of the original Muncie Public Library, which was closed in 1903, and of the new Carnegie Library, which opened its doors on January 1, 1904, shortly before the second period of the diary begins. When she authored the first part of the diary, Norene was just twenty years old, turning twenty one on February 16, 1899; in the second part, she reached the age of twenty-seven and, significantly for a young woman in a small city at that period, remained single.

Hawk's diary provides a picture of life in downtown Muncie in the era that Ned Griner aptly dubbed the "Gas Boom Years," so named because the nearby discovery of natural gas in the 1880s transformed Muncie from a sleepy agricultural community into the industrial city that it was for most of the twentieth century.[20] Though the 1890s preceded the advent of the automobile as the primary American mode of transportation, there is much in the Hawk diaries to suggest that the people of Muncie sensed that major changes were in the offing. And rather than being resistant to these, they (or at least those of Norene Hawk's generation) seem to have greeted with alacrity the technological innovations, which they perceived correctly as heralds of greater change. In her 1898–99 diary, she refers to the acquisition at the office of "a new Rem-Sho typewriter" (November 28, 1898)—Remington Scholes had introduced this in 1896; it was the first to employ a QWERTY keyboard and cost about $100— and six weeks later, she mentions putting "in an hour or so on a Caligraph Typewriter, trying to get used to it" (January 11, 1899). Elsewhere, she records her enthusiastic employment of a Kodak camera (a novelty first introduced in the late 1880s), noting, for instance, "[I] had eleven new plates put in my camera today" (January 2, 1899). Although it would be a few years—and a new century—before the advent of the motion picture, she records that she and a suitor "went out . . . to see the Cinematographic Exhibition" that was visiting Muncie in June 1899 (June 3). On another occasion, she describes being able to look through at the bones of her hand using X-ray plates (March 31, 1899), a process devised by Wilhelm Röntgen in Germany only three years earlier and (paralleling Freud) popularly seen as revealing our hitherto hidden inner selves. At home and in the office, the telephone had become an essential accompaniment, and even in 1898, almost all her friends seem to have had access to one.[21] Telegraphy, however, still remained the primary means by which Muncie communicated with the wider world, and her 1898 diary includes visits to the telegraph office (November, 25, for example). In the 1905 diary, she notes, "Papa and Adam . . . got the Graphophon[e] playing" (July 26), an early form of gramophone that had been introduced a few years earlier. Within town, when she didn't catch the "car" (the local electrical street car service having been introduced in 1892), she whizzed around on her "wheel," bicycling being particularly popular among young people. The impression that we get from the diary is of a young woman no less plugged in for her age than her equivalents today with their smartphones and text messaging. The young people of Muncie, it seems, tried to emulate the latest cosmopolitan trends that we might more readily associate with life in such cities as New York and Chicago.

Yet there was still much that was comfortably traditional about this small city. There were visiting circus performances (May 1, 1899; "Barnum & Bailey's," June 9, 1905) and of Buffalo Bill's Wild West Show, with excursions to the city by big crowds from all around (August 4, 1899). In early June, there was the annual "great street carnival," which also brought all and sundry to the city of Muncie (June 5, 1899). Throughout the diary, there are frequent references to stopping by at the candy shop to buy taffy and other such small confectionery treats. At the opera house, there were new performances of plays and musical events through most of the year. Among Norene's favorites were *The Sewanee River*, "a very interesting play" though drawing only a "light crowd" (April 17, 1899), and a dramatization of *Dr. Jekyll and Mr. Hyde*, which she "enjoyed very much" (September 4, 1905).[22] (From her borrowing data, we do know that she had already read Robert Louis Stevenson's novella, which she took out in November 1900.[23]) Norene also records a meeting of her graduating class of '96 in which she and her schoolmates planned for "a seven course banquet at the National Hotel [in Muncie] as a reunion" (December 9, 1898), though, feeling unwell on the day, she backed out from attending the event itself. At home, she and her family often spent the evening or weekends playing such popular Victorian parlor games as euchre, progressive pedro (Tuesday, January 17, 1905), and muggins (February 5, 1905), a form of dominoes.[24] Sometimes too she would occupy herself with crocheting a doily (December 9, 1898) or with sewing, as did many others by this time; the Hawk household possessed its own sewing machine (April 14, 1905).

However, if we were to look for Norene Hawk's favorite pastime, there is little question that above all, reading preoccupied this intelligent and articulate young woman. The diary is a record of her avid love of books. To begin with, she was an active member of the "American Literature Coterie" (February 6, 1899, and other entries), a reading and discussion group that was centered on her church. In February 1899, it fell upon her to lead the discussion, and she "spent part of the day writing an essay on Longfellow" (February 20). In her later diary, she reveals that she also wrote poetry (July 15, 1905), though neither that nor her piece on Longfellow has come down to us. It turns out that almost all her reading choices—or at least those she records in her diary—were works of fiction, and here, her picks were often dictated more by what was available to her than by her wanting to read the very latest book.

As mentioned, the first part of Norene Hawk's diary, covering November 1898 to August 1899, is the only one that accords in time with the surviving borrowing data for the Muncie Public Library. On several occasions during this period, she refers specifically to borrowing books from the library. For instance, on Sunday, January 15, she records that she "got a book from the Library, [J. M. Barrie's] 'The Little Minister'" (1891), a popular fiction that tells of the love of a young Scottish pastor for a wild gypsy girl, who predictably perhaps turns out to be of noble birth. The following month, also on a Sunday, she reports that she "got [Martha Farquharson's] 'Elsie Dinsmore' out of the Library," reading it the next day, "having nothing else to do" (February 26, 27). By the day after, she had finished it. *Elsie Dinsmore* (1867) was the first in a series of twenty-eight popular books by Farquharson (the pseudonym adopted by Martha Finley), all of which are centered on an eponymous heroine who finds solace from her trials and tribulations in her piety and strong religious belief. Both of these books were stocked by the Muncie Public Library and proved immensely popular; Barrie's book was borrowed 215 times between its acquisition by the library in 1894 and the end of our records in 1902, and *Elsie Dinsmore*, taken out or renewed 237 times in the ten years from 1892, topped that figure. In fact, a second copy of the book was added to the library in 1894, and that was borrowed 184 times. The vast majority of the time, female readers checked out the Farquharson books. The library held several other titles in this prolific series in duplicate copies. With an estimated 5 million copies of her Dinsmore series having sold when she was in vogue, Martha Finley has since become one of the largest black holes in our knowledge of popular literature of the late nineteenth century.[25] By comparison, Nathaniel Hawthorne's *The Scarlet Letter* (1850), already deemed an American classic by the 1890s, was borrowed 95 times during the period of our records, and an acclaimed new novel by Henry James, *The Spoils of Poynton*, acquired in 1897, the year of its publication, had but 54 borrowings.

Having found that Norene Hawk borrowed books like *The Little Minister* and *Elsie Dinsmore* from "the Library," we tried to collate these diary entries with our database records of borrowings from the Muncie Public Library. It came as a little bit of a shock and, at first, a letdown to discover that there was *no* record of her borrowing these individual books on January 15 and February 26, 1899, the dates respectively recorded in her diary for each of these. Our borrowing records show that Mrs. Kate B. Patterson, the wife of the proprietor of the Muncie Foundry, had taken out *The Little Minister* on January 3, and it was not borrowed again until February 16. Similarly, Iva Buckley, the daughter of Claude H. Buckley, a local carpenter, had borrowed the first copy of *Elsie Dinsmore* six days earlier and Donna Lane, the wife of a Muncie furniture dealer, had the second, taken only three days before. The absence of a record for Norene Hawk's loan of either of these books begged the question of whether the surviving data from the borrowing ledger may have been patchy or incomplete from the time of first recording. Were some books borrowed and the transaction omitted by default from the ledger? Could this have been by design? Was there significant missing information here that, given the passage of years, would no longer prove retrievable? The eventual actual answer to these worrisome questions was a simple one!

Both books were borrowed on a Sunday, and, given that they could not have come from the Muncie Public Library, since other readers had already taken out the copies available there, it appears that the copies of these two faith-based books were loaned to Norene Hawk from the library of the Baptist church of which she was an active member. Some records of the church have survived and are held in Archives and Special Collections at the Bracken Library, Ball State University, and it remains possible that we may still discover further information about its library there. At the very least, we now know for sure that the public library was not the only communal book repository in late-nineteenth-century Muncie.

Borrowing books from friends and individual book ownership were also common. A friend of Norene's lent her a copy of Marie Corelli's *Wormwood: A Drama of Paris* (1890), a book absent from the Muncie Public Library. *Wormwood* is a polemical novel written against the evils of absinthe drinking and its corrupting effect on French society. Norene describes it as "a wild strange book and not one adapted to a person [i.e., herself] subject to the blues" (March 29, April 5, 1899). Most of her comments on books that she read, if she made comments at all, are terse. Thackeray's *Vanity Fair*, which she read in 1905, strikes her as "anything but a cheerful book" (January 31); she found Indiana author Booth Tarkington's *Cherry* (1903) "very amusing" (March 1); after finishing reading Kendrick Bangs's *House-Boat on the Styx* (1895), also a copy from outside the Muncie Public Library, she confesses to feeling "very lonesome and blue" (May 2, 1899). None of her comments on individual books can be deemed profound, and they are more often indicative of the variety of moods created by her reading.

Although there are references to the many books that she read in the extant volumes of her diary, only a single one coincides precisely with the book records in our database. On Tuesday, August 8, 1899, she writes: "Went to the Library this morning and got 'The Fair Maid of Perth.'" Our borrowing record for that day shows that Sir Walter Scott's novel was borrowed on that day, though the library identification states that the book was lent not to Norene but to her brother, Winton. According to the diary, at this time Winton was quite seriously ill in bed at home. It was not unusual for family members to use their borrowers' numbers quite indiscriminately. Whether Winton was in a fit state to read is unclear, though we strongly suspect that the reader here was Norene. Looking at the records of her reading in the database and in the later 1905 diary, there is no question that she was an avid and committed reader, who could count Shakespeare, George Eliot (*Romola*), George Sand (*Consuelo*), Edward Bellamy (*Looking Backward*), and Victor Hugo (*Les Misérables*) among the "serious" authors that she borrowed, not to mention Marie Corelli, Rider Haggard, and E. P. Roe among the creators of Victorian potboilers.

Christine Pawley devotes a late section of *Reading on the Middle Border* to diaries as a key to individual reading. The single diary she was able to locate for her study of reading habits in Osage, Iowa, is that of Charles Miller, which she describes as both "laconic" and "erratic." In Miller's diary, according to Pawley, "any purchase warranted special mention," and the document is valuable as a record of stationery and newspapers that he bought.[26] Without undue modesty, we can say that Norene Hawk's diaries, studied in conjunction with the What Middletown Read database, provide us with far richer and more revealing material.

Our hope is that further research will illuminate many more such reading experiences, as well as insights into the role of the library in the lives of its users. As Norene Hawk's diary shows us, the public library was not the only source of reading material in turn-of-the-century Muncie. Nevertheless, a detailed accounting of who borrowed what books from such an institution gives us a valuable glimpse of that most elusive of historical figures: the individual reader. We anticipate that the What Middletown Read database will make possible a host of new insights about readers, reading, and libraries during the era of American industrialization. Ironically, present-day privacy legislation will prevent researchers a century hence from using American public library records to explore the reading habits of our own generation. Except by chance or sly deliberation, those records will have long been destroyed by law-abiding librarians. The uniqueness of the Muncie data as a rare palimpsest of midwestern reading habits during the 1890s should not be understated.

Notes

1. Muncie Public Library Board Minutes and Reports 1874–1902, February 4 and March 3, 1896. The specific book Winton Hawk donated is unrecorded in the minutes but can be traced through the accessions ledger. It is book number 9679, an edition of John Milton's "L'Allegro," "Il Penseroso," and "Lycidas." Milton was studied in the senior year at the Muncie High School.

2. Our evidence shows that library patrons perceived individual membership as extending to the family and often used cards belonging to other family members.

3. A fourth part of the archive consists of librarians' written monthly and annual reports, including indices of books borrowed, divided by subject, several ledgers recording fines and petty charges, and the detailed minute book of the meetings of the library board over the final quarter of the nineteenth century. Among other surviving accoutrements are early subscription bonds to the library. The original idea of creating it as a subscription library did not work and was very soon abandoned. Although this fourth part of the archive is integral to the whole, the present essay will concentrate on the first three.

4. We do not have the day-to-day borrowing records of the successor Carnegie Library, so that fully detailed before-and-after comparison is beyond our present capability.

5. Christine Pawley, *Reading on the Middle Border: The Culture of Print in Late-Nineteenth-Century Osage, Iowa* (Amherst: University of Massachusetts Press, 2001).

6. Robert Lynd and Helen Lynd, *Middletown: A Study in American Culture* (New York: Harcourt, Brace & World, 1929).

7. The MPL also allowed Ball State University Libraries to digitize several diaries from their collection, including Norene Hawk's, that contain entries about use of the public library during the period covered by the ledgers. They are available in the Digital Media Repository along with diaries from the University Libraries' Archives and Special Collections.

8. The 1890 federal census manuscript is not available, having been largely destroyed by a fire.

9. *Catalogue of Books in the Muncie Public Library* (Muncie, IN: Central Printing, 1905).

10. It also appears that the two ledgers were used at MPL up through the 1930s. Under the date field, multiple times (usually in red ink) the de-accession date was written over the accession date, information that is recorded in the What Middletown Read database. These ledgers were clearly used by the MPL for record-keeping purposes for at least forty years.

11. Sheila M. McGarr, "Snapshots of the Federal Depository Library Program," *Administrative Notes: Newsletter of the Federal Depository Library Program* 15, no. 11 (August 15, 1994): 6–14. This designation is confirmed by the frequent citing of either the secretary of the interior or the Department of the Interior as the source for government documents. Entries in the accession catalogue suggest that the MPL was part of two other depository programs. The library was a geological depository,

receiving U.S. Geological Survey monographs and bulletins, and was also a patent gazette depository.

12. These results and those presented in the following four paragraphs are taken from the What Middletown Read database. Occupational groupings are taken from a long-established, commonly employed system devised by Alba M. Edwards. See Alba M. Edwards, "A Social-Economic Grouping of the Gainful Workers of the United States," *Journal of the American Statistical Association* 28, no. 184 (December 1933): 377–87. See also Stephan Thernstrom, *The Other Bostonians: Poverty and Progress in the American Metropolis, 1880–1970* (Cambridge, MA: Harvard University Press, 1973), 289–302. For comparable results, see Pawley, *Reading on the Middle Border*, 69–77.

13. On the difficulty of distinguishing skilled workers from clerical workers and the petite bourgeoisie in this era, see Robert D. Johnston, *The Radical Middle Class: Populist Democracy and the Question of Capitalism in Progressive Era Portland, Oregon* (Princeton, NJ: Princeton University Press, 2003), 3–17.

14. Pawley, *Reading on the Middle Border*, 91–105; Wayne A. Wiegand, "The American Public Library: Construction of a Community Reading Institution," in *A History of the Book in America*, vol. 4, *Print in Motion: The Expansion of Publishing and Reading in the United States, 1880–1940*, ed. Carl F. Kaestle and Janice A. Radway (Chapel Hill: University of North Carolina Press, 2009), 431–51.

15. The contents of *Harper's* are available through the *Harper's Magazine* archive, http://www.harpers.org/archive/1895.

16. *Biennial Report of Fred A. Sims Secretary of State of the State of Indiana* (Indianapolis: Wm. B. Burford, Contractor for State Printing and Binding, 1906), 154.

17. [William Eidson], "First Baptist Muncie: History," http://fbcmuncie.org/about /history.

18. Pawley, *Reading on the Middle Border*, 128.

19. G. W. H. Kemper, *A Twentieth-Century History of Delaware County, Indiana*, 2 vols. (Chicago: Lewis Publishing Company, 1908), 1:277.

20. Ned H. Griner, *Gas Boom Society* (Muncie, IN: Minnetrista Cultural Foundation, 1991).

21. According to David E. Nye, *Electrifying America: Social Meanings of a New Technology* (Cambridge MA: MIT Press, 1990), "local citizens organized the Muncie Bell Telephone Exchange, securing a franchise from the city in February 1880 and starting operations the next month with forty subscribers" (2). By the 1890s, although owning a telephone had become far more commonplace, the novelty had not worn off.

22. We have not so far been able to identify *The Sewanee River* precisely, though we wonder whether it may have contained a precursor of the song later popularized in the "talkies" by Al Jolson.

23. The Muncie Public Library was given a copy of Robert Louis Stevenson's novella (which had made its first appearance in 1886) in 1897. It was borrowed sporadically about twenty times in the following five years.

24. Lynd and Lynd, in *Middletown*, remark that, along with dancing, card games were "the standard entertainment of Middletown," with pedro being popular "among

the workers and bridge among the others." They also point out that "playing cards on Sunday . . . [was] tabooed by many people" (281). According to Emily Kimbrough, *How Dear to My Heart* (New York: Dodd, Mead & Company, 1944), on Sunday, Presbyterian families in Muncie proscribed even children's games such as hide-and-seek and hopscotch during the early years of the twentieth century (173).

25. A useful though not entirely reliable website on her may be found at http://www.readseries.com/auth-dm/finley1.html. For a recent defense of Martha Farquharson, see Jackie E. Stallcup, "Stamping the Coin of Character: Elsie Dinsmore and the Power of Christian Wealth," *The Lion and the Unicorn* 33, no. 3 (September 2009): 300–323.

26. Pawley, *Reading on the Middle Border*, 205–7, quotation on 206.

"Story Develops Badly, Could Not Finish"

*Member Book Reviews at the
Boston Athenæum in the 1920s*

ROSS HARVEY

In the 1920s, the Boston Athenæum implemented a system for members to comment on books they read. A slip pasted into new fiction invited readers to record their opinions for the guidance of others. Readers were seldom unanimous about a book and argued vigorously about some books. This essay examines and comments on a sample of these reviews and uses other Athenæum records to describe the scheme, an early peer-to-peer book review system among members of a socially exclusive library. It draws comparisons with online reviewing programs, such as the Athenæum website's recommendations, Facebook's "We Read," and LibraryThing.

The Boston Athenæum is a venerable institution, having celebrated its two-hundredth birthday in 2007, and is often perceived as conservative, perhaps on account of its age. It is also seen as elitist, probably because it is a private subscription library. It states on its website that "today, it remains a vibrant and active institution that serves a wide variety of members and scholars."[1] In 1851 its mission was "to be a foundation, at which all, who choose, may gratify their thirst for knowledge. . . . The Athenæum will contain a variety, adapted to the diversity of the dispositions, views, and characters of its patrons and visiters [*sic*]. Every class of readers must derive profit and pleasure from a constant access to the foreign and domestic journals, and the periodical publications and pamphlets of the day."[2]

One consequence of this mission has been a strong emphasis on providing popular fiction as an aspect of its users deriving "profit and pleasure." Katherine Wolff suggests that an early decision by Joseph Buckminster (the Athenæum's first official book scout and longtime friend of the Athenæum's first librarian, William Smith Shaw, who held office from 1807 to 1822) to purchase "popular and useful books" was a key factor in the library's flourishing.[3] The popularity of fiction in social libraries is well documented and, according to Thomas Augst, was so well established by 1852 that the Trustees of the Boston Public Library "had perhaps learned from social libraries the importance of institutionalizing reading as a practice of leisure rather than study."[4] Adding fiction to the collections of social libraries and public libraries was tolerated, rather than embraced, as a way to encourage reading and eventually to lead the reader to "books belonging to high-culture canons in order to elevate the public taste and educate citizens," as Wiegand notes.[5] It can be conjectured that fiction was included in the Boston Athenæum's collection from an early date, and indeed, Wolff provides some evidence for this but also provides a caution with the comment "Real reading habits . . . are difficult to ascertain."[6]

Some of the popular fiction in the Athenæum's collection contains printed slips inviting readers to provide their reviews of the book to which they are affixed. Although the reviews are not in themselves particularly significant and seem unlikely, from a current perspective, to have been of value to other readers, annotations and reviews reflect the tastes and interests of a period and of a social group and are therefore worth investigating. They are also evidence of an early peer-to-peer book review scheme among members of a library. Most of the research into reading in libraries in the United States is in the context of public libraries, so this description of the Athenæum's book review program sheds some light on the question of whether social libraries, with their socially exclusive membership, differed from public libraries and, if so, how they did. This investigation also attempts to engage with Wayne Wiegand's argument that library history ought to be about "the library in the life of the user" rather than, as is more frequently the case, about "the user in the life of the library."[7]

It is fortunate that the Athenæum has kept most of its records and makes them available to researchers. These provide a unique perspective on the library's users. This chapter uses some of the Athenæum records to investigate the inception of the review scheme, to note the reasons for it, and to describe its context. The call for papers for "Library History Seminar XII: Libraries in the History of Print Culture" (Madison, Wisconsin, September 10–12, 2010), at which a presentation based on this research was given, notes that "library records provide a particularly fruitful avenue into the history of print culture" and allow libraries to be investigated as "both a site and a source of regulating processes. The interactions of multitudes of authors and readers are shaped in part by the meta-texts of the library's operations."[8] The Athenæum's attempt to provide a mechanism for readers to communicate with other readers and share opinions about specific books is an example of the library providing a regulating process that facilitates interactions among users.

In 2009 Mary Warnement, William D. Hacker Head of Reader Services at the Boston Athenæum, noted in a short piece in the Athenæum members' newsletter the presence of book review slips in some of the fiction.[9] She provided an illustration from Edward C. Booth's *The Doctor's Lass*, published in 1924. At the top of the slip were printed these words: "Readers who care to express an opinion of this book for the guidance of others may do so below. An opinion should contain not more than five words and should be followed by the initials of the reader."

Warnement's short piece raises many questions. How many of these slips were present in the Athenæum's books? Were they placed only in works of fiction? When did the practice of inserting them begin? When did it end? What did this practice indicate about the management of the Athenæum? Where did the idea come from? Might the comments provide insight into the thinking of the Athenæum's readers? These and other questions called for a search for more slips in the books in the Athenæum's collection.

The first step was to define the start and end dates, to determine when the printed slips were first added and when they stopped. In conversation, Warnement provided a starting point by observing that the classification PZ3 (used for fiction in English in the Library of Congress Classification system) would be a fruitful ground, as would the VEF sequence (fiction in English in the Cutter Expansive Classification system, developed by Charles Ammi Cutter during his employment at the Boston Athenæum). This proved the case, and details were recorded of a sample of 6,295 books in these classification sequences, most of them in the PZ3 sequence. The data recorded for each book were call number, author surname, book title, date (year only) received by the Athenæum, the presence of any annotations, and a transcription of comments and initials of the annotator, if there were any.

Of the books examined, 140 had printed slips inserted, not all of which had comments added—in fact, only 81 of them were annotated. The slips (four inches wide and six and a half inches high, but sometimes trimmed to fit in smaller books) were pasted into books that had been added to the Athenæum's collection between 1920 and 1929. We can be precise about this date range because it was, and continues to be, the Athenæum's practice to note in the book the date it was added to the collection. Only two books examined and found to have printed slips pasted into them did not have the dates of their addition to the collection noted, and these had no publication dates, either. Some other books among those examined were found to have annotations made before or after the 1920s, but these do not contain the printed slips examined in this chapter.[10]

The number of annotations on a single printed slip ranges from none to eleven. About 70 percent of annotators provided their initials, as requested. The direction to use "not more than five words," which 80 percent of the annotators adhered to, was too restrictive for some: forty annotations exceeded the limit, with their annotations ranging from six to eighteen words.

The annotations display a wide range of comments, from useful to irrelevant, from informative to biased. Sometimes there is agreement among them. H.C. considered Samuel Hopkins Adams's *From a Bench in Our Square* 1922 (PZ3.A217 Fr) to be "So good there's nothing to say but 'Read it,'" a view supported by Esta[?], who comments: "Excellent." H.C.'s comment that Algernon Blackwood's *The Bright Messenger* 1922 (PZ3.B5683 Br) was "Interesting to lovers of the guitar, and there's too much of it" was corroborated with a "Ditto" from W.A.S.[?]. Both reviewers of Richard Washburn Child's *Fresh Waters* 1924 (PZ3.C4372 Fr) agreed: "Rubbish," from S.A.M. and "Much attempted, futile result," from C.Y.

Sometimes the annotators' opinions are diametrically opposed. Unsigned comments of "No" and "Good" appear on Sherwood Anderson's *Poor White* 1926 (PZ3.A55 Po). G.W.V. wondered of H. C. Bailey's *The Master of Gray* 1921 (PZ3.B152 Ma), "Why was it written?," but P.R. disagreed, considering this book "Well done—interesting." Eden Phillpotts's *Circe's Island* 1926 (PZ3.P547 Ci) was thought to be "dull" by C.Y. but "charming" by E.H. Annotator V.B. left Hilaire Belloc's *Mr. Petre* 1925 (PZ3.B4193 Mi) unfinished ("Story develops badly, could not finish"), whereas J.H.C.J. presumably did finish reading it and so was able to make the comment "Illustrates same author's 'A Contrast.'"

Single annotations are common, representing 38 percent of the sample. Reactions were of confusion ("What is it all about? I can't tell," writes G.H.N. of Eden Phillpotts's *The Treasures of Typhon* 1925 [PZ3.P547 Tre]), were considered judgments (C.Y.'s judgment of E. Œ. Somerville's *French Leave* 1928 [PZ3.S6962 Fr] as "Not equal to their last"), and were at times somewhat ambivalent (R.L.'s view that "Cesare Borgia [was] praised to [the] limit" in Rafael Sabatini's *The Justice of the Duke* 1926 [VEF.Sa11.j]).

Three annotations were found in a single book rather less frequently, occurring in only 10 percent of books in the sample with pasted slips. Hilaire

Readers' annotations for Hilaire Belloc's *Mr. Petre.*
(Boston Athenæum)

Belloc's *Pongo and the Bull* 1925 (PZ3.B4193 Pon) was variously "Stupid" (unsigned), "Not stupid at all" (H.S.), or "Good satirical fooling—first class" (again unsigned).

All reviewers agreed about Rafael Sabatini's *The Hounds of God* 1928 (VEF.Sa11.h); C.Y. considered it "Interesting, but thrice too long," a view corroborated by an anonymous "Most interesting" and "Vivid story" from M.C.T.[?]. Slips with four annotations make up 10 percent of the books in the sample with printed slips. C.T.'s comment that George A. Birmingham's *Gold, Gore, & Gehenna* 1927 (PZ3.B536 Gol) was "'Much ado about nothing' dull" is amply outweighed by the other three reviewers, who considered it "Subtle, delicious wit" (N.C.T.[?]), "Delightful" (M.N.N.), and "inventive, fantastic, entertaining" (S.A.[?]). Another of George A. Birmingham's books, *The Lady of the Abbey* 1926 (PZ3.B536 Lad), fared worse; it was "Poor: very weak brew" (initials indecipherable), "Wretched! Unworthy of the author" (J.M.H.), and "Very dull" (C.T.[?]); but W.H.V.A. disagreed, keeping within the five-word limit and calling it a "Delicious satire on Irish 'republic.'"

At the other end of the scale, some (about 3 percent) have nine or more annotations. John Buchan's *Prester John* 1927 (PZ3.B851 Pr) attracted mixed reviews, including a comment that is exceptional because the annotator has added a date: "Very like R.L.S. therefore excellent" (C.T.[?]), "Improbable adventure, well told" (S.Y.[?]), "A mighty good yarn" (S.W.P.), "Rather like Haggard" (H.F.F.), "Wow" (J.G.M.), "The best of Buchan" (F.A.J.), "You lose your awareness of time" (R.B.), and "Very good and worth reading" (B.F.). The sole dissenting view was written in capital letters—"UNMITIGATED RACISM KAM 2005" and is an interesting comment for its perspective on changes in reading fashions and on the influence of political correctness on readers. *Prester John*, first published in 1910, tells the story of a young man leaving Scotland to seek his fortune in South Africa, where he uncovers and foils a general uprising against the white administration, along the way becoming seriously rich. Written as a boys' adventure story and functioning as "imperial initiation manual," *Prester John* displays the imperialistic racism typical of the period.[11] In it, Buchan presents a view of ordinary Africans that is patronizing in the extreme by the standards of the 2005 annotator, whose

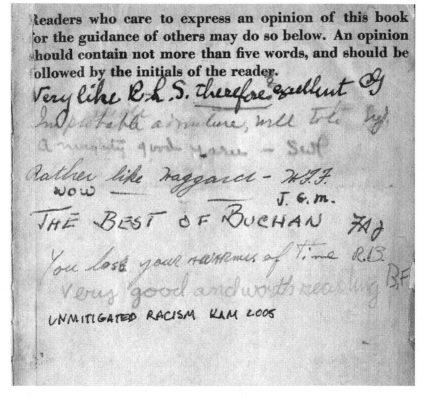

Readers' annotations for John Buchan's *Prester John*.
(Boston Athenæum)

response to the following excerpt from chapter 22 could be expected to differ from that of an Athenæum reader in the 1920s: "That is the difference between white and black, the gift of responsibility . . . and so long as we know this and practice it, we will rule not in Africa alone but wherever there are dark men who live only for the day and their own bellies." Unfortunately, that annotators typically did not date the comments they wrote on the slips does not allow further conjecture on these points.

As noted, most annotators were disciplined or skillful enough to meet the "not more than five words" request. Of the total number of annotations, 80 percent were five words or fewer; if we include annotations of six words, the total rises to 90 percent. Some of the longer annotations are of ten words ("Rather a beautiful romance = hero a very normal English gentleman" by C.R.U., in J. C. Snaith's *What Is to Be* [PZ3.S669 Wh]), fifteen words ("A good picture of how the poor lived in New York City in the nineties" by M.E.S. in O. Henry's *The Four Million* [PZ3.H3964 Fo]), and eighteen words ("Very good [except love-story], creates a character that is a stroke of genius, in the Little Scout" [by M.B.] in Gene Stratton-Porter's *The Keeper of the Bees* 1928 [PZ3.S8994 Ke]).

Readers who recorded their opinions frequently, as indicated by the signed annotations (70 percent of the total number of annotations), are "G.H.N." with ten annotations and "C.Y." with fourteen, thoroughly eclipsing others in this sample, who mainly provide one or two annotations. Only one annotator, Lisa Koch, has provided her full name. A considerable number of annotators' initials are difficult or impossible to decipher, making any further deductions from this sample unhelpful. Four annotations are dated, one in 1925 and the others later (one in 1951 and two in 2005, both of which were signed "KAM").

The slip in one book has many annotations that are particularly evocative, small masterpieces of compact expression that keep within the five-word limit. John Cowper Powys's *Wolf Solent* 1929 (PZ3.P8758 Wo) generated strong feelings: "Bologny!," thought M.A.D.; N.A. suggested, "For antidote, read Havelock Ellis." They were followed by strongly worded gems: "Morbid, better burn both volumes" (C.B.J.[?]), and "Sewer-gas bottled as perfume" (E.L.[?]). On the other hand, "D" thought it "Beautifully written—rather long."

The annotations indicate the reactions of readers to these books and to the scheme. The reaction of the Athenæum's librarian is available in the library's records. In two of the annual reports prepared by the librarian for the Boston Athenæum's Proprietors are comments on the book review scheme. The 1921 report, covering activities of 1920, notes that it was implemented "at the suggestion of one of our Proprietors" and commented: "It is said that the sale of a successful novel is due far more to commendation by readers than to advertisements. The impulse to recommend a novel that has given pleasure can by this sheet be made serviceable to a large number of shareholders."[12] The 1927 report, covering events in 1926, provides a comment about the recommendations and an example. "Users of the library," the librarian contends, "sometimes think the judgment of those who direct the purchase of books falls far short of the ideal. In other words, they cannot see why certain books are purchased and others rejected, as if there must be an absolute standard in selection." However, the readers themselves were "not always unanimous in their verdicts," and the librarian used the comments made on the review slips—"It is well known that each new novel bears a slip, on which readers are invited to register approval or disapproval of the book when read"—to show this. The comments about May Sinclair's *Anne Severn* were the example selected, and in reporting them "it seemed best to omit the initials that follow the comments." They ranged from forceful condemnation ("Make firewood of this book") to a more positive view ("A triumph for literature").[13]

The 1929 report similarly illustrates, again through examples, the lack of unanimity to illustrate the point that the readers "are as reliable as the critics and much more entertaining." Some of the comments noted on novels in 1928 are

The Wages of Virtue, by P. C. Wren: "How can one write such stuff"; "Very exciting!"

Inspector French's Greatest Case, by F. W. Crofts: "Very good until the weak ending"; "No" (twice); "Yes"; "Yes—better than most of them"; "Very good and surprising *dénoûment* [*sic*]"; "Very poor"; "Fair" (twice); "Not bad."

The Runaway Bag, by A. P. Terhume: "Poor"; "Good—while you're reading it"; "A wretched sample of a wretched type"; "Perfectly rotten"; "Burn it!"; "A well written adventure story," "Good"; "Preposterous"; "Foolish. Not worth reading."

Lost Ecstasy, by M. R. Rinehart: "Not worth while"; "Very much worth while"; "*Very* good"; "Worth reading twice and then some!"; "Decidedly worth reading"; "Impossible, sordid and banal and uninteresting."

The librarian concludes: "Much of our current fiction might be described as 'Good—while you're reading it.'"[14]

The evidence presented by the annotations and the Athenæum's comments leave us in no doubt that some readers participated energetically in the review scheme. It is not possible, however, to determine just what percentage of the Athenæum's users participated. As noted, 30 percent of the annotations are not signed, and the initials that form the signatures on many annotations are difficult, sometimes impossible, to decipher. The contemporary researcher must also be aware when reading these comments, made by Bostonians during the 1920s, of the censorship debates of the period. Boston, notes Paul Boyer, was "a major battleground in the 1920s" on which this debate raged.[15] It would be surprising if some element of the debate were not reflected, in miniature, in the annotations in the Athenæum's books.

Some of the questions posed near the start of this essay have been addressed, albeit rather partially. We have a better understanding of how many of the printed slips are present in the Athenæum's books and when the practice of inserting them began and ended. The annotations provide limited insight into the thinking of the Athenæum's readers.

Not addressed are questions about the management of the Athenæum and the origins of the scheme. Can the review mechanism demonstrated in the Athenæum's printed slips be situated in a broader context? Was it unusual, or perhaps even unique? If not, what may have prompted the idea? Were the Athenæum's librarian or trustees being influenced by activities elsewhere? It has already been noted that the suggestion came from a proprietor. In an entry dated October 4, 1930, the Athenaeum's Librarian and Library Committee Records give only the barest detail of the decision to implement them:

Present Messrs Wendell, Stockton & Greenough.

Voted: To insert this notice in novels.

"Readers who care to express an opinion of this book for the guidance of others may do so below.

An opinion should contain not more than five words and should be followed by initials of the Reader."[16]

Reading the *Library Journal* for 1919, 1920, and 1921 does not provide any leads to further information about the practice or the Athenæum's decision. If we assume that contributors to the *Library Journal* were progressive professional librarians, they appear not to have felt any need to comment on the use of printed review slips to gather readers' opinions, at least in the years examined. And we cannot, of course, assume that the Athenæum's librarian and other staff read and were influenced by the *Library Journal*. There is more investigation to be carried out on this point.

What useful comment can be made about all of this? The first is that the mechanism demonstrated in these review slips demonstrates a change in the relationship between the library and its readers. Readers are being acknowledged as having opinions and are provided with a mechanism that allows their opinions to be publicly shared so others might take them into account when choosing what they read. The model changes from the library as center of authority, from which knowledge flows downstream to its patrons, to one in which there is peer-to-peer knowledge flow and value is placed on patron expertise and knowledge. Formal peer-to-peer communication among users was unusual at the time (although it must be acknowledged that Athenæum members would have conversed about the books they read), and it has only been since the development of this century's Internet-hosted social-networking tools that the mechanisms that enable its effective flow have been readily available.

The traditional view was that the library mediates between book and reader, for example through the process of selecting books to add to its collection. The process had at its base the "'library faith'—a conviction in the library profession . . . that without an informed and educated citizenry democracy cannot exist," which inspired members of the profession to develop libraries as "emporiums of culture and citadels of scientific inquiry, broadly termed."[17] This approach, definitely prevalent in the 1920s, has no place for reader input, no means by which the reader can play a role in selection except, perhaps, by complaining loudly. The Athenæum's review slips, however, can be viewed as evidence of a differing reality, in this library at least, in that the librarian's imposed view was open to influence by readers.

The second comment is conjecture: did this peer-to-peer knowledge flow model arise because the Boston Athenæum was a social library and therefore different from public libraries? An answer to this question awaits a more detailed examination and deeper understanding of social libraries.[18]

The Athenæum provided the means for readers to communicate with one another through annotations, to advise each other about the merit (or otherwise) of a book. This appears to run directly counter to the motives of librarians, prevalent during the 1920s, of providing advice to improve the quality of what was being read through the mechanism of the readers' advisory.[19] The history of the readers' advisory may provide a context for more investigation. Brendan Luyt suggests that the advisory "at its heart was a project aiming to legitimize a body of knowledge presumed to be held by the advisors" and that "fundamental to the relationship to the readers' advisor and the patron was a belief that people needed help both in choosing what to read and how to read it." This view reinforces the expert and superior role of the library as center of authority, upstream in the information flow, as it were—indeed Luyt quotes the 1928 words of Charles Compton of the St. Louis Public Library that "in the far distant future—we shall have a public that will be sufficiently intelligent to select its own reading."[20] How far the history of the readers' advisory may help in explaining the Athenæum's scheme for fiction is not clear: Crowley reminds us that for adult readers' advisory services "*nonfiction* was the intellectual gold standard."[21]

The Boston Athenæum's printed review slip mechanism of the 1920s invites comparison with today's social-networking mechanisms. In fact, Warnement's short piece in the Athenæum's member newsletter was written to bring to the attention of members the book recommendations on a new page on the Athenæum's website.[22] The Athenæum's request for annotations to be no more than five words also invites a comparison with Twitter's 140-character limit. Many social-networking sites provide the means of posting book reviews and recommendations and commenting on postings; Facebook's weRead, Twitter's thebookclub, Goodreads, Shelfari, and LibraryThing are among the best known. These mechanisms are clear demonstrations of peer-to-peer knowledge flow, where value is placed on reader expertise and knowledge, definitely refuting Compton's skepticism that there will ever be "a public . . . sufficiently intelligent to select its own reading."[23] Conventional book reviewing has also changed and reflects the input of readers; indeed, it has been overtaken almost completely. As one commentator has noted, "Over the last 15 years, the book review landscape has changed seismically" with the result that "the golden age of the authority-driven review has been challenged by the conversation the Internet facilitates."[24]

This investigation has left unanswered more questions than it addresses. No analysis has been attempted of the relationships among the annotators, the annotations, and the books annotated. Censorship in the environment of 1920s Boston is probably a significant aspect of this set of questions. This book review scheme may have been prompted, at least in part, by concerns about the nature of books being added to the Athenæum's collection, and making readers' comments available can be explained as a device to forestall challenges to books. Nor is there any analysis of the effect of the annotations on reception: did their presence affect the reader, and if so, how? Some of the annotations constitute what might be a conversation among readers. And to what extent did the annotations help create and reinforce a community of readers? Another set of questions is about how the scheme operated at the Boston Athenæum. Was a printed slip inserted in all fiction acquired in the 1920s? Answering this will involve comparing acquisition records, available at the Athenæum, with the books. Did the Athenæum expand this scheme to books other than novels? The records make no mention of this, but some checking of other genres is required. Sampling of a small number of travel books shows no evidence of slips. Other questions revolve around the origins of the scheme. Was it unusual, or perhaps even unique? If not, what may have stimulated the idea? Were the Athenæum's librarian or trustees being influenced by activities elsewhere? Perhaps the most interesting question is whether the peer-to-peer knowledge-flow demonstrated in the Athenæum's scheme developed (assuming it was unique) and could thrive because the Boston Athenæum was a social library and therefore different from public libraries.

NOTES

I am grateful to Marika Cifor for carrying out the bulk of the sampling and investigation of the Athenæum's records, to Rachel Salmond for also participating in the sampling, to Tim Spalding (LibraryThingGuy) for comments on contemporary examples, and to Mary Warnement for providing advice and a starting point. I gratefully acknowledge the support of the Emily Hollowell Research Fund, Graduate School of Library and Information Science, Simmons College.

The quotation in the chapter title is taken from an annotation in a book in the Boston Athenæum's collection, Hilaire Belloc's *Mr. Petre* 1925 with the call number PZ3.B4193 Mi.

1. Paula D. Matthews, "Welcome to the Boston Athenæum!," http://www.boston athenaeum.org/node/41.

2. Josiah Quincy, *The History of the Boston Athenæum, with Biographical Notes of Its Deceased Founders* (Cambridge: Metcalf and Company, 1851), 30–31.

3. Katherine Wolff, *Culture Club: The Curious History of the Boston Athenaeum* (Amherst: University of Massachusetts Press, 2009), 49.

4. Thomas Augst, "Faith in Reading: Public Libraries, Liberalism, and the Civil Religion," in *Institutions of Reading: The Social Life of Libraries in the United States*, ed. Thomas Augst and Kenneth Carpenter (Amherst: University of Massachusetts Press, 2007), 158.

5. Wayne A. Wiegand, "The American Public Library: Construction of a Community Reading Institution," in *A History of the Book in America*, vol. 4, *Print in Motion: The Expansion of Publishing and Reading in the United States, 1880–1940*, ed. Carl F. Kaestle and Janice A. Radway (Chapel Hill: University of North Carolina Press, 2009), 449.

6. Wolff, *Culture Club*, 57.

7. Wayne A. Wiegand, "Tunnel Vision and Blind Spots: What the Past Tells Us about the Present: Reflections on the Twentieth-Century History of American Libraries," *Library Quarterly* 69, no. 1 (1999): 24.

8. "CFP—Libraries in the History of Print Culture," http://libprofdev.wordpress.com/2009/06/01/cfp-libraries-in-the-history-of-print-culture/.

9. Mary Warnement, "Seeking Member Book Recommendations," *Boston Athenæum Member Newsletter* 3, no. 11 (2009): 3.

10. Two from 1915 have printed slips of another kind. The wording on these reads: "This book is now temporary. The reader who feels strongly that it ought to be made permanent should place initials below." The Athenæum librarian and proprietors considered some books purchased in this period, although of interest to readers at the time, not worthy of adding to the Athenæum's permanent collection. Reader input into this decision was invited through these printed slips. An entry for October 11, 1915, in the Athenæum's Librarian and Library Committee Records (held in the Archive of the Boston Athenæum) probably refers to these printed slips: "Votes . . . A note on the back pocket of novels was approved." The Proprietors' Reports from 1921 to 1929 (covering events in the preceding year) note the number of fiction books purchased that were "considered of temporary interest only." They range from 230 in 1920 (noted in the 1921 report) to 435 in 1930 (noted in the 1931 report).

11. John A. Stotesbury, "A Critical Reassessment of Gender in John Buchan's *Prester John*," *Nordic Journal of African Studies* 2, no. 1 (1993): 111.

12. Boston Athenæum, *Report to the Proprietors for 1920* (Boston: Boston Athenæum, 1921), 2–3.

13. Boston Athenæum, *Report to the Proprietors for 1926* (Boston: Boston Athenæum, 1927), 2–3. The librarian quoted these other annotations about this book: "Should not have been bought"; "Singularly indecent"; "A moving love story, charmingly told"; "Must be an O.M. who wrote above Tale of woman's steadfastness"; "Test of Life. How we face Realities."

14. Boston Athenæum, *Report to the Proprietors for 1928* (Boston: Boston Athenæum, 1929), 3–4.

15. Paul S. Boyer, "Gilded-Age Consensus, Repressive Campaigns, and Gradual Liberalization: The Shifting Rhythms of Book Censorship," in *A History of the Book in America*, vol. 4, *Print in Motion: The Expansion of Publishing and Reading in the United States, 1880–1940*, ed. Carl F. Kaestle and Janice A. Radway (Chapel Hill: University of North Carolina Press, 2009), 294.

16. Boston Athenæum, Librarian and Library Committee Records.

17. Wayne A. Wiegand, "Community Places and Reading Spaces: Main Street Public Library in the Rural Heartland, 1876–1956," this volume, <000>; Alistair Black, "Introduction: The Public Library in Concept and Reality," in *The Cambridge History of Libraries in Britain and Ireland*, vol. 3, *1850–2000*, ed. Alistair Black and Peter Hoare (Cambridge: Cambridge University Press, 2006), 22.

18. It seems relevant here, however, to give a recent example of a dialog among public library patrons. In 2010, I was shown a book from the Cambridge Public Library (John Green's *Looking for Alaska* [New York: Speak, 2008]) about adolescence and its challenges. Annotations fill three blank pages at the end of the book. The first starts with these words: "Dear reader, Listen for I am telling you all you will need to know in life, don't be freaked im just a kid trying to help out other kids. After you read what I have wrote it will be your turn. In these last blank pages right something, a word of advice or an idea you have about humanity. Ill go first." Responses, often lengthy, appear in four different hands. I thank Associate Professor Amy Pattee, my colleague at Simmons College, for bringing this user-initiated dialog to my attention.

19. See Melanie A. Kimball, "A Brief History of Readers' Advisory," in *Genreflecting: A Guide to Popular Reading Interests*, ed. Diana Tixier Herald and Wayne A. Wiegand (Westport, CT: Libraries Unlimited, 2006).

20. Brendan Luyt, "Regulating Readers: The Social Origins of the Readers' Advisor in the United States," *Library Quarterly* 71, no. 4 (2001): 451, 452.

21. Bill Crowley, "Rediscovering the History of Readers Advisory Service," *Public Libraries* 44, no. 1 (2005): 38.

22. Warnement, "Seeking Member Book Recommendations."

23. Luyt, "Regulating Readers," 452.

24. Barbara Hoffert, "Every Reader a Reviewer: The Online Book Conversation," *Library Journal* 135, no. 13 (September 1, 2010), http://www.libraryjournal.com/lj/re viewsbook/886292-421/every_reader_a_reviewer_the.html.csp.

"A Search for Better Ways into the Future"

The Library of Congress and Its Users in the Interwar Period

JANE AIKIN

"I always regarded LC, in spite of its responsibilities to Government and in spite of its scholarly and museum-like characteristics, to be in essence a public library—the pinnacle of the library system of the country indeed, but of the library system viewed rather as a public library system than anything else," Verner Clapp recalled. During the early years of his employment at the Library of Congress, Clapp worked at the public service desk in the Reading Room, and he retained more than an impressionistic view of its character and clientele.[1] His recollections of that period, together with the observations of other library staff, illustrate the extent to which the library had a "public" character as 1920s prosperity gave way to the Depression.

The Library of Congress chiefly has served Congress and the federal government but is open as well to scholars, researchers, and the general public. For the years before 1913, its archives contain little detailed information on library use.[2] However, beginning with 1914 there is a long file of the reports of the chiefs of divisions.[3] Their reports were never published, but the chiefs often wrote of matters not included in the librarian's official annual report: for example, they discussed staffing and space problems, commented on interdivisional operations, and sometimes described library use and library users.

Before the United States entered World War I, the chiefs wrote more about building the collections than about reader services, and for good reason: the library's specialized divisions at that time acquired and processed most of their own material. It was a period of steady collection growth through copyright deposits, gifts, exchanges, federal documents deposits, transfers from other federal libraries, and bequests. From 1870 forward (when copyright deposit began), the library rapidly amassed a massive book collection that, from about a million volumes around the turn of the twentieth century, would double by 1912 and reach 4 million by 1930. And that total takes no account of the maps and charts, music, and prints collections, much of which also arrived through copyright deposit. By 1930, the nonbook collections amounted to more than 2.5 million additional items.[4] In 1933, Librarian Herbert Putnam announced to Congress that with over 4.8 million volumes, the Library of Congress had become the world's largest.[5]

As the staff continued to build the collections, during the 1920s and 1930s, library use increased rapidly, notably including American and foreign scholars, government agencies and officials, officers and staff members of foundations and organizations, and students at all levels. Whereas 132,576 readers entered the Reading Room during 1910, a level of use that did not change much before or during the World War I years, the number suddenly increased to 172,549 in 1919 and began a steady upward climb, in 1924 reaching a peak of 236,415. It then dipped back by around fourteen to eighteen thousand readers, remaining rather static for the next few years, but in fiscal 1930 (which included the October 1929 stock market crash), use again increased, reaching a higher level than ever before, at 278,512 and rising during most of the Depression years, until in 1939 the Reading Room staff reported 421,878 visitors.[6]

There were a number of reasons, in addition to overall collection growth, for postwar increases in library use. In 1925, Congress accepted Elizabeth Sprague Coolidge's offer to construct an auditorium and endow music-related activities and then established the Library of Congress Trust Fund Board to enable the library to accept gifts and endowments. During the late 1920s, gift followed gift, enabling the library to acquire more materials and hire staff consultants to systematically build the collections in specialized collecting areas such as aeronautics, American history, the fine arts, and Hispanic literature. Then in 1930 the congressional decision to purchase the three-thousand-volume Vollbehr Collection of incunabula, including a perfect Gutenberg Bible, drew international attention and brought new distinction to the library's rare book holdings. All these were customary areas of interest for a national library, but not all the new initiatives represented high culture. Begun in the late 1920s, a project to record or otherwise collect American folk songs represented an important commitment to an area of popular culture. It brought to the collections tunes familiar to Appalachian rural dwellers, dockworkers, state-prison inmates, and African American farmhands, thus prospectively extending the library's reach to minority and immigrant groups. Also in the area of popular culture, inexpensive books such as dime novels entered the national collections for the first time.[7] While both folk songs and cheap fiction fitted with the library's commitment to amassing Americana, it was the recognition that these areas formed parts of the American experience that mattered—not just increasing the collections but also broadening the library's role as a cultural institution.

During the interwar period, the main facility for users was the Reading Room, open from 9:00 a.m. to 10:00 p.m. six days of the week and from 2:00 to 10:00 p.m. on Sundays, plus most holidays as well. There also were other, smaller, reading areas—for periodicals and newspapers, manuscripts, maps, music, fine arts, and the Smithsonian collection—but after these closed at 5:00 p.m., the Reading Room staff served all users. Uniting the circulation and reference functions, they supplied library materials to members of Congress and their staffs, congressional committees, other federal agencies and offices, general readers within the library building, and, by interlibrary loan, libraries outside the District of Columbia. They also answered telephone, mail, and in-person inquiries from Congress and the public at large.[8] There was no limit on the number of items a user could request, a policy that encouraged readers to make extensive use of the collections.

There are only a few eyewitness accounts of Reading Room service in those days. Clapp, who began working at what was called the "Central Desk" in 1923, recalled:

> We knew everyone. We were on our feet continuously. There was much physical labor involved, going around servicing the pressure tubes for the slips, getting the books off the carriers, locating newspapers or delivering the books themselves, giving readers instructions on use of the catalog, giving instructions to the catalogers, going anywhere in the Library to get the material or information. It was a leg-work job, and it was exciting. We all had the feeling that we were engaged in service. . . . At the Central Desk there were two alternating forces. We worked from 9 to 10 six days a week.[9]

In addition to the two overlapping weekday shifts, other staff covered the central desk on Sundays.

Reading Room superintendent Frederick Ashley's account of services for library users reinforces Clapp's memories of a demanding workplace. "The term 'reading room' calls up a mental picture of a quiet place where a few persons of leisure sit idly turning the pages of the late reviews," he wrote.

"Reading room" does not connote a hundred miles of shelving packed with millions of books in scores of languages; it does not imply tension, stress, haste; the need to translate at sight a thrice-relayed call from the floor of the House for Dickinson's "Notes" into "American Notes" by Charles Dickens; the wit to send instanter "The four horsemen of the Apocalypse" to fill a written order for "The Tom Horsement of the Afolca Type." "Reading room" is not likely to evoke a mental picture of reference work by long-distance telephone from New York; telephone calls from a thousand offices in the Capitol, the House and Senate Office buildings, the executive departments, books going out by the wagon-load to the scientific bureaus, inter-library loans ordered by radiogram from Honolulu, by cable from Berlin, by mail from Vancouver; daily dealings of sorts with the ends of the earth.[10]

Between increased use and steady collection growth during the postwar years, space for readers was at a premium. In 1919 Ashley began reporting crowded conditions, and three years later he noted the shortage of special study tables for readers pursuing lengthy projects and the lack of facilities for those wanting to use typewriters or give dictation.[11] As the publishing business revived and thrived, books on new subjects—relativity, bolshevism, the League of Nations, submarine warfare, and aviation—jammed the shelves. The staff double-shelved books and piled newspaper volumes on the floor; but by 1925 readers had to wait for a place to sit on busy Sunday afternoons.[12] While Ashley speculated that the opening of the new southeastern branch of Washington's Carnegie Public Library might ease the crowding, over time it seemed to make little difference.[13]

Work on a new book stack in the northeast courtyard, begun in December 1925, was completed by March 1, 1927. With a capacity of 1.8 million volumes, or about 51.3 miles of shelving, the addition also included twenty-five new individual study rooms and forty-seven study tables and provided much-needed space for the library's rare books. Yet, a month after the rooms became available, all were occupied and there was a waiting list. And the growing collection of course begat a growing card catalog: after adding 1,344 drawers in 1918, it became necessary in 1927 to install 1,344 more. The catalog cabinets displaced sixteen readers' desks and two tables, forcing the staff to add chairs in the alcoves and rescore Reading Room desks to accommodate more readers.[14]

Looking back in mid-1930, when yet another addition provided more space for readers pursuing special projects, Superintendent Martin Roberts described the situation: "A decade ago," he wrote,

the percentage of those who desired to use the Reading Room for purposes
of research was very much less than at present. Aside from the service to the
Congress and the executive establishments, the chief function of the staff consisted in meeting the needs of a recreative reading public. With the exception of
a few serious investigators desiring research facilities the need was not difficult
to meet. American scholarship had not at that time reached its present development through endowments and other means. And besides American scholars
had not realized that the Library of Congress was rapidly developing into the
National Library primarily concerned with the problem of serious research.[15]

By the mid-1920s, however, both Roberts and Carl Engel, chief of the music
division, were commenting on how comprehensive the collections had become,
with Roberts going so far as to state that in many fields "no serious scholarly
work can be prepared without consulting the source material that we have."[16]

Thus significant changes in library use antedated the Depression: the sky-
rocketing use statistics during the Depression continued a pattern that had
emerged in the 1920s. Of course, after World War I federal agencies greatly
increased their activities—activities that reflected the prosperity of the 1920s.
But increased use of the Reading Room also came from scholars, foundation
and organization-funded projects, and growth in education in general; as Ashley put it, this increase came from those "whose requirements for the successful
prosecution of their studies are obviously greater than those of casual readers."[17]

The annual report data on Reading Room users and outside borrowers do
not connect individual readers with the exact books they used, but the staff
did record use by book classification, thus providing a simple tally of what
parts of the collection and which subjects were most in demand. Produced
yearly as part of the superintendent of the Reading Room's annual reports,
these statistics provide a long-term review of users' priorities and interests,
from those privileged to draw books for home use, to the general traffic in the
Reading Room, to the long-term users assigned study tables or study rooms.

Those authorized to borrow directly from the library for home use included
members of Congress, their families, and their staff members; officials of the
executive branch and the judiciary; foreign diplomats; and others specially
authorized.[18] Demands from these direct borrowers differed in one very significant respect from those of other readers: the importance of fiction. Between
1925 and 1939, the number of volumes of fiction loaned for use outside the
building varied between a low of 24,968 in 1927 and a high of 36,268 in
1930. Despite the proximity of the District of Columbia Public Library and

its branches (where novels were readily available to borrowers), fiction was the largest class of books borrowed for outside use, far outdistancing every other part of the classification. Evidently many outside users called on the library to satisfy their tastes for best-sellers and romance, adventure, western, and mystery novels, probably reveling in the popular novelists' works that the library received on copyright deposit—Zane Grey, E. Phillips Oppenheim, Sinclair Lewis, Mary Roberts Rinehart, Booth Tarkington, Edna Ferber, Lloyd C. Douglas, James Hilton, Edgar Rice Burroughs, and Margaret Mitchell, to name just a few.

Reading Room users, however, had other priorities. Having ranked in eighth place in 1926, their fiction requests fell to twentieth place in 1939. In the years just after the stock market crash, calls for fiction in the Reading Room dropped to fourteenth and fifteenth place. This pattern contrasts, for example, with the Middletown (Muncie, Indiana) Public Library, where Robert and Helen Lynd found that an increasing share of adult reading from 1929 through 1933 was fiction.[19] But Superintendent Ashley thought he saw a trend even earlier, writing in 1927: "This growing interest in serious books is nation-wide. A comparison of book production statistics for 1914 and 1923 shows an increase of 55 percent in literature, 98 percent in religion and philosophy, 163 percent in history, to mention but a few; whereas there was a decrease of 25 percent in the production of fiction."[20] And a few years later, Arthur E. Bostwick, director of the St. Louis Public Library, similarly commented on the trends he saw shaping library use: a growing number of readers and increases in publishing output—with much of it directed not toward scholars and specialists but to an interested population of lay readers.[21]

Among the most requested classes of material in the Reading Room was the C-CT classification, which includes genealogy—a subject that drew a large subset of library users (see table below). As early as 1927, Ashley began planning to establish "more direct contact" with this group of readers by bringing genealogical materials together in one area with a trained assistant to help them; and two years later Roberts referred to the experiment as a prototype for expanded public service. By 1935 this group of readers, including both amateur and professional genealogists and estimated at more than three hundred readers per week, was requesting so much specialized assistance that a reading area for American local history and genealogy opened on one of the decks off the main Reading Room, staffed by two assistants.[22] With the addition of this specialized service, the library formally recognized an increasing public absorption that affected not only the acquisition of materials but also daily operations.

Library of Congress Classification Outline

Classification	Subjects
A	General works
B-BT	Philosophy; Psychology; Religions
BV-BX	Practical Theology; Christian Denominations
C-CT	Auxiliary Sciences of History, including Genealogy
D-DB	General History; Great Britain and Central Europe
DC-DX	History: Europe, Asia, Africa, Australia, Oceania
E	History of the Americas
F	History of the Americas: U.S. Local History; Canada; Latin America
G	Geography; Anthropology; Recreation
H-HC	General Social Sciences; Statistics; Economic Theory; Demography; Economic History and Conditions
HD-HG	Industries; Land Use; Labor; Transportation; Communications; Commerce; Finance
HJ-HX	Public Finance; Sociology; Socialism; Communism; Anarchism
J	Legislative and executive papers
JA-JX	Political science; Public administration; Government; International law
K	Law
L	Education
M	Music
N	Fine Arts
P-PN	Philology; Linguistics; Ancient and modern languages; General literature
PQ	Romance literatures
PR-PS	English literature; American literature
PT-PY	Other national literatures
PZ	Fiction
Q	Science
R	Medicine
S	Agriculture
T-TK	Technology; Engineering; Construction; Electronics
TL-TX	Aeronautics; Mining and metallurgy; Chemical technology; Photography; Arts and crafts; Home economics
Z	Bibliography; Library science

Source: Annual Report of the Superintendent of the Reading Room, 1929–39, Library of Congress Archives, Manuscript Division, Library of Congress.

Main Reading Room readers also used materials in the HD-HG classes very heavily, which resonated with President Calvin Coolidge's adage, "The business of America *is* business." Books from this classification were in considerable demand from 1925 through 1939, though in the earliest years the H classification statistics were not broken down to separate business books from HJ to HX. Between 1929 and the end of 1939, calls for business material rose from seventh place to second place in 1932. By 1935 HD-HG had become the most heavily used part of the collection; it would hold this rank for the rest of the decade.

Readers also called for materials that formed part of the library's traditional collecting strengths. U.S. history and American local history usually were among the top five, while European history had lesser but still significant use. Representative of traditional academic interests were the P-PN and PR-PS literature classifications. But also important were B-BT and BV-BX, philosophy and religion. Two classes that varied more than the others in use patterns were L and Q. Science books were served to in-building users at a higher rate in the 1920s than in the 1930s, when Q dropped out of the ten most-used classes after 1931. Education, however, first appeared among the ten most popular classes in ninth place in 1928 and rose to fifth in 1931 before dropping below tenth by 1936.[23]

There was always demand for special facilities for long-term readers: even before World War I the staff was assigning table space. But the requests increased in the early 1920s, and by 1925 more tables had to be added—in the alcove galleries of the Reading Room, between bookcases in the North Curtain, in the Smithsonian Division, and around the outer rim of the Reading Room. The new stack completed in 1927 provided study rooms and more table space, and a special Study Room Reference Service was established to assist these users.[24]

A late 1920s profile of the intensive users included individuals from six nations and twenty-nine states: 34 percent requesting political science material; 22 percent, economics; 19 percent, history; 9 percent, biography; 3.5 percent, technology; 3.5 percent, literature; 3.5 percent, finance; 3 percent, agriculture; and 2.3 percent, psychology. A group of sixteen foreign scholars sponsored by the Laura Spelman Rockefeller Memorial Fund requested materials on American economics, constitutional law, sociology, and psychology, while a group sponsored by the Social Science Research Council spent three weeks working through several thousand volumes to compile an annotated bibliography on crime. One hundred twenty faculty members from fifty-seven different

American universities used the collections, and eight federal agencies maintained staff at the library. Subjects of research were varied, including the American highway system, history of American labor organization, the British Parliament and North America, civil service in the United States and Britain, Chinese drama and literature, European treaties bearing on American history, intergovernmental financial relations, German literature in British magazines, Henrik Ibsen, Irish arts and crafts, medieval towns, Norwegian American history and bibliography, history of the pan-American movement, economic development of the South since 1865, political theories of Sun Yat-Sen, Turkey in world politics (1914–23), John Wesley, the legal position of women, and history and bibliography of yellow fever.[25] Judging from this list, the late-1920s long-term users were immersed in a wide variety of projects, and federal agency use was not predominant.

In addition to emphasizing the intellectual vigor of the 1920s, some of these varied interests stemmed from the growth of private sector research during the period. Herbert Hoover pursued ties to the private sector during his wartime administration of food relief and as secretary of commerce; then as president he promoted efforts to employ voluntarism and private resources for federal planning and development. The growing cooperation between the government and foundations and between foundations and university researchers originated in what Barry D. Karl has called "progressivism scientifically conceived," the conviction that scientific expertise and research should be harnessed to promote an informed government. Research also became more closely directed toward the social and economic sciences, marked by the establishment of independent research institutions such as the Brookings Institution (1916), the Twentieth Century Fund (1919), the National Bureau of Economic Research (1920), and the Social Science Research Council (1923).[26] And the national capital, of course, was a magnet, drawing public interest organizations, headquarters of national associations, and other groups in addition to private research organizations.

More evidence of advancing research activity appeared in fiscal 1930, which saw a 22 percent increase in the number of readers in the Reading Room, including 260 faculty members from ninety-three American universities, and 33 from eighteen foreign universities; in all, investigators came from eleven different foreign countries. Moreover, increased federal demands antedated the New Deal, with forty-two researchers from twenty-three different agencies, while an additional sixty-two came from learned societies. Noting the increase in the number of scholars, both domestic and foreign, during the previous year, Roberts had observed that the thirty-one investigators from abroad who came on Rockefeller scholarships were chiefly interested in studying conditions in the United States and predicted not only that an international exchange of ideas with American scholars might result but also that "such studies when interpreted to their own nationals may have far reaching results."[27] And there were other types of users as well, some of them unmentioned in official reports: for example, a vignette on some library users of the early 1930s appeared in the *Washington Post* after a reporter visited the Reading Room during the last part of a week in May 1931 and found "ministers of all denominations, their desks piled high with books and papers, their backs bent to their task, and their brows knitted in thought." After commenting on the reading habits of several noted Washington clerics, the reporter concluded, "This, I wot, is where the sermons come from."[28]

Three years later, in the depths of the Depression, the number of books issued in the Reading Room was double the 1928 total. Superintendent Roberts reported, "During the past winter one could see large groups forced to the necessity of examining books while standing and this despite the addition of several hundred chairs. . . . On a single Saturday there were four times as many readers as study desks." The special congressional session President Roosevelt called from March to June 1933 brought huge demands; the phone rang every two minutes on average, and the staff doubled the number of study tables on two decks and in the gallery alcoves, installing them even in the aisles of the book stacks. As Roberts explained, they resorted to crowding to avoid keeping a waiting list for reading space, and he noted that the staff had even "seriously contemplated recommending the placing of study tables in the visitors' gallery of the Reading Room." By 1935, readers could be admitted only when there were vacant desks, and with material in all classifications overflowing the shelves, the staff was again double- and triple-shelving volumes and storing books in the cellar.[29] Often, more than a thousand readers entered the Reading Room between 9:00 a.m. and 10:00 p.m. But Thomas Blair, a staff member who delivered books to readers' desks, could detect no particular agenda in the requests, which ranged from travel literature to books on various hobbies and from literature to mathematics. Nor was there a dominant class of readers; there were students intent on their assignments, scholars working on their own books, researchers compiling facts, and many individuals simply absorbing books that interested them.[30]

Students' use of the library had increased so markedly by the mid-1930s that the Reading Room staff made a special effort in 1936 to analyze that class of users. It found that the heavy use came less from university students than secondary school and teachers' college students. The staff reserved approximately fifty seats for this class of users, which, in a February 1936 snapshot, comprised 8 percent of all readers. About one-fourth were reading literary works and 22 percent history, with lesser numbers requesting books on science and technology, education, social and political science, philosophy and religion, and psychology. Roberts observed with some surprise that "there was an observable tendency to draw large quantities of books and to send for everything listed in the Catalogue under the subject in hand." And he speculated, "This might have been the result of a laudable desire to exhaust the subject, or of ignorance of the bibliography." On scrutinizing call slips more closely, staff found that probably two-thirds of the books that one teachers' college student used should have been available in her own college or public library, and this pattern was observed in other cases of heavy use. Thus, Roberts concluded that "their use of the Library was more habitual and less from a special quest of unusual books."

The staff members who analyzed student use commented that the most serious problem was multiple use of the same books: "A total of 404 titles were used no less than 1,074 times; 31 titles were requested 5 times or more; one book (*The Canterbury Tales*) was used 18 times during the month. . . . Such use of our collections, arising from class assignments, will quickly call from our shelves all the editions—the old and scholarly as well as the most recent—and cause in a brief space an amount of wear which should never occur to the collections of the National Reference Library." Yet they found that the students were, after all, pursuing their reading with a serious purpose. There was no evidence that they were requesting "objectionable" reading; in fact, there was "little observable tendency to stray from the strict path of assigned study."[31]

The concerns about collection wear and tear, though well founded, now seem less important than what the flood of students represented: the expansion of the school population during the period and significant increases in both secondary and higher education. During the Depression, the proportion of seventeen-year-olds who finished high school rose, from 29 percent in 1930 to 50 percent in 1940, the greatest advance in U.S. history, while the number of college graduates increased 55 percent (following on a nearly 50 percent increase during the 1920s).[32] More students needing more books (and many of them perhaps needing books they could not afford to buy) translated into more library use.

In addition to the varied requests of Depression-era readers, the library served the demands of the Roosevelt administration's new federal agencies: the National Recovery Administration, Farm Credit Administration, Agricultural Adjustment Administration, Federal Farm Board, Tennessee Valley Authority, and National Emergency Administration of Public Works. Equally, government and private researchers continued to draw on Library of Congress resources for projects, such as a U.S. Bureau of Mines treatise on diamonds, editorial work on the papers of William Howard Taft, the National Park Service's documentation of battlefields and landmarks, the American Historical Association's Commission on Social Studies in the Schools, a Eugenic Research Foundation study on fecundity, the inquiries of the American College of Surgeons on industrial medicine and workmen's compensation, and research for the World Monetary and Economic Conference.[33] The variety of projects and numbers of researchers testified to the depth of the collections but also perhaps to shrinking library budgets elsewhere: the Library of Congress remained the place where users could rely on copyright deposit to ensure the continued growth of up-to-date book, map, music, print, and other collections serving the needs of nearly all disciplines.[34]

Long-term users assigned to study rooms or study tables included researchers from government agencies and those engaged in special projects. Among the ten most-used classes of books in the study rooms during the 1930s, business books were nearly always the most-used group from 1932 to the end of the decade, with U.S. history and American local history always among the top five. But there are some shifts in use patterns as well. In 1929, the most-used classes were K, Law and JA-JX, Political Science. Both these remained among the heaviest requested by study room users, but beginning in 1932 they yielded the top rank to books in the HD-HG classes. Readers served by the special study room reference service hailed from states and countries worldwide, but over the Depression decade readers from colleges and universities and societies and foundations increased in numbers. Most striking was the growing demand from government agencies: the number sending staff to work at study rooms or tables rose from twenty-three agencies in 1930 to forty-seven in 1939. In his 1933–34 report, Roberts noted that many long-term users were concentrating on "domestic social trends," while those from abroad centered on "the recent economic situation."

Three years later, the superintendent wrote again about user needs, this time emphasizing the heavy federal use during the Depression: "It is the common experience of libraries, everywhere," he noted, that use has multiplied in proportion to growth, and in our own case, some of the stimuli may be identified with the growth of the contents of the library from about 3,500,000 volumes and pamphlets in 1927, to more than 5,400,000 today. Other factors have also given impetus to our activity: the development of special facilities for research (including the work of the consultative staff), the provision of adequate quarters for the administration and custody of rare book collections, and the expansion of our bibliographical apparatus. But a more apparent (as it is a more immediate) explanation is found in the widening recognition of the importance of research to the functions of government. Whereas, in the recent past such agencies as concerned themselves with research were limited to pure and applied science, our post-war economic structure has called into being a number of bureaux charged with fact-finding responsibilities, and, as a result, government investigations have extended to the social, the political, and even the historical sciences. The number of government organizations with which we have loan relations has more than doubled since 1934, whilst for the decennium, 1927–1937, more than 800 representatives of most of these agencies have conducted research on the premises. Indeed during this most literate of decades 8,785,188 books have been issued to 3,167,565 readers.[35]

Soon after, Acting Superintendent David Chambers Mearns commented, "It is a sign of health, then, that so much of the tremendous increase in the use of our collection in the past two decades has resulted, not only from an increasing study of past events for their own sakes, but from a search for better ways into the future. It is incontrovertible that never before has government demanded so much from libraries and books (and been so dependent upon them) as during the last decade."[36]

In the interwar period, although the library's responsibilities to the Congress and the federal government remained the highest priority, users' needs and cultural trends also affected its collections and services. The library mounted initiatives to collect more widely and in new fields. New services such as the Reading Room's genealogy service and the special assistance provided to associations, foundations, and research organizations responded to increasing pressures and intensive use.

Post-1930 use of the library's collections built on the public-sector-oriented research activity of the previous decade and general modernization trends of the interwar period. The Depression intensified these use patterns. From the unemployed seeking recreation or reinvention, to the general readers intently following their own interests, to the businessmen plumbing prospects for recovery, to the students who stayed in school rather than join the ranks of the jobless, people used libraries as both refuge and resource, and the Library of Congress did not differ in that respect from other libraries. In its 1930s use patterns, we encounter the comforting rhythm of traditional research needs overlain with the imprint of vigorous efforts to restore individual, corporate, and governmental economic health.

NOTES

The opinions expressed in this essay are my own and do not reflect the views of the National Endowment for the Humanities or the United States government.

1. Verner W. Clapp to John G. Lorenz, August 12, 1965, box 8, Verner Clapp Papers, Manuscript Division, Library of Congress.

2. In 1905, Librarian Herbert Putnam announced his decision to stop publishing use statistics because such statistics provided only a partial indication of actual use; see U.S. Library of Congress, *Annual Report of the Librarian of Congress* 1905, 83; and 1920, 99 (hereafter *ARLC*). No further use statistics appeared until 1936.

3. All years are fiscal years: fiscal 1914, for example, covered the period July 1, 1913–June 30, 1914.

4. For statistics, see John Y. Cole and Jane Aikin, eds., *The Encyclopedia of the Library of Congress: For Congress, the Nation, and the World* (Washington, DC: Library of Congress, in association with Bernan Press, 2005), 513–14.

5. Jane Aikin Rosenberg, *The Nation's Great Library: Herbert Putnam and the Library of Congress, 1899–1939* (Urbana: University of Illinois Press, 1993), 129.

6. Statistics of main Reading Room use are recorded in the reports of the superintendents during the interwar period (except the 1936–37 report, which omits the statistics), Library of Congress Archives, Manuscript Division, Library of Congress (hereafter LCA).

7. See Elizabeth Jane Aikin, "High Culture, Low Culture: The Singular Duality of the Library of Congress," in *Libraries as Agencies of Culture*, ed. Thomas Augst and Wayne A. Wiegand (Madison: University of Wisconsin Press, 2003), 43–61.

8. Annual Report of the Superintendent of the Reading Room, 1924–25, Library of Congress Archives, Manuscript Division, Library of Congress (hereafter ARSRR). The library was closed only on July 4 and December 25. For a general history, see Josephus Nelson and Judith Farley, *Full Circle: Ninety Years of Service in the Main Reading Room* (Washington, DC: Library of Congress, 1991).

9. Marlene Morrissey to Verner Clapp, June 5, 1970, with notes on Clapp's remarks to the Library of Congress Professional Association, May 27, 1970, box 9, Clapp Papers. For the reminiscences of Harry Eastman Lower, another Reading Room assistant, see ARSRR, 1928–29.

10. ARSRR, 1923–24.

11. ARSRR, 1918–19, 1921–22.

12. ARSRR, 1922–23, 1924–25.

13. ARSRR, 1924–25; the new branch opened in 1925 at 403 7th Street Southeast; in 1932 a northeastern branch opened at 330 7th Street Northeast. Both libraries seem to have been much concerned with the need for children's materials; see http://www.dc .library.org.

14. ARSRR, 1926–27; *ARLC* 1927, 11, 167–71.

15. *ARLC* 1930, 6–10; ARSRR, 1929–30.

16. Annual Report of the Chief of the Music Division, 1923–24, LCA; ARSRR, 1928–29.

17. ARSRR 1938–39.

18. ARSRR 1923–24. Library employees also had limited borrowing privileges; see General Order No. 585, November 25, 1924, box 158, Central File, LCA.

19. Robert Staughton Lynd and Helen Merrell Lynd, *Middletown in Transition* (New York: Harcourt, Brace, 1937), 252–53, 570.

20. ARSRR, 1926–27.

21. Arthur E. Bostwick, "The Library's Place in a Changing World," *Library Journal* 58, no. 22 (December 15, 1933): 6.

22. ARSRR, 1926–27; 1928–29, 1935–36; Martin Roberts to Herbert Putnam, February 17, 1936, box 159, Central File, LCA.

23. Lesser use of some Library of Congress collections was undoubtedly due to the specialized collections available elsewhere in the area, notably, the Surgeon-General's Library (now the National Library of Medicine), the Department of Agriculture (now the National Agricultural Library), and the U.S. Geological Survey Library. By the mid-1930s, too, the Library of Congress's Smithsonian Division had extended hours to 10:00 p.m. on weekdays and offered weekend service, shifting some of the demand for science materials to that division.

24. ARSRR, 1924–25, 1926–27, 1938–39.

25. ARSRR, 1926–27, 1927–28.

26. Ellis Hawley, *The Great War and the Search for a Modern Order: A History of the American People and Their Institutions, 1917–1933*, 2nd ed. (New York: St. Martin's, 1992), 43–44; Barry D. Karl, "Foundations and Public Policy," in *Encyclopedia of the United States in the Twentieth Century*, 4 vols., ed. Stanley I. Kutler et al. (New York: Charles Scribner's Sons, 1996), 3:493–99.

27. ARSRR, 1928–29.

28. *Washington Post*, May 23, 1931, 4.

29. ARSRR, 1932–33; *ARLC* 1935, 270. The opening of the Annex Building (now the Adams Building) on April 5, 1939, helped to remedy the acute space problems.

30. Thomas H. M. Blair, "I See You Read: A Glimpse into the Library of Congress," *Library Journal* 62 (February 15, 1937): 157–59.

31. ARSRR, 1935–36.

32. James T. Patterson, *America in the Twentieth Century: A History*, 5th ed. (Fort Worth, TX: Harcourt College Publishers, 2000), 186; Kenneth J. Lipartito and Paul J. Moranti Jr., "The Professions," in Kutler et al., *Encyclopedia of the United States*, 3:1419; Hawley, *Great War*, 116.

33. ARSRR, 1932–33.

34. A survey of more than six hundred libraries covering 1930–32 revealed reduced budgets nationwide in medium-sized and large libraries and noted the increased demands for library services. Book budgets were cut by approximately 12 to 19 percent. See Douglas Waples, Leon Carnovsky, and William Randall, "The Public Library in the Depression," *Library Quarterly* 2 (October 1932): 321–43.

35. ARSRR, 1936–37. Between 1920 and 1929, nine new federal bureaus were established. Between 1930 and 1939, the total rose to sixty-one new agencies, fifty-six of which were established between 1933 and 1939. The first burst of New Deal legislation, between 1933 and 1936, established thirty-four agencies. See Solomon Fabricant, *The Trend of Government Activity in the United States since 1900* (Millwood, NY: Kraus Reprint, 1975), 69–70, and Caroll H. Woody, *The Growth of the Federal Government, 1915–1932* (New York: McGraw-Hill, 1934), 547–51.

36. ARSRR, 1938–39.

PART 2

Public Libraries, Readers, and Localities

Going to "America"

Italian Neighborhoods and the Newark Free Public Library, 1900–1920

ELLEN M. POZZI

"I have been down to America today." Enrico Sartorio overheard this phrase more than once in the early decades of the twentieth century, uttered by Italian women who had ventured a few blocks outside of the ethnic enclave where they lived.[1] Lillian Betts studied Italian immigrants in the Mulberry Street area of New York City in the early 1900s and noted that "within this limit of territory . . . all worked, all their social affiliations were established and it was all of America they knew."[2] Sartorio saw this isolation as a form of self-preservation; "as soon as they step outside of the Italian colony they are almost as helpless as babies, owing to their lack of knowledge of the language, customs and laws of this country."[3]

In *The Practice of Everyday Life*, Michel de Certeau describes immigrants to France using tactics to adapt their neighborhoods to their needs. "A North African living in Paris or Roubaix (France)," he says, "insinuates *into* the system imposed on him by the construction of a low-income housing development or of the French language the ways of 'dwelling' (in a house or a language) peculiar to his native Kabylia. He . . . creates for himself a space in which he can find *ways of using* the constraining order of the place or of the language." Forced into poor living conditions in cities by both economics and prejudice, Italian immigrants adapted to the constraints placed on them. They re-created the familiar elements of the villages and towns of their home country; established bakeries, macaroni shops, stores that sold Italian wine and oil; and re-created rituals, such as religious festivals and processions that honored patron saints.[4]

Even behavior patterns were transplanted to the new world. Observed one inhabitant, "People do exactly as they did in Cinisi. . . . [I]f someone varies, he or she will be criticized."[5] According to de Certeau and Pierre Mayol, "as a result of the practical everyday use of this space" the public space of the neighborhood becomes a *"private, particularized space."*[6] The public streets and shops became a private space that extended immigrants' limited living spaces. According to Pozzetta, "streets were the meeting places providing a setting for an intricate network of social relationships."[7]

Inside the boundaries of the ethnic enclave, and within the private, public spaces that provided the physical space for the creation of networks, there existed a conceptual space for gathering information, coexistent with the geographical enclave, or what can be called an information neighborhood.[8] The Italian neighborhoods of Newark, New Jersey, in the early 1900s contained the various sources, or information nodes, that comprised an information neighborhood, including print and oral material available in libraries, bookstores, newspapers, and religious or other institutions; from social support services; passed on by friends, acquaintances, or community leaders; and circulated through ethnic communication networks. Situating the library within the information neighborhood creates a framework for understanding the library in the life of immigrants and answering Wayne A. Wiegand's call to write about the "role of the library in the life of the user" rather than the "role of the user in the life of the library."[9] Exploring the information neighborhood provides a way to approach the study of immigrant library users from their perspective.

ENCLAVES

As Italian immigration to the United States burgeoned in the 1880s and continued to grow in the early twentieth century, enclaves known as Little Italies began to appear in cities, including Newark, New Jersey. From the 1880s to the 1920s, the Italian portion of Newark's population grew from one of the smallest to one of the largest, outpacing even the earlier German settlement, and by 1920 the city had the fifth-largest Italian population in the United States, even though Newark was not ranked in the top ten most populated cities; only New York, Philadelphia, Chicago, and Boston had larger Italian populations.[10] The Italians near the business center of Newark settled in three main enclaves as shown in a map produced in 1911 detailing their locations and sizes.[11] The First Ward was the home of the first Italians who settled in Newark. Another large enclave along the Passaic River was nicknamed the Ironbound or Down Neck section. The smallest neighborhood, home to later arrivals, only a few streets wide and deep, was referred to as the 14th Avenue enclave.[12] In Boston's Italian enclaves, "one can find in the Italian colony a

Sicilian, a Calabrian, a Neapolitan, an Abruzzian village, all within a few blocks, and each with its peculiar traditions, manner of living, and dialect," and this was also true of Newark's Italian neighborhoods.[13]

An Italian immigrant writing in 1906 observed, "The statement of an Italian carries more weight with his fellow-countrymen than that of ten Americans put together."[14] This cognitive authority was granted more easily to those from same region or village in Italy, which would more often have been found within the familiar social settings constructed by immigrants within their neighborhoods.[15] Within immigrants' localized worldview, the most-trusted sources were those who operated within the "private, particularized space" that was created within enclaves.[16] The information neighborhood within these enclaves contained a variety of sources of information, or information nodes, which ranged on a continuum from formal to informal and from print to oral. Within this conceptualization of the Italian information neighborhood, the library, the immigrant press, friends and family, religious institutions, the padrone system, and other institutions that acted as information sources—such as stores, saloons, and societies or organizations—were all information nodes.

INFORMATION NODES

In 1889, the city of Newark established the Newark Free Public Library in the building that formerly housed a subscription library known as the Newark Library Association. The newly founded free public library opened its first deposit stations in 1891 but ended the experiment five months later. Reporting the closures, library director Frank Hill noted requests for reestablishment of the service and said, "The matter is deserving of consideration, as to attain its highest degree of usefulness the library should reach all classes and give equal facilities to all sections of the city." By 1894 six deposit stations had been reopened, and the library system continued to grow until in 1911 it included the main building of the Newark Free Public Library, seven branches, including one designated as the Foreign Branch, and eleven deposit stations. Overlaying the locations of the main library, its branches, and its deposit stations in 1911 onto a map of immigrant enclaves in Newark generates a diagram of the institutional space of the library at this particular point in time and illuminates its relationship to the Italian neighborhoods. The larger First Ward did not contain any branches or deposit stations, although the main library building was situated several blocks to the south, and a deposit station in Galloway & Company and the Clark Street Branch were located on the northern border of the enclave. Another branch was located a few streets to the west of the First Ward, housed within the high school.[17]

The Ironbound section was the only Italian enclave to have a library presence—both a branch and a deposit station—within its borders. The Ferry Street Branch was within the borders of the enclave as depicted on the 1911 map but east of the neighborhoods of the Ironbound most heavily populated by Italians.[18] Despite its location within the footprint of the Italian neighborhood, a floor plan of the Ferry Street Branch at this time identifies a "high case for German Polish and Lithuanian books" but does not indicate a section for Italian books.[19] The deposit station in the Ironbound section was located in a settlement house not far from the branch but still outside the area with the densest Italian population. The Business Branch was west of this enclave, and another deposit station was south. The 14th Avenue enclave was the smallest of the three Italian neighborhoods, and the library did not have a presence within its confines. The Foreign Branch was located several streets southeast. The boundaries of the area served by this branch (as defined by the library) included the 14th Avenue enclave in its entirety, and Italians were part of the reported "70,000 people from other countries" within its service area.[20]

The first foreign books in this branch were German but "soon urgent requests poured in from several nationalities for books in their own language." The branch director, Catherine Van Dyne, reported, "When the first Yiddish and Hebrew books were placed at the branch . . . their use was amazing. The use of the library by adults was greatly increased. . . . The Yiddish are the most popular of all the foreign books and the collection has been gradually increased so now there are about 600 volumes in use."[21] Not surprisingly, the 1911 map reveals the branch was located directly within the (only) Jewish neighborhood in Newark. However, at the time of the 1911 map, the Foreign Branch did not contain any Italian books, and would not until 1914. Italian-language books moved among the main library and branches over the years. In 1907 Italian books were located on the third floor of the main library. In 1909 Italian-language books from the children's collection were relocated with other Italian books in the main library. For a brief period in 1910, Italian books were available at the Foreign Branch, but in 1911 they were back at the main library, along with some German and French books. In 1914, Italian books were moved to the Foreign Branch, then the second biggest branch in terms of collection size, containing ten thousand books.[22] While this branch served some foreign populations well, particularly the residents of its Jewish neighborhood, Italian immigrants who did not choose to leave their enclaves would find the library outside of the trajectories of their everyday lives.

When the lack of library branches and deposit stations within Italian neighborhoods made "going to America" a necessity for, and a possible barrier to, acquiring books and other material from the library, there were alternative information sources within the neighborhoods. The print culture within the communities included newspapers printed in Italian as well as books and newspapers published in Italy and sold in bookstores and by newsagents within the enclave. Oscar Handlin recognized the immigrant press as the source of information, noting that "in the new world there was no life without some kinds of knowledge" that could be acquired in this press and newspapers were the "instruments through which the immigrants learned to interpret the issues and events of the larger American society within which they were situated," although Charles Jaret argues that the Italian press more often included articles from the home press and about events in Italy than about American events.[23] Fourteen Italian papers were published in Italian in Newark between 1894 and 1920. Some were issued for a month or two; others were published for many years; and *La Montagna*, a weekly paper printed in the First Ward, was published continuously until 1920.[24] *La Frusta*, issued from 1900 to 1914, published letters to the editor, advertisements, news from the neighborhood, news from Italy, notices of community events, and serialized novels.[25]

The immigrant press provided a vehicle for the dissemination of information to the literate population of immigrants and, through the oral culture of the neighborhood, to nonliterate members. One of Newark's English papers reported this oral culture in action:

> The gangs of Italians start work at 7 o'clock in the morning and work in the sun until noon. It is a remarkable scene during the meal hour. There is not covering enough to accommodate half of them, and each selects his favorite pile on the dump, and rain or shine, calmly disposes of his food. One will pull out a ragged copy of an Italian paper and will soon be surrounded by a crowd of eager listeners. . . . After the half-hour allowed for lunch the men and women return to their various jobs and labor until 5 o'clock.[26]

The Italian paper referred to could have been published in Italy and purchased in the enclave from Domenico Orgo, who sold general, literary, political, scientific, and humor papers of Italy.[27] Or it could have been one of the Italian papers published in Newark, such as *La Frusta*, which carried Orgo's

advertisements in several of its 1903 issues. The main branch of the Newark
Free Public Library had available donated copies of *La Frusta* and *L'Ora*.[28]
Also, a member of the Italian community, Mr. Magnano, Newark's Italian
consul, donated four Italian daily newspapers from Milan, Naples, Palermo,
and Rome to the library, and patrons could read these by requesting them
from the librarian; they were not freely available in the reading room.[29]

Orgo was also a bookseller and advertised the availability of novels, or *il
romanzo mensile*, Italian translations of English and French novels published
in Italy, and printed in journal form. Several Romanzo Mensile publications
were serialized in *La Frusta* in 1903 and 1904.[30] George Pozzetta provides
a sample of other items that were available in the "bookstalls and small
libraries [that] abounded in the Mulberry district" of New York. The material
included "great literature classics . . . comic sheets and Neapolitan dialect
love songs . . . and innumerable tragic or amorous novelettes by Carolina Inver-
nizio and other popular writers."[31] Robert Ferrari, whose father immigrated in
1872, reports that as a young man he went to the Mulberry Street Book Store
in New York for his Italian books, where he found Galileo's *Dialogues*;
Goldoni's complete works, including the Venetian dialect comedies; *The Satires
of Juvenal*; many translations from the Latin and Greek; Manzoni's *I Promessi
Sposi* (The betrothed); and three or four volumes of Edmondo D'Amici's
novels and his *L'Idomia Gentile* (Cultivated usage).[32]

Family, friends and *paesanos* were also part of the network that existed
in information neighborhoods in the United States but also extended back to
the home country. Often, it was through these networks that immigrants
heard of opportunities in the Americas, and the networks continued to operate once immigrants were established in their new homes. A pioneer immigrant to Newark, like Angelo Mattia, thought to be one of the first Italians
to immigrate to the First Ward in 1873, did not have a network of family and
friends when he arrived. Mattia's wife joined him in 1874, and her brother,
Alfonso Ilaria, also came to Newark at the same time, providing the beginnings of a web of connections. Ilaria became a source of information for later
settlers, helping them find jobs and lodging in a boarding house he co-owned
with a German woman.[33] Gerardo Spatola, another early Italian settler in the
First Ward, also assisted later waves of immigrants. Some newcomers arrived
with only a piece of paper with Spatola's name written on it.[34] The name
on the paper was that immigrant's keyword that allowed him to access information stored in Spatola's web of connections and experiences, which would
provide access to jobs and places to stay.

Alfonso Ilaria was part of the padrone system, another node in the information neighborhood. *Padroni* operated as a point of contact between immigrants, particularly those who did not speak English, and employers. In Sicily, a padrone was a person who owned something, or worked independently, or someone "who controlled the work of or 'owned' the social loyalties of another person." "Boss" is not an accurate translation, according to Donna Gabaccia, because it carries the implication of employment, which was usually not the relationship between padrone and immigrant.[35] In the United States the padrone's role was that of a labor agent, acting as an intermediary between employer and employee, and he was not always part of the social network of friends and family but came from within the Italian community and therefore was trusted as a source of information. His role providing information leading to jobs and to places for immigrants to live put him at the center of an important information network for those just arriving in Newark.

An Italian immigrant who had been born in Italy recalled his role as a padrone and banker for Italians in his Newark community. In an interview conducted in the late 1930s for the Federal Writers' Projects' New Jersey Ethnic Survey, this anonymous Newark resident described how he learned English more quickly than his *paesanos* and was able to secure employment for fellow countrymen. He lent them money, provided lodgings for newcomers, and served as a banker.[36] In his study of the padrone system, Luciano Iorizzo notes, "It was through the *padroni* that many Italians could find a place to eat and sleep, get a job, save money, bring their families over, return to the old country for a vacation or permanently, and enjoy the company of their countrymen."[37]

Padroni were not always benign sources of information. Some operated under an indentured servant model, and even those who didn't often charged excessive prices for lodgings or may have cheated their customers when operating as bankers.[38] However, they were often trusted because they were from within the neighborhood and were Italian. Sartorio's observation about the worth of an Italian's word over an American's is evident in the trust of padroni. However, padroni formed an essential node for some Italian immigrants looking for work and lodging in the United States.

Religion was an integral part of Italian life. In Newark, as each of the Italian enclaves grew the community established an Italian Roman Catholic church. Along with their clerical duties, priests acted as information sources and intermediaries. In an unpublished memoir, Italian immigrant Salvatore Castagnola describes how Italians were timid when they had to deal with American institutions but trusted their priests. "Hence Father Vogel was not only the spiritual advisor but the general information bureau for the community. The church became the civic center, the charitable mother, and the 'abriga faccende' or clearing house for all sorts of trouble."[39]

The effectiveness of religious institutions probably depended on the nationality of the priest or pastor. Peter DiDonato and Jerre Mangione wrote fictionalized autobiographical books about their experiences of life in Italian communities in the early part of the twentieth century; these describe ethnicity as a factor in the priest's ability to connect with his parishioners. Mangione presents the church as a peripheral institution in the community because the priest was Irish, not part of the Italian community. In DiDonato's *Three Circles of Light*, the priest was Italian and related to individuals in the neighborhood, and therefore was an integral and trusted part of the information neighborhood.[40] Although most Italians were Catholic, Newark also had Italian Methodist and Presbyterian congregations. The First Presbyterian Church of Newark established an Italian mission with an Italian pastor. It had 125 Italian members, who lived within six blocks of the church, while only a handful belonged to the larger church, located farther away.[41] The location of this church and the ethnicity of the pastor seem to have filled a need within the community, regardless of its denomination.

Other public social places were also information spaces for Italian immigrants. Marie Jastrow, writing about her own immigrant mother, says, "the grocery store was the first place where . . . [she] got much necessary information (for example where to look for a better apartment), and then there were helpful neighbors and friends from the old country that her mother made in time."[42] Grocery stores, streets, and saloons provided spaces for the exchange of information. Alfonso Ilaria's saloon at 31 Boyden Street became the focal point of the First Ward colony in Newark: "his saloon, known as the Bee Hive, was a haven for Italians and a source of news."[43] In the Ironbound section, social worker Willard D. Price reported in 1912 that 114 of 122 saloons in the district had "tables and chairs for social purposes"; thus, men found them "a convenient meeting place, work and wages are discussed, political arguments are frequent and recent immigrants discover it an admirable school in which to learn English rapidly and gain an acquaintance with things American." The saloons were also used as meeting places for social and political associations, and Price deemed them to "fill a real and vital social need."[44]

Mutual benefit societies provided places for the exchange of information and establishing social networks. Other social societies included Italian Republican clubs, the Columbian Guards, and various societies that advertised picnics held in halls and parks in Newark.[45] All of these facilitated the informal exchange of information within neighborhoods and among Italian immigrants.

INSTITUTIONAL VIEW

The subtitle of an article in the *Newarker* in 1912 describing the Foreign Branch is "What One Branch Is Doing to Help Make Several Thousand New Good American Citizens," indicating the focus of the branch's work from the library's perspective. The article was pitched to the ears of the business leaders in the city as a plea for a new building because the branch's limited space was so heavily used. As the article appears in a publication produced explicitly for the business community, its implicit assumption is that the idea of creating good citizens out of poor and immigrant workers appealed to businessmen, who would then support funding for the library.[46]

After describing the size of different foreign book collections, and the demand for these books, the branch manager asserts, "All these collections are proof of the foreigner's desire to read." The article continues, "New foreign books are not added unless the need is very urgent on account of the expense and labor of buying and cataloging foreign books and the recognized claims of the American reader." The demand for books in foreign languages rebutted the idea of illiterate immigrants and is a vivid picture of immigrants' agency in asking for books in their native language, even though the library's emphasis was on providing those resources that "make good new American citizens."[47] Beatrice Winser, assistant library director at Newark Free Public Library, demonstrated the concern over the purpose of books acquired for immigrants; a newspaper reported her response to the donation of one hundred Italian-language books from members of the community: "It is not the function of the public library to keep alive Italian and Austrian customs, but the books presented to the library for this collection do not tend to do that. We are Americans, and we want to make American citizens of them. These books will not hinder that effort, for they number among them some of the best Italian classics, though a few modern novels have also been received."[48]

The librarians acknowledged that "foreigners and their children are insatiable readers."[49] Although the demand was high, there were limited resources available for foreign-language readers, as might be expected, given the policies articulated on the purchase of foreign books. In 1913 only 750 Italian books were in the library system, when more than 25,000 Italians were living in Newark.[50] These books also had the highest circulation per book of any of the foreign-language books.[51] The few Italian books in the system were being read, even though most access points for library material were located outside the enclaves in "America."

One explanation for this may be gleaned from clues in the *Newarker*. In a photograph of the Foreign Branch in a 1913 article, many children are lined up in front of the branch, anxious to get into the library.[52] The article mentions that due to the overcrowding of the library, children were only allowed in the branch during certain hours. Abigail Van Slyck notes children were likely to use the public space of the library as part of the space of their neighborhoods, in much the same way they used the streets as extensions of their living spaces.[53] Immigrant children (both those born of immigrant parents and those arriving from Italy) were influenced by their experiences in public schools, another educational and Americanizing institution. Their everyday trajectories brought them into contact with individuals and institutions outside the neighborhood. They acted as a bridge, connecting their parents in the privatized public space of the ethnic enclave with the public sphere of the library.

Newark Free Public Library developed an extensive system of "libraries," boxes of forty or fifty English-language children's books that were sent to the city's public schools.[54] The library's annual report for 1903 comments that "very often a teacher receives a note from a parent asking that she may have, for her own enjoyment, some book which her child has mentioned as being in the class library [traveling library]. In this way we are reaching both old and young."[55] Although Italian-language books were not available through this channel, access to library material was provided through children. Children became familiar with the institution and the public space of the library. The demand for Italian books may be explained by the willingness of children of immigrants to cross the boundaries of the immigrant enclave and reach out to the formal information nodes in the form of the public library.

CONCLUSION

Given the importance of Little Italies and other ethnic enclaves in the lives of immigrants during the Gilded and Progressive eras, understanding the role of reading and libraries in their lives requires an examination of these neighborhoods. Reconstructing the information neighborhood of Italian immigrants within the ethnic enclaves of Newark helps peel back the institutional focus of library history to reveal the role of libraries within the private, particularized space that contained other information sources used by Italian immigrants. This research contributes to the larger project Wiegand suggested—exploring the role of the library in the life of the user—by situating the library in the larger context of the information ecology of Italian immigrants, one in which the library was one source of information among many.

Library branches were not well situated within the Italian enclaves in Newark, and other sources of information were available within the trajectories of their residents' everyday lives. However, based on reports of the use of and demand for books, libraries were able to draw some immigrants outside of their enclaves, either directly or indirectly through children's access to the library. However, libraries did not respond to the demands of their Italian patrons or grant the same importance to foreign-language books as they did to English books, and they did not situate their services within the Italian communities, even though they recognized the importance of locating the Foreign Branch near foreign communities. Those immigrants who wanted to become American citizens or who were interested in assimilating might have sought out the library, even though it was outside their neighborhood. But the library may not have played a large role for those Italian immigrants who wanted other things from it, such as fiction in their own languages, and for those who did not want to go to "America."

NOTES

Research for this essay has been supported by a grant from the Immigrant History Research Center at the University of Minnesota, and a Eugene Garfield Doctoral Dissertation Fellowship from Beta Phi Mu.

1. Enrico Sartorio, *Social and Religious Life of Italians in America* (Boston: Christopher Publishing House, 1918), 19.

2. Betts quoted in George E. Pozzetta, "The Mulberry District of New York City," in *Little Italies of North America*, ed. Robert F. Herney and J. Vincenze Scarpaci (Toronto: Multicultural History Society of Ontario, 1981), 25.

3. Sartorio, *Social and Religious Life*, 18.

4. Michel de Certeau, *The Practice of Everyday Life*, trans. Steven Rendall (Berkeley: University of California Press, 1984), 30; Herbert Gans, *The Urban Villagers: Group and Class in the Life of Italian-Americans*, updated and expanded ed. (New York: Free Press, 1982), 4; Michael Immerso, *Newark's Little Italy: The Vanished First Ward* (New Brunswick, NJ: Rutgers University Press, 1999).

5. Pozzetta, "Mulberry District," 19.

6. Michel de Certeau, Luce Giard, and Pierre Mayol, *The Practice of Everyday Life*, vol. 2, *Living and Cooking*, trans. Timothy J. Tomasik (Minneapolis: University of Minnesota Press, 1998), 9.

7. Pozzetta, "Mulberry District," 24.

8. The information neighborhood is a multinodal infrastructure that encompasses the information sources available in an individual's or a group's circuit of everyday

living. Thanks to Marija Dalbello for her inspiration and guidance in the development of the articulation of this conceptualization of the information neighborhood.

9. Wayne A. Wiegand, "Tunnel Vision and Blind Spots: What the Past Tells Us about the Present: Reflections on the Twentieth-Century History of American Librarianship," *Library Quarterly* 69 (January 1991): 24. Wiegand credits Douglas Zweizig for this concept.

10. William Bolen, "The Changing Geography of Italian Immigrants in the United States: A Case Study of the Ironbound Colony, Newark, NJ" (PhD diss., Rutgers, The State University of New Jersey, 1986), 76.

11. A. W. MacDougall, *The Resources for Social Service: Charitable, Civic, Educational, Religious, of Newark, New Jersey: A Classified and Descriptive Directory* (New York: Knickerbocker Press, 1912). The map's legend reads: "This map, the only one of its kind, was commissioned by the leaders of the Presbyterian Church in Newark in 1910 as a part of a study of the city's health needs."

12. The early settlement of the neighborhoods in Newark is described in Bolen, "Changing Geography"; Charles W. Churchill, *The Italians of Newark: A Community Study* (New York: Arno, 1975); Immerso, *Newark's Little Italy*; and Willard Price, *"The Ironbound District": A Study of a District in Newark, N.J.* (Newark: n.p., 1912).

13. Sartorio, *Social and Religious Life*, 18; Churchill, *Italians of Newark*; Immerso, *Newark's Little Italy*.

14. Sartorio, *Social and Religious Life*, 43.

15. Patrick Wilson, *Second-Hand Knowledge: An Inquiry into Cognitive Authority* (Westport, CT: Greenwood, 1983).

16. Writing about another population within a constrained environment, Elfreda Chatman notes that prisoners have a "localized worldview, centered on everyday concerns." Within this localized worldview, "information is credible because the provider is trusted." Elfreda Chatman, "A Theory of Life in the Round," *Journal of the American Society for Information Science* 50, no. 3 (1999): 215.

17. Newark Free Public Library (NFPL), 1891 Annual Report, 15; NFPL, 1892 Annual Report, 31; NFPL, 1894 Annual Report, 16–17. On the location of deposit stations and branches in 1910, see *Newark City Directory* (Newark, NJ: Price & Lee Company, 1911); enclave map from MacDougall, *Resources for Social Service*. Digital Sanborn Maps (detailed fire insurance maps that include every street name and house/business address) were used to determine locations of the branches and deposit stations based on address, then both were manually superimposed onto the trolley map of Newark published in the *Newarker* (hereafter 1911 map). It was not possible to reproduce the 1911 map here, but see Ellen M. Pozzi, "The Public Library in an Immigrant Neighborhood: A Case Study of Italian Immigrants' Information Ecologies in Newark (NJ), 1889–1919" (PhD diss., Rutgers University, 2013).

18. This is based on 1915 census map reproduced in Bolen, "Changing Geography," 161.

19. "Floor Plan of the Ferry Street Branch," *Newarker: A Journal Published to Introduce a City to Itself and to Its Public Library* 4 (December 1914): 27.

20. L.H.M., "The Foreigners in Newark" (December 1913), rpr. in *Three Years of "The Newarker": A Journal Published to Introduce a City to Itself and to Its Public Library*, 3 vols. (Newark, NJ: Essex Press, 1914), 3:424.

21. Catherine Van Dyne, "The Springfield Avenue Library" (September 1912), rpr. in *Three Years of "The Newarker,"* 2:178.

22. Newark Free Public Library Staff Notebooks, 1903–12, November 18, 1907, 86; July 19, 1909, n.p.; November 10, 1910, n.p.; April 13, 1911, n.p., Charles F. Cummings New Jersey Information Center, Newark Public Library.

23. Oscar Handlin, *The Uprooted: The Epic Story of the Great Migrations That Made the American People*, 2nd ed. (Philadelphia: University of Pennsylvania Press, 2002), 160, 161; Charles Jaret, "The Greek, Italian, and Jewish Ethnic Press: A Comparative Analysis," *Journal of Ethnic Studies* 7 (Summer 1979): 47–70.

24. William Wright and Paul A. Stellhorn, eds., *Directory of New Jersey Newspapers, 1765–1970* (Trenton: New Jersey Historical Commission, 1977).

25. Few copies of the Italian-language papers published in Newark are available. The New Jersey Historical Society in Newark has issues of *La Frusta* published in 1903–4 in their archives.

26. *Newark Evening News*, May 18, 1902. Quoted in Bolen, "Changing Geography," 171.

27. *"I giornali d'Italia utlimi arrivati di ogni genere, letterarii, politici, scentifici ed umoristici,"* *La Frusta*, advertisement, 1903.

28. NFPL, 1904 Annual Report, 65.

29. Newark Free Public Library Staff notebook, n.d., 117, between pages dated May 1908 and June 8, 1908.

30. *La Frusta*, advertisements, 1903.

31. Pozzetta, "Mulberry District," 24–25.

32. Robert Ferrari, unpublished autobiography, Robert Ferrari Papers, 1912–65, Italian American Collection, Immigration History Research Center, University of Minnesota.

33. Immerso, *Newark's Little Italy*.

34. Gerard Zanfini and Michael D. Immerso, First Ward Italian Collection (photographs), 1997, n.p., Charles F. Cummings New Jersey Information Center, Newark Public Library.

35. Donna Gabaccia, *From Sicily to Elizabeth Street: Housing and Social Change among Italian Immigrants, 1880–1930* (Albany: State University of New York Press, 1984), 5, 7.

36. David Cohen, *America, The Dream of My Life: Selections from the Federal Writers' Projects' New Jersey Ethnic Survey* (New Brunswick, NJ: Rutgers University Press, 1990), 63–67.

37. Luciano John Iorizzo, *Italian Immigration and the Impact of the Padrone System* (New York: Arno, 1980), 99.

38. Iorizzo claims early padroni (before 1910) were paid for the workers they brought to jobs, and then paid laborers from that income, often short changing them,

thus acquiring a bad reputation. He explains that this changed after 1910; padroni became organizers of laborers, and immigrants were paid directly.

39. Salvatore Castagnola, unpublished autobiography, Salvatore Castagnola Papers, 1893–1909, Italian American Collection, Immigrant History Research Center, University of Minnesota.

40. Jerre Mangione, *Mount Allegro: A Memoir of Italian American Life* (New York: Harper & Row, 1982); Pietro DiDonato, *Three Circles of Light* (New York: Julian Messner, 1960).

41. First Presbyterian Church, *Manual of the First Presbyterian Church of Newark, NJ: By Order of the Session, January 1911* (Newark, NJ: The Church, 1911).

42. Anca-Luminta Iancu, "Visible Invisibility: Literacy Practices of Non-English Speaking European-American Immigrant Women (1835–1930)" (PhD diss., University of Louisville, 2009), 142.

43. Immerso, *Newark's Little Italy*, 6.

44. Price, *"Ironbound District,"* 9.

45. *La Frusta*, various articles and advertisements, 1903–4.

46. Catherine Van Dyne, "Springfield Avenue Library" (September 1912), rpr. in *Three Years of "The Newarker,"* 1:177–79.

47. Ibid., 178, 177.

48. "Italians Give Books," *Newark Daily Advertiser*, Newark Free Public Library Clippings Scrapbooks, October 10, 1905, Charles F. Cummings New Jersey Information Center, Newark Public Library.

49. John Cotton Dana, "Library Report for 1913" (February 1914), rpr. in *Three Years of "The Newarker,"* 3:456.

50. "Books in Foreign Languages in the Library" (August 1913), rpr. in *Three Years of "The Newarker,"* 2:360.

51. "Fiction Room" (February 1914), rpr. in *Three Years of "The Newarker,"* 3:462.

52. John Cotton Dana, "Springfield Avenue Branch Readers: They Need a Library Building" (December 1913), rpr. in *Three Years of "The Newarker,"* 3:426.

53. Abigail Van Slyck, *Free to All: Carnegie Libraries & American Culture, 1890–1920* (Chicago: University of Chicago Press, 1995), 202.

54. NFPL, 1898 Annual Report.

55. NFPL, 1903 Annual Report, 27.

"A Liberal and Dignified Approach"

The John Toman Branch of the Chicago Public Library and the Making of Americans, 1927–1940

JOYCE M. LATHAM

Abram Korman, chief of the foreign-language department of the Chicago Public Library (CPL), expressed his philosophy of service to the foreign born in an unpublished 1935 article titled "Present and Future Status of Foreign Language Work in Chicago." He observed that 27 percent of the city's population was foreign born, with another million residents first-generation Americans. He wrote that in

> serving the needs of these various elements of a cosmopolitan community . . . [w]e are not interested in rushing the Americanization of the foreigner by curtailing his reading of foreign books, by directing his reading to English literature, or by plying him with lists of juvenile books on language and American history. The Library's resources, both in English and in foreign literature, are open to him, and he is free to read what he will. . . . We find that the interests of true Americanism are best served by this liberal and dignified approach to the needs of our foreign population.[1]

Chicago was second only to New York in its concentration of immigrant populations. Based on data drawn from the 1920 census, it had a population of 2,701,705, which accounted for over 40 percent of the population of the state of Illinois.[2] Of the 2 million plus city residents, 805,482 were "Foreign born white"; residents classified as "foreign or mixed parentage"—one parent was a "foreign born white"—totaled 1,140,816. Only 642,871 residents were characterized as "Native white." Nonwhites accounted for 112,536.[3] This concentration of ethnic diversity incorporated German, Russian, Polish, Italian, and Czech populations in high numbers, as well as Irish and British, among others. Chicago was also a destination for southern African Americans during the Great Migration of the 1920s and 1930s.

Motivations behind Americanization reflected the various agendas of the agencies and institutions engaged in the practice. Classes offered by the dominant corporate industries, such as the Ford "Five Dollar Day" incentive program, sought to develop compliant workers, while classes such as those offered by the Women's Trade Union League sought to encourage educated workers.[4] Some programs drew on interpretations of patriotism, while others promoted Americanization as a means of achieving economic justice. Philanthropic organizations, such as the Carnegie Corporation of New York, supported Americanization efforts with grants and subsidies. The American Library Association's Committee on Work with the Foreign Born advocated a tolerance for foreign cultures while making the means of Americanization available.[5] Whatever the purposes behind these various strategies, most represented a top-down approach to immigrant reorientation and citizenship. Public libraries engaged in a variety of strategies, incorporating, modifying, and resisting these multiple initiatives. Libraries were among the many institutions that emerged as negotiated spaces through these programs, whether addressing issues of ethnicity, nationality, race, or class. Through outreach, programming, and collection development, public librarians engaged the question of "American" as a fluid identity.[6]

The tensions between the definitions of American identity and the re-memorization of root cultures surfaced vividly in the John Toman Branch of CPL, as the Old Settlers of the Lawndale-Crawford community affirmed their identity in response to the promotion of a Bohemian Czech culture ascendant in the city. A review of departmental- and branch-level institutional records housed in the Chicago Public Library special collections department, supplemented with the American Library Association archival collection, supports a presentation of an urban community actively engaged in multicultural repositioning through and within the local public library.

Carlton Joeckel and Leon Carnovsky, in their study *A Municipal Library in Action*, described the foreign department of the Chicago Public Library as "the headquarters for all matters concerning library materials in languages other than English . . . responsible for the selection, cataloging and classification, and allotment to the various service agencies of all foreign books. It compiles foreign book lists and handles reference questions in foreign languages. . . . The chief of the department is active in promoting the use of the foreign collections of the library and in making contacts with foreign population groups and numerous national organizations."[7] Korman wrote that the actual focus on a coherent service model addressing immigrant groups began in Chicago around 1922–23, when the library created a centralized department dedicated to selecting, cataloging, annotating, and disseminating foreign-language materials. The departmental collection had grown from twenty thousand foreign books in 1923 to approximately a hundred thousand books in twenty-seven languages on the open shelves in 1932; another ten thousand volumes were housed in reference collections.[8] The foreign-language collection was small, however, relative to the broader collection and to collections in similar urban centers.[9]

Korman struggled to expand the collection and maintain the department. His 1932 report for the service year 1931 indicates that the library spent $7,562 to add 7,708 volumes in fifteen different languages. For the first time, the circulation of foreign-language materials had surpassed the half-million mark and the increase in foreign-language circulation was greater than the increase in general circulation. He considered "how much of that increase is due to the larger proportion of foreign unemployed and how much to the growing interest and activity with the foreign born. . . . It seems to me that the increasing interest in foreign work is due less to a growth of civic consciousness among the foreign born than to a hopeful change in our attitude to the foreigner." More materials were being distributed to branch libraries, and he highlighted the "remarkable work" done in the John Toman, Douglas, and Hild Branches with various national groups. For CPL and its small collections, the focus was on outreach and engagement with immigrant communities.[10]

Korman did use his reports to advocate for a change in the approach of the administration to the foreign-language department. While the report on 1931 activities highlighted the addition of two junior assistants fluent in German, by February of 1934 he was arguing for the retention of his more experienced assistants who were at risk of removal as temporary employees, one of whom had served for ten years. He requested civil service tests and appointments for the staff to enable their transfer to full-time permanent positions. Two of the employees scored well enough to qualify for appointments, but the city was slow to fund these permanent positions.[11] In the later 1930s, Works Progress Administration (WPA) workers provided some additional support, but the failure to honor civil service practice in the hiring and retention of city employees was an issue for the library, one Korman himself challenged. He organized the CPL staff union in 1937 as a local of the emerging State, County, and Municipal Workers of America, a Congress of Industrial Organizations public employee union. The foreign-language chief was a natural bridge between the worker class and the professional class, the immigrant and the native-born Americans.[12] Korman was also representative of that leadership within the library profession, which favored cultural pluralism and open borders.[13]

The 1920s were a particularly restless decade in the history of immigration in the United States, as the 1910s were a particularly active one for workers. There was a constant drum of labor events: the Triangle Shirtwaist fire in New York City in 1911; the Lawrence, Massachusetts, mill strike in 1912; the Ludlow massacre in Colorado in 1914. The International Workers of the World—the IWW, or Wobblies—launched a work slowdown in the lumber camps of the American Northwest in 1917; also that year, Congress passed the Espionage Act to enable a federal campaign against the IWW. All this activity culminated in the great strikes of 1919—the Boston Police strike; the national steel strike, led by labor organizer John L. Lewis; the Seattle general strike organized by the IWW; and the great coal strike in Oklahoma. The American Labor party organized in New York, and John Fitzpatrick, the Irish leader of the Chicago Federation of Labor (CFL), organized the Labor Party of Cook County in Illinois.

While the worker uprisings confronted corporate America, the U.S. government countered these challenges. The Palmer raids, conducted by Attorney General A. Mitchell Palmer from 1918 to 1921, targeted largely immigrant labor groups and deported many of the nonnative activists; these raids enjoyed popular support. Nativists further called for a restriction on the policy of open borders, backed by the mainstream American Federation of Labor. In 1921, the U.S. government passed the Emergency Quota Act, followed in 1924 by the Immigration Act (National Origins Act). The Immigration Act tempered Americanization fever, as it limited the immigration of southeastern European and Italian nationals in particular, as potential sources of labor unrest. It could not, however, control the broad disparities in wealth that existed within the country or the impact of economic failure after the Crash of 1929 that revitalized radical resistance.

Chicago incorporated a sizable Slavic population due to the employment possibilities that existed in the city. The Lawndale-Crawford community, on the city's southwest side, was ringed by seventy-three various businesses, such as Western Electric, International Harvester, Liquid Carbonic, and Kimball Piano, which employed more than twenty-six thousand people combined.[14] The area became the home of a large Bohemian community, and the John Toman Branch (Toman) of CPL became a local center of Czech culture.

Toman opened in 1927 in the 2700 block of Pulaski Road. According to the branch reports maintained by the head librarian, Helena Hamel, the library was designed to serve a four-square-mile area. The Toman Branch Library replaced the small Shedd Park Branch and was the first building erected as part of a five-year construction program developed by CPL administration. At the time of its completion in 1927, it was the eighth largest branch in the system of forty-five locations. The building was named for John Toman, a former CPL employee (served 1889–1912), outspoken alderman, and local sheriff. In 1925, he called for Chicago to secede from the state of Illinois, as the city was underrepresented at the level of state government.[15] While Hamel, the former head of the Shedd Park Branch, was named the branch librarian at Toman, Edith Wolinsky served as the deputy branch librarian, before moving to the South Chicago Branch Library in the early 1940s. These two women encompassed the immigrant culture within their library service model while also supporting the original establishing population—the Old Settlers.

The neighborhood in 1927 was "of lower middle class . . . made up largely of the Slavic races, Bohemia predominating." Hamel further noted that the "Slavic races are home-loving people with simple tastes and few outside interests."[16] Yet by 1932, the library was a vibrant cultural center, host to a significant discussion forum organized and presented through active community participation. The partnership between the librarians and the community reflected an intentional collaboration in the creation of a socially pluralist neighborhood.

While Toman Branch head Hamel initially characterized her Czech patrons as a people of "simple tastes and few outside interests," Eleanor Ledbetter, librarian of the Broadway Branch of the Cleveland Public Library and chair of the American Library Association Committee on Work with the Foreign Born, provided more detail. A 1923 article that was part of a series of writings on the work of libraries with foreign-born populations presented an overview of Czech history, religious observance, and popular Czech written materials. Czech immigration began in 1848, continued to grow until 1870, and then rose quickly into the first decade of the 1900s. Ledbetter wrote that "the Czech immigration has always been largely one of families, coming here for permanent settlement. Its intellectual character is indicated by the general level of education and training—less than two per cent of illiteracy being the average record, and many skilled workmen being included in the number." They were the first of the Slavs to come to America.[17]

In Chicago, the Czechs had gained significant visibility. The Bohemians, a regional group within the larger Czech population, began their migration to

Lawndale-Crawford in 1900, with a large number moving east from the city's
Pilsen area. They replaced many of the original settlers of Dutch, German,
Irish, and Scotch backgrounds, and within a few years the community represented the largest settlement of Czechs outside of Prague.[18] Anton Cermak,
the thirty-fifth mayor of Chicago, was born in Kladno, Czechoslovakia, in
1873, although his family moved to the States within the year. Historians
credit his election with the creation of the "house for all peoples," the original
Democratic machine that forced the dominant Irish to recognize other ethnic
groups. While Cermak died in 1933 as the unintended victim of an assassi-
nation attempt on Franklin D. Roosevelt, the Democratic Party's dominance
was established in the city, and German, Polish, Czech, and Jewish leaders
joined the Irish in access to government and the patronage it allowed.[19]

Three main resources advanced the Bohemian image in the Lawndale-
Crawford community: a community discussion forum, the Bohemian Room
in the library itself, and the Jan Masaryk Collection.

THE TOMAN LIBRARY FORUM

The Toman Branch Forum was a defining characteristic of the John Toman
Branch, as it achieved a high degree of visibility beyond even the city of
Chicago. The forum was the result of an art appreciation event the Bohemian
Arts Club of Chicago offered at the library in 1931. The exhibit promoted the
work of "internationally known Czech artists," according to Hamel, and its
success led to requests for other similar activities of a cultural nature.[20] As a
result, three members of the arts club, along with Hamel and Wolinsky, established a committee that planned an English-language discussion forum, originally devoted to Czech topics. It was similar to a lecture series Ledbetter had
developed at the Broadway Branch in Cleveland.[21] As Hamel explained to
the CPL administration in her proposal, there was no "settlement house" of
any significance in the Lawndale-Crawford community, and the Depression
was negatively affecting materials collections, so the staff members were less
busy. With the developing interest in adult education, the forum was a natural
means of incorporating that focus, and it "would prove an excellent publicity measure, keeping the library constantly before the public and linking it
actively with community life."[22]

Educational forums were familiar events in the 1930s. They built on the
practices of the lyceum and Chautauqua movements for personal improve-
ment and drew on the strategies of the worker education programs offered
by various unions and worker advocacy groups. The League for Industrial

Democracy, based in New York, sponsored traveling programs addressing issues such as the unionization of white-collar workers, war and empire, the technological revolution, and socialized medicine.[23] There was also the "American Way," a national initiative launched by John W. Studebaker, commissioner of education in the Franklin D. Roosevelt administration. In response to the many intellectual challenges to the sustainability of a capitalist democracy that emerged in response to the Great Depression, the federal government launched "an experiment in mass education for civic literacy." It was an expansion of a statewide program Studebaker had developed as superintendent of the Des Moines (Iowa) school system in cooperation with the American Association for Adult Education, with funding from the Carnegie Corporation. The basic premise of the forums was that discussion would lead to positive action yet avert radical challenge. While the national program encouraged local control through the public education systems, the program itself was highly structured, with trained facilitators and timed progressions through the discussions of the topics of the forum events.[24] An independent committee recommended a series of public affairs pamphlets to the Office of Education; this covered such topics as "Agricultural Problems," "Labor Problems," and "War and Peace Issues."[25] The American Library Association also produced a guide to review articles about the use of pamphlets and civic education.[26] One trenchant critique of the national program was that "the intelligentsia" shaped the debate.[27]

John Chancellor, assistant to the ALA Committee on Adult Education, evaluated the Des Moines, Iowa, forums in 1934. He wrote, "The Des Moines Public Forums are under the control and direction of the Board of Directors of the Des Moines Public Schools" and the forums made use of "expert interpreters of the crucial problems."[28] Chancellor noted that the forum facilitators made extensive use of library services, but the libraries did not benefit from their participation in the forums—specifically, the project did not fund reading materials to support the discussion topics at the local level. In October 1936, Chancellor met with Chester S. Williams, assistant administrator of the U.S. Department of Education Public Forum Project, to discuss a study of a national library-education forum model. His November report of the meeting indicates that the increase in new forums was "rapid" and expected to grow further. He sketched the role of the "'forum librarians,' relief workers," who had the task of lending materials, taking enrollment at the forums, and selling the topical pamphlets collected by the education department. While Chancellor promoted the pamphlet list to the state libraries, there is no indication that the proposed partnership between the ALA and the Office of Education actually materialized.[29]

The John Toman Branch Forum, however, emerged from the community itself. The forum committee began with five members, but its success quickly attracted others. Over the many years of the forum, the committee included such men as Harvey Mitchell, editor of a local paper; Otto Oplatka, a lawyer; Anton Brosche, a gardener and art collector; Charles Vetter, an American Federation of Labor official; and Thomas Cermak, a merchant (and no relation to the mayor, Anton Cermak). Hamel described the group in 1936 as "well-balanced politically: two being conservative, two radical and three liberal." She further observed that the discussions during the planning meetings were often lively and the selection of lectures diversified.[30] The only women to serve on the committee from 1932 to at least 1941 were affiliated with the branch library directly; women as speakers were also in a distinct minority. While the Bohemian Women's Civic Club established itself in 1931 and did partner with the library for other events, there is no indication that it was involved with the lecture series.

Roderick A. Ginsburg was the major player in planning the forum. He was born in Czechoslovakia in 1899, and his family immigrated to Chicago in 1910, where he attended the University of Chicago and completed his bachelor's degree after service in World War I. Ginsburg was a strong lecturer, and since he was bilingual, he was popular as a speaker and a radio announcer on the first Czech-language programs on stations WSBC, WEDC, and WHFC in Chicago. He was an advocate of Czech writing and the Great Books program, which he offered at Toman for more than four years in the 1940s. Hamel wrote, "It was due to his efforts that the Toman Library Forum was started in the early 1930s."[31]

THE SCOPE OF PROGRAMS

With the approval of the CPL Board of Directors, the Toman committee planned its schedule: alternating Fridays, with the forty-five-minute lecture beginning at 8:00 p.m., and fifteen minutes for questions and discussions. The first program, held on January 22, 1932, presented the Czechoslovak consul general Jaroslav Smetanka speaking on "Present Conditions in Czechoslovakia"; 108 attended. The last program of the year featured Ladislav Urban, the Czechoslovak vice consul general, who spoke on music, with the assistance of a string trio and vocalist; 225 attended. For the first half year, Toman offered eight programs or lectures, with a total attendance of 837.

The programs offered through the Toman Branch Forum varied, but politics was the general theme of most offerings. During the second season, a debate on "Restriction of Immigration" drew an audience of 254, while a program on "Diet in Health and Disease" (illustrated with slides) drew 345. These are large crowds for a branch library, and, as Hamel explained, the library presented the programs even though it had no convenient facilities. Without a proper meeting room, the lectures began in the story room associated with the children's department, but the attendance sometimes spilled over into the main library area. For the first two years, the branch depended on local undertakers to share their chairs, then the CPL Board supplied the funds for additional seating.[32]

Also during the first two years, the organizers of the forum were able to draw on city officials for programming, so M. S. Szymczak, the city comptroller, spoke on the financial situation of Chicago, and Fred G. Minor, from the World's Fair Committee, came to speak on the "Century of Progress Exposition." According to the librarians' reports, the second season of the Toman Library Forum, 1932–33, offered twelve lectures, with a total attendance of 2,181.[33]

Other speakers came from interested supporters of the forum, such as the Chicago adult education council, settlement houses, speakers' bureaus, and area universities. Edith Wolinsky, for example, contacted Maynard C. Kruegar, an assistant professor of economics at the University of Chicago, for suggestions of speakers.[34] The branch offered no honorarium until 1937, and, as Hamel reported, speakers sometimes refused because of it. The library also surveyed the community to identify topics of interest. Despite the original preference for topics with a Czech theme, the branch staff found that the "majority wanted lectures on current economic, social and political problems." The scope of topics allowed members of the community to explore "American" identity as affected by different ideological perspectives and social values and then determine for themselves what was most relevant to their own understanding. Hamel wrote that while the committee tried to avoid controversial topics, some just demanded attention.[35]

The 1933 season began with a "Political Symposium Addressing the Topics of 'Rooseveltism,' 'Socialism,' 'Fascism,' and 'Communism.'" Ginsberg organized the program, which 248 attended. A program on "Russia" in January 1934 attracted 285, and all subsequent programs that focused on Russia drew high attendance, which suggests Russian immigrants were participating in the Forum. Beginning in 1935, the number of attendees began to drop, but the lowest attendance for the year, for the topic of the "National Youth Administration," still drew fifty-three people.[36] The forum also stimulated interest beyond the library system, as the WPA offered to take over the series in 1936; however, the committee rejected the offer, preferring to retain local control.[37]

One significant program was the presentation by labor lawyer William E. Rodriguez of the [Chicago] Civil Liberties League on "The Dangers of Fascism in the U.S.," which featured a viewing of a film of the South Chicago Steel Strike, also known as the Memorial Day Massacre (1937). The film was banned in the city, as the Chicago Police Department tried to control the story about its response to the southside strike at Republic Steel in which ten demonstrators were killed and scores wounded. Charles Vetter, a labor official who served on the forum committee, arranged for the film to be shown at the March 4, 1938, meeting; 179 attended. Even in the face of such government control, the community itself determined what it would consider as relevant to its understanding of America.[38]

The *C.P.L. Union News* reported in January of 1939 that the forum came under attack by "isolated disgruntled individuals" who objected to discussion topics. A delegation comprised of the Toman Branch and community leadership addressed the board relative to the challenges. Ginsburg presented a history and overview of the policies for the forum and argued for the right of free speech, exercising a claim on American values. The CPL Board affirmed that right and indicated that it applied not simply to the Toman forum but to the entire Chicago Public Library.[39] This decision reinforced the intellectual freedom resolution passed by the board in 1936 when the foreign-language department had faced charges of being "Communistic and pornographic." As the newsletter article noted, in 1936, the CPL Board of Directors voted that "the Library asserts . . . its rights and duty to keep on its shelves a representative selection of books on all subjects of interest to its readers . . . including all books on all sides of controversial questions."[40]

The board of directors, in keeping with its 1936 precedent, confirmed the forum participants' right to uncensored speech. The decision expanded the scope of the original declaration of the library's duty to represent all views in the collection and ensured that all locations of the Chicago Public Library were sites of free speech. Library patrons were now assured of not just the right to access information but also the right to share it. The board also established the right of the institution of the library to function as an independent social agency despite its relationship with city government.

The Toman Library Forum subsequently presented two CPL Board members as speakers: community newspaper publisher Leo Lerner in March 1939, and Dr. Preston Bradley, pastor of the People's Church of Chicago, in March 1941. The committee arranged conservative programs as well. James P. Ringley, former American Legion state commander, spoke on "America, Last Hope of Civilization" in November 1939; Charles S. Braden, of the America First Committee, debated Maurice Criz, of the Committee to Defend America by Aiding the Allies, on the topic of "How Much Aid to Britain" in January 1941.

Paul H. Douglas, the University of Chicago professor who went on to become a popular U.S. senator from Illinois, drew 401, the largest crowd in the ten-year period under review, when he spoke on the "Role of Czechoslovakia in Central Europe" in April 1938, just before the Nazi challenge to Czechoslovak autonomy. Charlotte Carr, director of Hull House, was another notable; she spoke on labor organization in 1939. Using names as an inexact indicator of gender, it appears that in 117 total presentations, only fifteen women spoke.[41]

The Bohemian Room and Masaryk Club

In the segment of her 1937 annual report titled "Work with the Foreign Born (Bohemian)," Hamel provided details of the expansion of the Bohemian influence in the branch. While circulation of foreign materials had decreased in 1936 due to a shortage, in part, of new materials, beginning in January of 1937, the library began receiving foreign titles again, 1,489 for the year. John Toman collected and donated $300 in 1938 to launch the Masaryk Collection, named in honor of the former Czech president. The original Bohemian Room, created in a small workroom in 1931, proved too small once the new collection began to arrive, so in March 1937 the materials were moved to the Peter Pan Room, displacing the children's collection. "Colorful Bohemian scenes were hung on the walls, and the two beautiful Bohemian encyclopedias were displayed in the cases," Hamel wrote. The new room and collection were announced in the Bohemian and English newspapers, and one reporter, Denni Hlasatel, promoted the collection via a daily column about new library acquisitions. The local Bohemian newspapers donated free copies of their publications, which also stimulated in-house use of the collection.[42]

To further promote the use of the collection, a group formed an ad hoc committee to arrange a Bohemian event. The men contacted speakers, secured a rare book collection for display, and arranged the publicity. Anton Vanek, a member of the CPL Board of Directors, was a featured speaker. The event itself, on November 12, 1937, was a success and it stimulated the creation that very evening of the Masaryk Club: Friends of the Czech Book. The officers elected that night included one woman, Mrs. Reichman, wife of the vice-president, J. J. Reichman; she was named secretary. The president was Dr. J. E. S. Vojan, noted scholar of Czech culture.[43]

Foreign-language department chief Korman wrote to Chief Librarian Carl Roden about the event. He noted that "the affair at Toman was an interesting and exhilarating experience from every angle, and a credit to the library, and to Mrs. Hamel and her assistants. . . . The entire affair had an air of intimacy and friendly neighborly feeling. We need more of that spirit in the Library." He left the branch building at 10:45, with others still behind engrossed in conversation. His assistant, Ben Hirsch, had attended a similar event at the Newberry Library, but he reported none of the excitement Korman found at Toman. The Newberry was not a community-based library.[44]

Dr. Vojan spoke at the next meeting of the Masaryk Club, on the poetry of Jan Neruda. Hamel wrote that a number of young people were present for the event, which pleased the organizers. The number of new library card holders pleased the librarians; all the books on Neruda were checked out after the event. As a result of the creation of the Bohemian Room, the Masaryk Club, and the new materials, circulation of the foreign titles increased by 1,715 over the same period in the previous year.[45]

Thomas Garrigue Masaryk (1850–1937) was the founder and first president of the country of Czechoslovakia. He made three visits to Chicago, the first in 1902. He visited again in 1907 to lecture at the Chicago Congress of Czech Freethinkers.[46] He was a visiting faculty member at the University of Chicago for the 1918–19 academic year and lived in the Lawndale-Crawford neighborhood. The Masaryk collection was launched by John Toman with his initial donation, which stimulated contributions by others; it expanded over time as Masaryk's government sent materials over to the library. The 1939 catalog of the collection indicates that the materials are by and about Masaryk himself. Eduard Benes, the second president of Czechoslovakia and head of the Czech government in exile during World War II, wrote the introduction to the catalog and indicated that Masaryk was "reputed to have one of the largest private libraries in Europe." The catalog's printing aligns closely to the Nazi takeover of Czechoslovakia in March 1939; the Benes foreword was written in May 1939, just two months later. The single date on the catalog is 1939, suggesting that the work was released as a means of affirming the continuity of the Czech identity in exile with the Czech government.[47]

Also, for the first time, the 1939 annual report contained news of the forum and the Masaryk Reading Club under the heading of "Adult Education Activities," reflecting a revived emphasis on adult education within library practice. The collection was eventually moved to the CPL Central Library in the Cultural Center on Michigan Avenue, circa 1975. While there was some discussion of relocating the materials to another Czech community, they remained with CPL; they currently reside at the Harold Washington Resource Center in downtown Chicago.[48]

THE OLD SETTLERS OF LAWNDALE-CRAWFORD

During the week of December 10–15, 1934, the Toman Branch housed a photographic exhibit titled "Historical Exhibit of Lawndale-Crawford." On December 13, thirty members of the Lawndale-Crawford community met to share stories about the origins of the community. From this first gathering, the Lawndale-Crawford Historical Association (LCHA) was established in 1934 and incorporated in 1935 "to commemorate persons and events of the earliest years of Chicago's westward expansion, to stimulate interest in the traditions of those primitive days and their preservation, and to afford occasions for renewing and maintaining acquaintance among those who lived in Lawndale and Crawford long ago."[49] It developed in parallel with the Bohemian Room and its associated cultural activities. Perhaps challenged by the cultural promotion of the immigrant population in the neighborhood, the Old Settlers launched an organization to celebrate their own established presence in the community.

The Old Settlers were as active as the Bohemians and as engaged with the Toman Branch Library and staff; Hamel was included in the first five-member board of the LCHA, as was her assistant, Marie Stampen. The board also included one other woman, Mary Newett Broadway, as vice president. The association held its meetings in the branch, and the branch housed the association's collection of photographs, manuscripts, printed items, and memorabilia gathered by the members. The association printed two directories: *The Old Families of Lawndale and Crawford* (1935) and *An Experiment in Friendship* (1937).[50]

The first event noted by Hamel in her 1937 annual report was Old Settlers Week, held September 21–26, 1937. The association held its annual meeting on September 25, and 170 attended.[51] The meeting included an exhibit of self-identified Old Settlers' accomplishments and featured such items as drawings by an architect, cartoons by a local cartoonist, books by local authors, and a picture of Clarence Darrow, a former Lawndale resident. The Lawndale-Crawford Centennial Jubilee was held from October 11, 1939, to November 11, 1939, in the John Toman Branch Library.[52] The LCHA materials were eventually relocated to the Special Collections Department of CPL and are now housed in the Harold Washington Resource Center.

An unattributed four-page report titled "Present Day Lawndale-Crawford" was written in 1939. It identified Lawndale-Crawford as "one of the leading Bohemian centers in the country. It is a district of clean streets and beautiful lawns. . . . [A]n atmosphere of the old world clings to many of the shops." The report characterized the John Toman Branch Library as the cultural center of the community and further noted, "There is a closely knit community spirit in Lawndale-Crawford. . . . There is much interchange of ideas and opinions. This is the reason, no doubt, that Lawndale-Crawford has become one of the outstanding communities of Chicago."[53] In 1940, reflecting that "closeness," a "friends of the library" group formed. It included Leonard Serdiuk and J. J. Reichman from the forum organizing committee; Larned E. Meacham, president of the Lawndale-Crawford Historical Association; and Anton Brosche from the Masaryk Reading Club.[54]

CONCLUSION

While the annual reports of library administrators will commonly acknowledge the activities of branch libraries, this is often in statistical terms: circulation, programming, visitation numbers. These data allow comparisons over time and place but do not provide the depth of understanding made possible through the active reporting of local relationships and the activities that emerge through those relationships. The official record of the Chicago Public Library Board of Trustees meeting for January 9, 1939, provides no discussion of the Toman Branch Forum petition for protection of its intellectual freedom, as no official action was taken. The newsletter of the CPL employees union, Local 88 of the State, County, and Municipal Employees, carried the report of the delegation's visit; union officers had attended the board meeting for the first time, as an "experiment in staff relations."[55] Given the close association of labor activists with free speech, it is understandable that the union members who attended the meeting—Abram Korman and Jeremiah Shay—would highlight the event in the local's publication.

Positioning library history through the lived experiences of frontline librarians challenges those discourses about public library history that emerge from reliance on bureaucratic representations of the library, academic interpretations of the role of the library, and images of the public librarian in popular culture.[56] The use of second-tier, internal reports and associational publications allows us to investigate a broader perspective—the institution in the community—and may lead to a deeper understanding of the practitioner at work.

The Foreign-language department of the Chicago Public Library during the period 1927–40 exemplified such active engagement with the communities it served; the department chief advocated to established authorities on behalf of those communities. The staff of the John Toman Branch during the same period both supported and expanded the traditional role of libraries beyond the conventional presentation of authorized cultural canons, as the women partnered with the grassroots leadership of all the engaged groups of Lawndale-Crawford to explore the various meanings of being "American." Both the Bohemian and the Old Settler communities appropriated the branch library to shape images of themselves in the history of their common neighborhood that they could share with each other and the broader city. The John Toman Branch enriched, and was enriched by, those it served.

NOTES

1. Abram Korman, "Present and Future Status of Foreign Language Work in Chicago," unpublished manuscript, 1935, 4, Chicago Public Library Archives.

2. "Population, By Race: No. 31—Population at Each Census, 1860–1920: By Color and Race, and by States and Geographic Divisions," in *Statistical Abstract of the United States 1922*, 45th number (Washington, DC: Government Printing Office, 1923), 42.

3. "Population of Principal Cities: No. 34—Cities Having 50,000 or More Inhabitants in 1920: Populations, by Color, Nativity, and Parentage, 1910 and 1920," in *Statistical Abstract of the United States 1922*, 55.

4. James R. Barrett, "Americanization from the Bottom Up: Immigration and the Remaking of the Working Class in the United States, 1880–1930," *Journal of American History* 79, no. 3 (1992): 996–1020.

5. Plummer Alston Jones Jr., *Libraries, Immigrants and the American Experience* (Westport, CT: Greenwood, 1999.)

6. Barrett, "Americanization from the Bottom Up," 997.

7. Carlton B. Joeckel and Leon Carnovsky, *A Metropolitan Library in Action: A Survey of the Chicago Public Library* (Chicago: University of Chicago Press, 1940), 133.

8. Korman, "Present and Future Status," 2–3.

9. Eric Novotny, "Library Services to Immigrants: The Debate in the Library Literature, 1900–1920, and a Chicago Case Study," *Reference and User Services Quarterly* 42, no. 4 (2003): 348.

10. Chicago Public Library, "Annual report to Carl Roden, April 13, 1932," Abram Korman binder, CPL Special Collections.

11. Correspondence between Abram Korman and Carl Roden, February 15, 1934, Abram Korman binder, CPL Special Collections.

12. See Joyce M. Latham, "'So Promising of Success': The Role of Local 88 in the Development of the Chicago Public Library," *Progressive Librarian* 30 (2008): 18–37, for a discussion of the development of the Chicago Public Library Local 88.

13. Jones, *Libraries, Immigrants and the American Experience*, 196. Jones identifies two camps in the Americanization movement within librarianship: the Anglo-conformist and the cultural pluralist, noting that neither of these philosophies was "motivated by racism or nativism."

14. Chicago Public Library, "Present Day Lawndale-Crawford," 1939, John Toman Branch binder, 2–3, CPL Special Collections.

15. John R. Schmidt, "The State of Chicago (6-25-1925)," Unknown Chicago, last updated June 25, 2010, http://www.chicagonow.com/blogs/unknown-chicago/2010/06/the-state-of-chicago-6-25-1925.html. The resolution passed unanimously and, while never actually acted upon, did resurface periodically.

16. Chicago Public Library, "Annual Report, 1930," John Toman Branch binder, CPL Special Collections.

17. Eleanor E. Ledbetter, "The Czechoslovak Immigrant and the Library," *Library Journal* 48 (November 1, 1923): 911–12.

18. Chicago Public Library, "Lawndale-Crawford Collection, 1875–1979, Finding Aid," Neighborhood Research History Collection, CPL Special Collections, http://www.chipublib.org/cplbooksmovies/cplarchive/archivalcoll/lccc.php.

19. Roger Biles, "Encyclopedia of Chicago: Machine Politics," http://encyclopedia.chicagohistory.org/pages/774.html.

20. Helena C. Hamel, "The John Toman Branch Library Forum," *Illinois Libraries* 17, no. 1 (January 1936): 53.

21. Jones, *Libraries, Immigrants and the American Experience*, 147.

22. Hamel, "John Toman Branch Library Forum," 53.

23. Harry W. Laidler, *Looking Forward: Outlines for Discussion and Action*, LID Pamphlet series (New York: League for Industrial Democracy, 1937).

24. Robert Kunzman and David Tyack, "Educational Forums of the 1930s: An Experiment in Adult Civic Education," *American Journal of Education* 111, no. 3 (May 2005): 320–40.

25. United States Department of the Interior, Office of Education, *Public Affairs Pamphlets* (Washington, DC: Government Printing Office, 1936).

26. American Library Association, "Democracy and Civic Education," 1936, Archives, Adult Education Board, Circular Letters, ser. 1, box 30/5/2.

27. Kunzman and Tyack, "Educational Forums of the 1930s," 329.

28. John Chancellor, "Cooperation of the Des Moines Public Library with the Public Forum," ALA Public Library Division, May 1934.

29. John Chancellor, "Reading and the Des Moines Forums: Together with Some Observation on Library-Forum Relationships in General," ALA Public Library Division, May 1934, 4.

30. Hamel, "The John Toman Branch Library Forum," 53.

31. Chicago Public Library, "Biographical Data Compiled from Various Sources by Mrs. Helena Hamel" [1967?], John Toman Branch binder, CPL Special Collections.

32. Hamel, "John Toman Branch Library Forum," 55.

33. Chicago Public Library, "Toman Library Forum," John Toman Branch binder, 3, CPL Special Collections.

34. Correspondence between Edith Wolinsky and Maynard C. Kruegar, [1935?], John Toman Branch binder, CPL Special Collections.

35. Hamel, "John Toman Branch Library Forum," 54.

36. Chicago Public Library, "Toman Library Forum," John Toman Branch binder, 4, 8, CPL Special Collections.

37. Chicago Public Library, "Annual Report, 1936," John Toman Branch binder, CPL Special Collections.

38. Joyce M. Latham, "Memorial Day to Memorial Library: The South Chicago Branch Library as Cultural Terrain, 1937–1947," *Libraries and the Cultural Record* 46, no. 3 (2011): 321–42.

39. "Report on Board Meeting," *C.P.L. Union News* (Chicago), January 1939, 4.

40. Chicago Public Library, *Proceedings (1924–1951)* ([Chicago]: Board of Directors, 1936), 71.

41. Chicago Public Library, "Toman Library Forum," John Toman Branch binder, 5, CPL Special Collections.

42. Chicago Public Library, "Annual Report, 1930," John Toman Branch binder, CPL Special Collections.

43. Chicago Public Library, "Annual Report, 1930."

44. Correspondence between Abram Korman and Carl Roden, November 13, 1937, John Toman Branch binder, CPL Special Collections.

45. Chicago Public Library, "Annual Report, 1937," John Toman Branch binder, 5, CPL Special Collections.

46. Chicago Public Library, "Collection Masaryk: A Catalog of the Books by and about Thomas Garrigue Masaryk Presented by the Honorable John Toman to John Toman Branch of the Chicago Public Library, 1939," John Toman Branch binder, 7, CPL Special Collections.

47. Chicago Public Library, foreword to Collection Masaryk, John Toman Branch binder, CPL Special Collections.

48. Correspondence between Galen Wilson and Laura Linard, June 1, 1989, John Toman Branch binder, CPL Special Collections.

49. Chicago Public Library, "Annual report, 1937, John Toman Branch binder, 5, CPL Special Collections.

50. Chicago Public Library, "Lawndale-Crawford Historical Association: Historical Note," Neighborhood Research History Collection, http://www.chipublib.org/cpl booksmovies/cplarchive/archivalcoll/lcha.php.

51. The records indicate September 25, but September 26 was the birth date of the area's original settler, Peter Crawford, and all other celebrations were held on the twenty-sixth.

52. Chicago Public Library, "Annual Report, 1939," John Toman Branch binder, CPL Special Collections.

53. Chicago Public Library, "Present Day Lawndale-Crawford," 1939, John Toman Branch binder, CPL Special Collections.

54. Chicago Public Library, "Annual Report, 1940," John Toman Branch binder, CPL Special Collections.

55. "Union Delegates Report on Board Meeting," *C.P.L. Union News* (Chicago), January 1939, 1.

56. Patricia Hill Collins, *Fighting Words: Black Women and the Search for Justice* (Minneapolis: University of Minneapolis Press, 1998), 49.

Counter Culture

The World as Viewed from Inside the
Indianapolis Public Library, 1944–1956

JEAN PREER

Observers of Indiana culture have long remarked on its social and political contradictions. From 1890 to 1920, the state experienced a literary renaissance in which every Hoosier was a potential author. Some of America's most popular and celebrated writers of the early twentieth century, including Booth Tarkington, Theodore Dreiser, and Gene Stratton-Porter, hailed from Indiana.[1] Yet Indiana lagged behind other northern states in literacy and high school graduation rates.[2] Located at the crossroads of America, Indiana wrestled with the conflicting traditions of Yankee and Appalachian settlers. Having sided with the North during the Civil War and sheltered runaway slaves on the Underground Railroad, in the 1920s Indiana had the largest state membership in the resurgent Ku Klux Klan. Known for its political conservatism and insularity, Indiana was home to socialist Eugene V. Debs and Republican and One World proponent Wendell Wilkie, unsuccessful presidential candidates whose philosophies and global visions extended far beyond the banks of the Wabash. And despite its staunchly anticommunist stand during the Cold War, Indiana had been home to Robert Owen's early-nineteenth-century utopian experiment that briefly flourished in New Harmony.

An embodiment of this cultural contradiction, Kurt Vonnegut, a more recently celebrated Hoosier author, lauded his Indiana roots while he skewered midwestern society. Proud member of a prominent Indianapolis family of German immigrants, Vonnegut praised his splendid high school and its demanding teachers, the city's wonderful symphony orchestra, and the beautiful buildings designed by his father and grandfather, both architects. In his fiction, however, Vonnegut portrayed heartland cities as intellectual wastelands with boring residents leading dreary lives. In *Breakfast of Champions*, he wrote:

Patty Keene was stupid on purpose, which was the case with most women in Midland City. The women all had big minds because they were big animals, but they did not use them much for this reason: unusual ideas could make enemies, and the women, if they were going to achieve any sort of comfort and safety, needed all the friends they could get.

So, in the interests of survival, they trained themselves to be agreeing machines instead of thinking machines. All their minds had to do was to discover what other people were thinking, and then they thought that, too.[3]

Midland City, Ohio, was said to be modeled on Indianapolis.

Speaking in Indianapolis in 1986, Vonnegut expressed disappointment that his hometown had failed to become the progressive and enlightened city it had promised to be at the close of World War II. Recalling an earlier visit, he said, "I would have felt more triumphant, I would have been happier, if this city had become what I thought it might become after the second World War. I thought this might become a marvelously liberal city because the potential was here."[4] Vonnegut's wartime experience as a prisoner of the Germans during the firebombing of Dresden, a horror recounted in *Slaughterhouse-Five*, transformed his world view and shaped much of his fiction.[5] He seems to have accepted the notion of his fellow midwesterners as poorly educated, provincial, and narrow-minded, although he, for one, was none of these. But during the last years of the war and into the early Cold War, the Indianapolis Public Library embraced ideas and sponsored programs that seem at odds with prominent aspects of Hoosier culture. In writings and interviews, Vonnegut scarcely mentioned the library, but had he viewed the world from inside the Indianapolis Public Library, he might have thought he had entered a parallel universe or landed on a different planet. In a culture that was said to disdain education and promote conformity and that regularly elected conservative if not stridently anticommunist politicians, Vonnegut might have been surprised at the library's promotion of critical thought and its expansive definition of Americanism.[6] Might the public library have been part of the city's promised postwar enlightenment?

Highly regarded among urban public libraries, the Indianapolis Public Library had developed under a succession of strong directors. Already a leader in adult education, the library in the late 1940s faced the challenges of a political and racial environment charged by anticommunist pressures and continuing racial segregation. Marian McFadden, director of the library from 1944 to 1956, established the library as a place where ideas counter to Hoosier culture

might be expressed and explored. One of a handful of women in her generation to lead a major public library, McFadden demonstrated administrative
ability and political savvy that enabled the library to take risks and maintain
a high visibility in perilous times.

As with Kurt Vonnegut, Indiana's cultural contradictions were manifest in
McFadden's life and career. Born in Shelbyville, thirty miles southeast of Indianapolis, McFadden was the daughter and granddaughter of small-town phys-
icians. According to family history, her grandfather, William G. McFadden,
was a staunch patriot. Goaded by neighbors who favored southern secession,
he impulsively enlisted in the Union army and served to the end of the war.
Later, having established a successful practice as the first doctor in Shelby
County, he amassed one of the finest medical libraries in the state.[7] McFadden
grew up in a house full of books but described herself as an avid user of the
public library from the time she could first scrawl her name.[8] Unusual for a
Hoosier woman of her time, she left Indiana to attend college in the East (as
Vonnegut would go east to attend Cornell) and graduated from Smith in
1926. After working for two years in the public library in Shelbyville, she went
east again to earn her BLS degree at Columbia University's School of Library
Service in 1929.[9] While a library student, she had dinner with the widow of
Andrew Carnegie, who recalled Carnegie's continuing gratitude to Major
Anderson for opening the world of books to him.[10] McFadden also sought to
share the joys of reading with young people. After graduate studies in child
psychology at Hunter College, she worked as a children's librarian in Queens-
boro, New York, and in Springfield, Illinois, where she boarded with a grand-
niece of Mary Lincoln.[11]

In 1934, McFadden joined the staff of the Indianapolis Public Library,
working at the West Indianapolis and Brightwood Branches. From the outset,
senior library officials noted her talent and potential. On yearly evaluations,
her supervisors particularly remarked on her wide reading. Although an early
review described her as aloof and reserved, later evaluations warned that unless she were given challenging work the library might lose her to a more
attractive position elsewhere. When asked what other library position might
better suit her, Carrie Scott, supervisor of work with children, wrote "Executive work at Central Library."[12] Luther Dickerson, library director since 1928,
and former head of Adult Education for the American Library Association,
spotted McFadden's ability and appointed her assistant librarian in 1942.[13] On
his recommendation, McFadden was named acting director in 1944, when
Dickerson stepped down, and director the following year.[14]

Indianapolis residents "reading" the library would have observed a highly educated young woman in a position of leadership. McFadden was only forty, then the youngest woman heading an urban public library system. Praising her selection, *Library Occurrent*, the journal of the Indiana Library Association, observed, "Her appointment now as librarian is a recognition of a decade of able service with the Indianapolis Public Library. It is also recognition for women in the library profession, few of whom attain administrative positions of such importance."[15] What was true nationally about the scarcity of women in the professions was even more the case in Indiana, although the Indianapolis Public Library had been headed by a woman from 1892 to 1927, when Eliza Gordon Browning, as director, had overseen the expansion of the library and the construction of the Beaux-Arts building of the Central Library.[16]

As all her supervisors noted, McFadden was an avid reader. In a portrait published on her appointment as head librarian, the *Indianapolis Star* reported that McFadden favored the works of Russian novelists and Charles Dickens for leisure reading; further, "Thomas Mann, she thinks, is the greatest living man of letters, and she has read his 'Magic Mountain' three times, getting something new out of it each time; and she regards Ernest Hemingway and John Steinbeck the best of the American Novelists."[17] McFadden was later outspoken in her opposition to the notion that the library should solely respond to reader demand. In 1955 she observed, "Actually, the expression 'give the people what they want' is used by librarians to mean just this: 'to satisfy one group of the people who read a type of book so quickly . . . that the turnover is great, the demand therefore greater, the selection of the material easier and the resultant amount of brain power needed, less.'" McFadden believed that the librarian's familiarity with books was like a doctor's knowledge of the body, the result of serious and continuing study. Viewing this intimate acquaintance with books as an essential element of the librarian's professionalism, McFadden urged her staff not to shy away from "the responsibility for selection of books and the responsibility of guiding the reading of people for whom the books are selected."[18]

While she upheld high standards for reading material, McFadden had an encompassing view of the library's community and the potential of its readers. In early 1945, she reported that 66 percent of the demand by readers was for nonfiction works, such as Sumner Welles's *Time for Decision* and W. W. Waller's *The Veteran Comes Back*, "reflecting an alert, serious-minded Indianapolis reading public." High-demand fiction included Irving Stone's *Immortal Wife*, Lloyd Douglas's *The Robe*, but also Lillian Smith's *Strange Fruit*, a controversial story of an interracial relationship, which various state courts later found obscene.[19] For the librarian to be able to guide readers to more serious works, McFadden sought to make the library a more welcoming community place. "Miss McFadden wants to get away from the idea that a library is an 'institution,' and all that somewhat forbidding term implies," the *Indianapolis Star* reported. "It seems to me that the most important thing for a library is not to lose the human touch," she said. "A library shouldn't be just a storage house for books. It ought to be a friendly place, where the person who wants a book meets the person who has a book to give."[20]

OPEN MINDS

With her predecessors, Marian McFadden was committed to the role of the public library as an agent of adult education. Inside the Indianapolis Public Library, education did not mean the stilted, boring, compulsory learning required by the state but a freely undertaken, lifelong exploration of ideas. As early as 1945, a Great Books discussion group met in Indianapolis, following the model developed at the University of Chicago by Robert Hutchins and Mortimer Adler, with the library hosting its organizational meeting.[21] In 1947, Indiana was chosen as a test state for an expansion of the program from campus to urban and rural areas. Marian McFadden served on the recruiting committee.[22] And in 1950 the library was designated the official Great Books coordinating agency in Indianapolis, with McFadden on the local board of directors.[23]

The library also undertook its own adult education initiative after an experience McFadden often recounted to demonstrate the urgency driving the effort. Listening to a local radio news broadcast, she was "shocked" by the results of a poll showing that a third of the people questioned knew nothing about the United Nations. At a time when many believed that the United Nations was a communist organization, McFadden oversaw a three-fold effort by the library to educate the community about it, using bookmarks, forums, and film discussion groups. Certain that library users were not among the uninformed (they discovered they were wrong about this), McFadden and her staff concluded that it was "necessary to reach farther beyond the library doors than we had ever attempted to reach before." The resulting campaign flooded the community with information about the United Nations and sought to enlist citizens in supporting and promoting it.[24]

Within the library, patrons could pick up one of twenty-thousand bookmarks that asked "DO YOU KNOW [about the United Nations]? It is your responsibility to find out." The library created a special desk in Central Library's circulation department to provide materials on the United Nations and posed a question of the month about the organization. Reaching out farther still, the library organized a series of forums on international affairs and film discussion groups that were widely advertised, heavily attended, and extensively reported.[25] Those who attended these events or read about them in the paper would have experienced a library neither staid nor book-bound. Showings of films on current affairs and countries around the world attracted large crowds to library branches, including more than a hundred intrepid viewers who braved a blizzard to attend the showing of a film about India.[26]

McFadden seems to have felt the same urgency about issues related to atomic energy and the atom bomb. The library's adult programming for 1948 included a showing of the film *Where Will You Hide?*, described in a press release as a film concerning the atom bomb and "the need for planning to prevent another world war." At the Spades Park Branch, a general discussion followed the film.[27] In a December 1949 profile of McFadden in the *Indianapolis Times*, reporter John Wilson recounted how McFadden and the library staff had been asked to compile a list of the hundred greatest books. At first limiting her choices to works published before 1940, McFadden changed her mind to include John Hersey's *Hiroshima*, "because we must know about the atomic age. Nothing has been written yet to tell that story completely," she said. "The book introduces the average man to the atomic age the way the people of Hiroshima were introduced to it in August of 1945."[28]

The library worked to open the minds of young adults as well. Hersey's book appeared on the library's 1948 book list, "Let's Read Books for Young People," along with *The Bomb that Fell on America*, and *The United Nations*. The booklist text read, "To a greater extent than ever before in history, we of high school age are asked to think in terms of the world, its problems, and the United Nations organization which will achieve peace. To accept this responsibility we must become receptive. Not many have had the advantage of travel through which to learn to know countries and to make friends with other peoples. But knowledge, understanding, friendship are necessary if we are to realize the universal hope of ONE WORLD with a functioning UNITED NATIONS ORGANIZATION."[29]

In a talk at the ALA Film Workshop and Adult Education Institute in 1948, McFadden described this effort as going far beyond the library's role in providing information. "At last," she said, "we in the library profession, [*sic*] are coming out of the neutral corners and plunging into controversial issues."[30]

Working in cooperation with the local League of Women Voters, adult activities librarian Pauline French conducted workshops to train leaders for film discussion groups on the United Nations. "The library's aim," French said, "is to spread information about the United Nations so that an informed citizenry can help the organization achieve its goals."[31]

A patron "reading" the Indianapolis Public Library in 1948 would have seen the library not only providing information on diverse points of view but also seeking to spark conversation. The United Nations bookmark that asked, "DO YOU KNOW? It is your responsibility to find out," went on to say, "Tell one another." The staff, wrote McFadden, counted on and hoped "that users of the library would feel the necessity of spreading the information." McFadden considered impromptu discussions among patrons an indicator of the effort's success. "It is good to know that democracy is still at work, with the library desk substituting for the proverbial cracker barrel."[32]

TOLERANCE

Marian McFadden personally embraced values of tolerance and respect and believed that they were furthered by discussion. In a letter to staff members following the death of President Franklin D. Roosevelt in April 1945, she reflected on the problems of the coming peace: "Where do the principles of the Atlantic Charter or Dumbarton Oaks begin? They begin wherever and whenever two individuals meet to discuss their differences and compromise those differences in such a way that the individual integrity of each is not destroyed. Tolerance, kindness, sympathy, and decent recognition of the rights of others, like charity, begin at home."[33]

Under McFadden's leadership, the Indianapolis Public Library followed a principled path on matters involving race relations and communist subversion. Often described as the northernmost southern state, Indiana had a complex history on race matters; it was home to both stations on the Underground Railroad and, in the 1920s, the Ku Klux Klan. Until discredited by the second-degree-murder conviction of Grand Dragon D. C. Stephenson, the Klan in Indiana had dominated Republican politics, winning both local and statewide offices. According to some historians, the Klan's revival in the Midwest in the 1920s was more directed at Catholics and immigrants than at African Americans or was simply a movement to recapture the family values and community spirit of a bygone era, but a strong racist current still coursed through Indiana.[34] As recently as 1930, the small community of Marion, Indiana, located about eighty miles northeast of Indianapolis, was the site of the last lynching north of the Mason-Dixon line, when two prisoners abducted from the county jail were beaten and hanged as a large crowd looked on. A third prisoner, James Cameron, escaped hanging and was later pardoned by the governor.[35]

In the late 1940s, Indianapolis remained a city divided along racial lines. Until 1949, Indiana state law provided that local school districts could decide whether elementary and secondary schools would be segregated. During the ascendency of the Klan, most urban schools, including those in Indianapolis, moved to partial or complete segregation.[36] Marian McFadden's predecessors, however, had committed the Indianapolis Public Library to service for all. As in other cities, the library had opened a branch in a predominantly African American neighborhood, but—unlike libraries in Louisville, Kentucky, and Richmond, Virginia—did not bar blacks from the main library. The Great Books program was open to all, with its promotional material stressing the diverse makeup of discussion groups.

In other cities, promotion of race relations was linked to communist agitation. In Peoria, Illinois, for example, the local American Legion post forced cancellation of a showing of the animated short *Brotherhood of Man*, in which a man awakes to find the whole world in his backyard.[37] Based on a Public Affairs Committee pamphlet written by anthropologists Ruth Benedict and Gene Weltfish and sponsored by the UAW-CIO, the film portrayed diverse races as part of one global family.[38] But in Indianapolis, the library observed National Brotherhood Week, organized exhibits and programming on race relations, and showed the film without objection.[39]

POSITIVE AMERICANISM

Marian McFadden's term as library director overlapped the beginnings of the Cold War and its most virulent manifestations. Outside the library, fear of communism spread. Inside, book offerings and programs suggested a more nuanced understanding of patriotism than the red-white-and-blue variety promoted by the American Legion. In 1919, the Legion had moved its national headquarters to Indianapolis, with the help of public funds, becoming a neighbor to the new Central Library building on what was to be called the American Legion Mall.[40] Having represented Indiana in the U.S. Senate since 1946, Republican William Jenner was an outspoken anticommunist, self-described redneck, and the closest legislative friend of Senator Joseph McCarthy of Wisconsin. Jenner called for the impeachment of President Harry Truman and claimed that the United Nations was infiltrating American schools. After Republicans took control of the Senate in 1952, Jenner became chair of the Subcommittee to Investigate the Administration of the Internal Security Act and Other Internal Security Laws. Indiana writer Irving Leibowitz observed that unlike McCarthy, Jenner was able to work with fellow legislators and added that the report of Jenner's subcommittee, *Interlocking Subversion in Government Departments*, sold almost as well in Washington as the Kinsey report on *Sexual Behavior in the Human Male*, another product of Indiana.[41]

Under McFadden, the library pursued a course of what she called "positive Americanism." On the one hand, the library adopted a formal policy on questionable materials that signaled its commitment to contain communist propaganda. On the other, the library produced reading lists on America that reflected an expansive view of the country's traditions and values. McFadden anticipated that fervent anticommunists might challenge the library. In her talk on the library and international relations in 1948 she observed,

> Obviously, it is ridiculous to consider having discussions, etc., unless the issues are important enough to have the element of controversy in them. Will we get into trouble? The answer is probably, "Yes." After all, A.L.A. couldn't discuss the Marshall Plan without being criticized by a newspaper, located not very far from Headquarters, geographically that is. Someone in your audience [missing word?] find an excellent chance to expound his theories of communism and the next morning it will be all over town that you sponsored a communist meeting. Such incidents are regrettable but are we, after long years of service, so weak and afraid that we cannot take the risks?[42]

Perhaps to forestall controversy or preempt action by the library's board, McFadden presented a "Statement on Questionable Materials," which she and staff members had drafted, to the Board of School Commissioners, the library's governing board. Adopted in November 1950, the statement reflected McFadden's commitment to intellectual freedom. Like other big-city public libraries, the Indianapolis Public Library received free propaganda materials promoting the Soviet cause. The policy provided that before the library added such publications to the collection, its staff would check with the FBI and the U.S. attorney general to determine whether any had been deemed subversive. If so, the material would be rejected.[43] This policy did not differ greatly from those adopted by the Detroit Public Library under Ralph Ulveling or the Carnegie Library of Pittsburgh under Ralph Munn and gained for the library such headlines as "Public Library to Weed Out Red Literature" and "City

Library to Censor Red Papers."[44] Nevertheless, the policy reaffirmed the Library
Bill of Rights, maintained the right of citizens to gain access to information
about communism, and declared the right of the library to hold such material for research purposes. Indeed, *The Communist Manifesto* remained in the
library's collection in multiple copies and in the Great Books first-year cur-
riculum. The policy provided that the works of blacklisted authors would
remain in circulation unless separately found subversive.[45] While it helped
shield the library from local critics, the policy emphasized access and had min-
imal impact on the library's collection practices.

As a counterweight to the questionable materials policy, the staff produced
a series of booklists recommending titles on the meaning of America. The first
in the series, *What Made America? Books Have the Answer*, appeared in early
1950. The foreword explained that the chosen titles "present a composite picture of what has gone into the making of these United States—what events
have built them (HISTORY), what kinds of leaders in all fields have led them
(BIOGRAPHY), what culture has evolved from them (FINE ARTS) and
above all, what forms of daily living their peoples have undergone which have
been so desirable that no sacrifice was too great to retain them (FICTION)."

Selections had to be entertaining as well as authentic. "Many great books,"
it explained, "which are ordinarily included in lists such as these have been
omitted deliberately because they lack the 'human touch.'"[46] Along with mainstream works recounting the lives of the Founding Fathers, the list also included biographies of African Americans and women, a labor leader, and a
surgeon. Employing its public relations know-how and community connections, the library put an exhibit of recommended books in the window of a
downtown department store. In her history of the library from 1945 to 1955,
McFadden noted that the booklist was mentioned in the *Library of Congress
Information Bulletin* and used by the State Department. Even Senator Homer
Capehart sang its praises: "This little booklet, small in physical aspect, is great
and large in its purpose. It should be a splendid contribution to one of the
nation's greatest needs of the day: A rededication to the principles and philosophies which made America great."[47]

The second volume, *What Is America? Books Have the Answer*, appeared in
October 1951.[48] Dedicated to the American Library Association on its seventy-
fifth anniversary, it received national circulation as part of ALA's American
Heritage Project. Its titles, drawn from the period 1945 to 1951, included works
by Stephen Vincent Benét, Norman Corwin, David Lilienthal; titles such as
The Death of a Salesman and *The Catcher in the Rye*, which Marian McFadden

compared to novels by Booth Tarkington; and works on the atom bomb, solar power, and world peace—a midcentury catalog of promise and perils. In 1952–53, the Indianapolis Public Library served as a test site for the Young People's American Heritage Project, where the meaning of Americanism was explored through a rich mix of ethnic stories in an overwhelmingly white community.[49]

COMMUNITY CONNECTIONS

McFadden sensed the importance of communicating the library's message to the public and proved adept at putting the library on the front page and on the airwaves. She was its best public face but was also one of the first library directors to employ a public relations professional. Soon after her appointment, she invited Wilbur Nagley, a reporter for the *Indianapolis Star*, to work part-time for six months to generate publicity for the library. At the end of the trial period, when the number of column inches about the library had doubled, McFadden brought him onto the staff full-time. Among the first such library publicists, Nagley pioneered the role and provided a model for other systems to follow.[50] Working together, McFadden and Nagley provided a constant stream of newsworthy events for the press to cover. In a photograph that accompanied her *Library Journal* article "Library Fights for an Informed Citizenry," McFadden is surrounded by representatives of the local press and broadcast media.[51]

McFadden also sought to protect the library by organizing an advisory group of prominent citizens, representing, as she said, "various faiths and organizations," to be ready to back up the library in case of trouble. As one member explained, "'We know the library has no axe to grind and is only helping us help ourselves.'"[52] She also reached out to numerous, diverse community groups to join the library's educational efforts, demonstrating the validity of Oliver Garceau's finding of the importance of fitting volunteer groups into the work of the library.[53] Nagley produced and hosted a radio quiz show, *Just for Fun*, on which members of local organizations answered questions about Indiana, giving them good publicity while drawing them into the library's orbit.[54]

Dignitaries who participated in the library's programs also benefited. Senator Capehart appeared on the panel on foreign aid on the eve of the Senate debate of the Marshall Plan. An advance headline in the *Indianapolis Star* announced, "European Aid Capehart Topic on Library Forum." Capehart could then claim credit for using the forum to gain citizen input on the issue.[55] The panel also included A. Wayne Murphy, vice commander of the 11th District, American Legion.[56] An article announcing the second forum on compulsory military training concluded, "The forums are part of the library's program to help stimulate public thinking and understanding of vital issues before the country."[57] This panel included representatives from Selective Service and the American Legion, the Congress of Parents and Teachers, and a minister from Richmond, Indiana, who also edited the *American Friend*, a Quaker publication. According to the *Indianapolis Star*, the library's first two forums "drew capacity audiences which took an enthusiastic part in the proceedings." The editorial boasted that the American Library Association planned to urge other public libraries to sponsor similar programs.[58]

In April 1948, in the midst of its forum programs, the Indianapolis Public Library observed its seventy-fifth anniversary. Stage-managed by Nagley, the weeklong celebration featured daily programs at the library, from a teen music group sponsored by the Junior Chamber of Commerce to a tea for the library's board. Pictures of each event appeared in the city's three daily papers. News releases were sent to dozens of community papers and corporate outlets. Downtown department stores put library exhibits in their windows and ran congratulatory messages in their ads. Busses and trolleys sported library bumper stickers. McFadden and other staff members did fifteen-minute radio broadcasts. Local papers ran cartoons, and columnists approvingly noted the occasion. A gala dinner featured an after-dinner speech by Librarian of Congress Luther Evans and honored eighty-nine-year-old Amelia Orndorff, one of the library's first five hundred card holders.[59] In her remarks, McFadden thanked the press for its coverage of the library. "I can honestly say that during the years I have been in this position, there has never been anything but a happy relationship with the press. And this goes for the reporters, the photographers, and right on up to the top." In response, the editor of the *Indianapolis Star* wrote to McFadden,

> On behalf of the news staff and any others who gave space in our paper to your 75th anniversary program, I will say that you are a most gracious lady. Bless your heart, it is part of our job to see that such important events are well covered. Please know that I am always happy to be of service to the library in any way I can.
>
> Sincerely yours, James A. Stuart.[60]

A patron "reading" the Indianapolis Public Library would have seen an institution that encouraged critical thought and provided multiple opportunities to acquire, share, and discuss ideas. Its campaign on behalf of the United Nations, its organization of public forums, its support of racial tolerance, its expansive view of Americanism, and even its nuanced policy on subversive materials all represented a world view at odds with the anti-intellectual, racist, and anticommunist strains of Hoosier culture. It is telling that when a protest letter appeared in the *Indianapolis Star*, the author criticized the library's questionable materials policy rather than its showing of *The Brotherhood of Man* or its holdings of *The Communist Manifesto*. Describing himself as a twenty-year-old about to be drafted, although too young to vote, Ned Rosen wrote, "Please, allow me the prerogative of examining all sides of the International mess, at least! Let me read the Communists' point of view. Our statesmen are not perfect. Let me find out what I am to fight for besides the traditions on which this country was founded. Let me determine my own answers to the foreign policy questions. As Robert Burns put it, 'Let us see ourselves as others see us.'"[61] Rosen had internalized the library's message of self-education and critical thought, and in his letter he reminded the library of its own best self.

As a professional librarian, Marian McFadden might well have agreed. As a Hoosier, she was sensitive to the currents in her community, steering the library through the rocky shoals of the early Cold War. How had she reconciled these contradictions? In part, her efforts to connect the library to diverse community groups helped buffer the library from the same organizations that challenged libraries elsewhere. Civic, educational, and religious groups had been involved in the library. The press had covered its activities; politicians and civic leaders had appeared on its programs. An advisory committee was in place to defend the library; a policy on questionable materials preempted charges of being soft on communism. McFadden played a large role: she was engaged in the community, a familiar face in the local papers. The American Legion had honored her efforts on behalf of returned veterans.[62] Her family's strong ties to Indiana, its solid social standing, and her own lifelong identification with the Republican Party further assured the community that the library was in good hands.

After twelve years as library director, Marian McFadden retired in 1956 at the age of fifty-two.[63] Shortly before her retirement, she reflected on the library's policy on subversive material and concluded that it had proven "effective and workable." Reiterating that "censorship is and ought to be abhorrent to librarians," she observed that the librarian was ultimately responsible only to the will of the community at large. "Note this does not refer to Mrs. White, not to Joe McCarthy, but to the ultimate will of the community at large. So much easier to cry 'Censorship' but to accept that responsibility so much more of a challenge." From Oscar Wilde she quoted an epigram that she believed dealt "swiftly and devastatingly with the topic of censorship . . . whether the question is one of subversion or the much older and persistent one of immorality." Wilde had written, "There is no such thing as a moral or an immoral book. Books are well written and badly written. That is all." McFadden heartily concurred, "Isn't that the perfect, the absolute criterion?"[64]

Two decades of fruitful engagement in her hometown of Shelbyville followed. She was unanimously elected to the school board, authored a history of Shelbyville, and volunteered in the local hospital.[65] In 1971 she wrote a commentary in *American Libraries* responding to the question "Why choose librarianship as a profession?" She recalled her own commitment to intellectual freedom: "I now quite knowingly step on precarious ground. No one acquainted with my work would, I believe, accuse me of being false to the concepts of freedom to read or be denied access to information they desire. I stood my job on the line for those principles and I stand for them today." But then she asked whether the library had another, as important, responsibility. "The question is that, even considering the many dangerous reasons for it, is there too much emphasis on 'freedom to read,' etc. while the quality of material the library has the responsibility of providing mostly from tax monies, is not given enough consideration?"[66]

Still committed to both the promotion of good reading and the protection of intellectual freedom, Marian McFadden died in 1975, having lived to see Kurt Vonnegut's great success with *Slaughterhouse-Five* in 1969 and *Breakfast of Champions* in 1973.[67] In her will, she left an outright bequest of $30,000 to the Indianapolis-Marion County Public Library Foundation, established by her successor, Harold Sander. An additional residual bequest to the library foundation brought the total to $152,042.69 (the equivalent of more than $500,000 today).[68] With the income from McFadden's bequest, the Library Foundation established an annual author lecture series in her memory.[69] Over the years, speakers invited to give the Marian McFadden Lecture have been both the best and most controversial writers of their day, including Saul Bellow, Norman Mailer, James Baldwin, and (twice) Kurt Vonnegut. In 1986, when Vonnegut expressed his unfulfilled hopes for Indianapolis, he was delivering the Marian McFadden Lecture. A packed auditorium heard him denounce President Ronald Reagan for never having read a book and Attorney General Ed Meese and the city of Indianapolis for campaigning against pornography.[70] Though lamenting his hometown's failures, by his presence at the podium Vonnegut honored the legacy of Marian McFadden.

NOTES

1. Using statistics compiled by Alice Payne Hackney, in *Fifty Years of Best Sellers, 1895–1945* (New York: R. R. Bowker, 1945), Purdue librarian John Moriarty calculated that Indiana had produced more bestselling authors from 1895 to 1945 than any other state except New York. In addition to Dreiser, Tarkington, and Stratton-Porter, Indiana's literary luminaries included Meredith Nicholson, James Whitcomb Riley, and George Ade. See John H. Moriarty, "Hoosiers Sell Best," *Indiana Quarterly for Bookmen* 3, no. 1 (January 1947): 7–14. These figures are corrected in R. E. Banta, *Indiana Authors and Their Books, 1816–1916: Biographical Sketches of Authors Who Published during the First Century of Indiana Statehood, with Lists of Their Books* (Crawfordsville, IN: Wabash College, 1949), xi; and Arthur W. Shumaker, *A History of Indiana Literature, with Emphasis on Authors of Imaginative Works Who Commenced Writing Prior to World War II* (Indianapolis: Indiana Historical Society, 1962).

2. Irving Leibowitz, *My Indiana* (Englewood Cliffs, NJ: Prentice-Hall, 1964), 242. The chapter "What Made Hoosiers Write" begins with a quotation from Hoosier novelist Meredith Nicholson, describing Indiana as "a state where not to be an author is to be distinguished."

3. Kurt Vonnegut Jr., *Breakfast of Champions: Or, Goodbye Blue Monday!* (New York: Delacorte, 1973). Over the years, Vonnegut maintained a love-hate relationship with his hometown. His appearance in 1986 signaled a reconciliation that climaxed two decades later with a citywide celebration of the Year of Vonnegut. An honor he much appreciated, it was cut short by his death, in April 2007, just as it began. Vonnegut enthusiasts in Indianapolis have recently established a Kurt Vonnegut Memorial Library in the city's center, not far from his old neighborhood. Melanie D. Hayes, "Memorial Library Illustrates Chapters of Vonnegut's Life," *Indianapolis Star*, January 30, 2011, B1. For more information go to http://www.vonnegutlibrary.org/.

4. Marcy Mermel, "Vonnegut Deplores Lack of City Change," *Indianapolis News*, April 19, 1986. The speech was not recorded. Another description can be found in Pam Morice, "Vonnegut Covers News," *Butler [University] Collegian*, April 21, 1986, 5.

5. Kurt Vonnegut Jr., *Slaughterhouse-Five: Or, The Children's Crusade, a Duty Dance with Death* (New York: Delacorte, 1969).

6. In *The Age of American Unreason*, Susan Jacoby uses an Indiana example to demonstrate the anti-intellectual strain in American history and the distrust of higher education. Susan Jacoby, *The Age of American Unreason* (New York: Pantheon, 2008), 11.

7. Lotys Benning Stewart, "They Achieve," *Indianapolis Star*, January 28, 1945 (no. 203 in the Women Who Achieve series).

8. Marian McFadden, "One Librarian?," *American Libraries* 2, no. 7 (July–August 1971): 687.

9. Marian McFadden, Staff Efficiency Card, McFadden-Miscellaneous folder, Marian McFadden Files, Indianapolis Marion County Public Library Special Collections (McFadden Files, IMCPL Special Collections).

10. Marian McFadden to Harold Sander, December 8, 1970, McFadden-Handwritten Correspondence folder, McFadden Files, IMCPL Special Collections.

11. Stewart, "They Achieve"; McFadden, "One Librarian?," 687.

12. Carrie Scott, Performance Evaluation of Marian McFadden, February 19, 1942, McFadden-Early Performance Evaluations folder, McFadden Files, IMCPL Special Collections.

13. Leonard J. Downey, *A Live Thing in the Whole Town: The History of the Indianapolis-Marion County Public Library 1873–1990* (Indianapolis: Indianapolis-Marion County Public Library Foundation, 1991), 50–55.

14. "Staff Member Approved as Acting City Librarian," *Indianapolis News*, October 11, 1944; "City's Acting Librarian," *Indianapolis Star*, October 13, 1944; Downey, *Live Thing in the Whole Town*, 57.

15. "Indianapolis Public Library, Marian McFadden, Librarian" [Interlaken Mills Library Outline, No. 82] *Library Journal* 71 (January 15, 1946): [65]; John Wilson, "Inside Indianapolis: Hoosier Profile [Marian McFadden]," *Indianapolis Times*, December 10, 1949; "Marian McFadden," *Library Occurrent* 15, no. 1 (January–March 1945): 348.

16. "Second Woman in Seventy-Two Years Chosen as City Librarian," *Indianapolis News*, February 28, 1945. See also Downey, *Live Thing in the Whole Town*; and S. L. Berry with Mary Ellen Gadski, *Stacks: A History of the Indianapolis-Marion County Public Library* (Indianapolis: Indianapolis-Marion County Public Library Foundation, 2011).

17. Mary E. Bostwick, "Books Everywhere, but New Librarian Too Busy to Read," *Indianapolis Star*, March 1, 1945.

18. Marian McFadden, "Librarians and Books," 3, Indianapolis Public Library Staff Day 1955 [n.d.], McFadden Talks-Internal folder, McFadden Files, IMCPL Special Collections.

19. "Demand at Library Reflects Serious Reading Public," *Indianapolis Star*, January 4, 1945.

20. Bostwick, "Books Everywhere."

21. Marian McFadden, *The Indianapolis Public Library: A Portrait against the Background of the Past Decade, 1945–1955* (Indianapolis: Indianapolis Public Library, 1956), 50; *Great Books in the Modern World: A Community Program of Adult Education* (Indianapolis: Indianapolis Project, with the Cooperation of the University of Chicago, 1946). For a retrospective look at the Great Books movement, see Alex Beam, *A Great Idea at the Time: The Rise, Fall, and Curious Afterlife of the Great Books* (New York: Public Affairs, 2008).

22. "Great Books Sets Goal of 4,000 Hoosiers," *Indianapolis Star*, August 6, 1947, 4.

23. McFadden, *Indianapolis Public Library*, 50.

24. Marian McFadden, "Library Fights for Informed Citizenry," *Library Journal* 73 (January 1, 1948): 14.

25. "Local Libraries Open 'Public Thinking' Drive" *Indianapolis Times*, October 15, 1947.

26. McFadden, *Indianapolis Public Library*, 25.

27. *Where Will You Hide?*, undated press releases, IMCPL Publicity Scrapbook 1948, IMCPL Special Collections.

28. Wilson, "Inside Indianapolis."

29. "Let's Read Books for Young People," IMCPL Publicity Scrapbook 1948, IMCPL Special Collections.

30. Marian McFadden, "Library Programs in the Field of International Relations," Remarks at Film Workshop and Adult Education Institute, American Library Association, Ambassador Hotel, Atlantic City, NJ, June 11, 1948, 11, typescript, McFadden-External Talks/Papers folder McFadden Files, IMCPL Special Collections.

31. "Library to Sponsor U.N. Workshop Course Here," *Indianapolis Star*, August 31, 1948; "Calling Attention to an Exhibit," *Indianapolis Star*, October 19, 1948.

32. McFadden, "Library Fights," 15.

33. Marian McFadden to Staff, April 16, 1945, McFadden-Work Memos, Reports, Correspondence folder, McFadden Files, IMCPL Special Collections.

34. Herbert Rissler, "David C. Stephenson and the Indiana KKK," *Indiana Social Studies Quarterly* 19 (1966): 29–39; Leonard J. Moore, *Citizen Klansmen: The Ku Klux Klan in Indiana, 1921–1928* (Chapel Hill: University of North Carolina Press, 1991). Moore argues that the Klan represented a populist movement, cutting across class lines, which sought to recapture community ties of the preindustrial era, restore family values, and enforce Prohibition. During the revival of the Klan, Indiana had the largest membership of any state. In the 1924 election, the Klan dominated the Republican Party, forcing out the Republican establishment and capturing most statewide and national congressional seats. Once in office, Klan members did little to promote a Klan agenda. In many localities, the Klan supported reform and anticorruption causes, and female Klan members were strong proponents of votes for women. Klan membership could not be described as either urban or rural but rather as a form of Protestant nationalism. For Indiana women in the Klan, see Kathleen M. Blee, *Women of the Klan: Racism and Gender in the 1920s*, rev. ed. (Berkeley: University of California Press, 2009).

35. For additional accounts of the Marion, Indiana, lynching, see James Madison, *A Lynching in the Heartland: Race and Memory in America* (New York: Palgrave, 2001), and Cynthia Carr, *Our Town: A Heartland Lynching, a Haunted Town, and the Hidden History of White America* (New York: Three Rivers, 2007). Carr is the granddaughter of a Klan member who participated in the Marion lynching.

36. Dwight W. Culver, "Racial Desegregation in Indiana," *Journal of Negro Education* 23, no. 3 (Summer 1954): 296–302.

37. David K. Berninghausen, "Film Censorship," *ALA Bulletin* 44 (December 1950): 447–48.

38. *The Brotherhood of Man*, screenplay by Ring Lardner Jr. (United Productions of America, 1946). The film can be viewed on YouTube: http://www.youtube.com/watch?v=2KLgDTGT-I. See Ruth Benedict and Gene Weltfish, *The Races of Mankind*, Public Affairs Pamphlet no. 85 (New York: Public Affairs Committee, 1943).

39. "Racial Relations Exhibit at Library," *Indianapolis News*, February 20, 1946; "Library to Show Free Films; Films to Follow Theme of Better Race Tolerance," press release, Library Public Relations, Indianapolis Public Library, March 25, 1949.

40. Leibowitz, *My Indiana*, 235–37.

41. Irving Leibowitz, "Senator William E. Jenner," in *Indiana History: A Book of Readings*, ed. Ralph D. Gray (Bloomington: Indiana University Press, 1994), 363; U.S. Congress, Senate, Committee on the Judiciary, Subcommittee to Investigate the Administration of the Internal Security Act and Other Internal Security Laws, *Report on Interlocking Subversion in Government Departments* (Washington, DC: Government Printing Office, 1953).

Kinsey was a faculty member at Indiana University whose research into human sexuality were funded in part by the Rockefeller Foundation. See Alfred C. Kinsey, Wardell B. Pomeroy, and Clyde E. Martin, *Sexual Behavior in the Human Male* (Philadelphia: W. B. Saunders, 1948). The way university president Herman B [no period] Wells protected Kinsey's academic freedom from foundation staff and hostile state legislators is well depicted in the film *Kinsey*, directed by Bill Condon (Fox Searchlight, 2004).

42. McFadden, "Library Programs," 11.

43. McFadden, *Indianapolis Public Library*, 75.

44. Ralph A. Ulveling, "Book Selection Policies," *Library Journal* 76, no. 14 (August 1951): 1170–71; Louise S. Robbins, "Segregating Propaganda in American Libraries: Ralph Ulveling Confronts the Intellectual Freedom Committee," *Library Quarterly* 63, no. 2 (April 1993): 143–65. Writing in 1953, McFadden noted that librarians had long distinguished collections in branches from that in the main library; see Marian McFadden, "Objectives and Functions of Public Libraries," *Library Trends* 1 (April 1953): 431.

"City Library to Censor Red Papers," *Indianapolis Star*, November 29, 1950; "Public Library to Weed Out Red Literature," *Indianapolis News*, November 29, 1950. The latter article began: "The Communists are going to have to figure out some other way of infiltrating the Indianapolis Public Library."

45. This meant, for example, that the library could continue to show *The Brotherhood of Man* although its screenwriter, Ring Lardner Jr., had been blacklisted as one of the "Hollywood 10."

46. *What Made America? Books Have the Answer* (Indianapolis: Indianapolis Public Library, 1950).

47. McFadden, *Indianapolis Public Library*, 47.

48. *What Is America? Books Have the Answer* (Indianapolis: Indianapolis Public Library, 1951).

49. McFadden, *Indianapolis Public Library*, 48. See also Hannah Hunt, "Young Americans Discuss Their Heritage," *Public Libraries* 7 (February 1953): 5–6; and Hannah Hunt, "It's Our America," *Library Journal* 78 (May 1, 1953): 777–82, 786–87. Hunt was a graduate of Earlham College, a Quaker school in Richmond, Indiana.

50. Bill Nagley, "Trained Publicity Writer," *Wilson Library Bulletin* 20, no. 3 (March 1946): 540; "They Really *Make* News," *Library Journal* 72, no. 10 (October 1, 1947): 1340–41.

51. McFadden, "Library Fights," 15.

52. McFadden, "Library Programs," 11.

53. Oliver Garceau, *The Public Library in the Political Process: A Report of the Public Library Inquiry* (New York: Columbia University Press, 1949), 128–29.

54. "Indianapolis P. L. Produces Quiz Show," *Library Journal* 70 (December 1, 1945): 1130–31.

55. "European Aid Capehart Topic on Library Forum," *Indianapolis Star*, November 9, 1948.

56. McFadden, "Library Fights," 15.

57. "Compulsory Military Training to Be Library Forum Topic," *Indianapolis News*, December 4, 1947.

58. "Our Library Takes the Lead," *Indianapolis Star*, January 8, 1948. The ALA "Great Issues" program provided reading lists on topics such as the Marshall Plan and encouraged libraries to organize discussions but did not provide either administrative support or funding for the initiative.

59. "Librarian of Congress Is Anniversary Speaker," *Indianapolis News*, April 8, 1948.

60. James A. Stuart to McFadden, 21 April 1948, Seventy-fifth Anniversary File, IMCPL Special Collections.

61. Ned Rosen, "Library Rule on Communist Propaganda Brings a Protest," letter to the editor, *Indianapolis Star*, December 3, 1950, 14.

62. Citation presented to Marian McFadden by the Robison-Ragsdale Post No. 133, American Legion, September 30, 1947, McFadden-Awards, Honors folder, McFadden Papers, IMCPL Special Collections.

63. "Well Done, Miss McFadden," *Indianapolis News*, July 21, 1956.

64. "McFadden, "Librarians and Books," 4–5.

65. Marian McFadden, *Biography of a Town: Shelbyville, Indiana, 1822–1962* (Shelbyville, IN: Tippecanoe Press, 1968).

66. Marian McFadden, "One Librarian?," 687–88.

67. "Miss McFadden, Ex-Library Head," *Indianapolis News*, September 9, 1975; "Necrology," *Library Occurrent* 25 (November 1975): 131.

68. Downey, *Live Place in the Whole Town*, 63.

69. For more on the Marian McFadden Memorial Lecture, see http://www.imcpl.org/mcfadden.

70. Rebecca Overton, "Vonnegut Blasts Reagan with Wit," *Indianapolis Star*, April 9, 1986.

PART 3

INTELLECTUAL FREEDOM

Censorship in the Heartland

Eastern Iowa Libraries during World War I

JULIA SKINNER

Early in 1918, Herbert Metcalf, secretary of the Iowa Council of National Defense, sent a request to public and academic libraries requesting that staff scour their shelves and remove materials sympathetic to the German war effort. While Metcalf's original letter does not survive, his records at the State Historical Society of Iowa include responses from a number of Iowa librarians, which largely report the removal of fiction and nonfiction materials considered "pro-German."[1] Whether their actions were spurred by a desire to avoid scrutiny or a patriotic endeavor to assist the war effort, many public libraries around the state chose to comply with pressures from government and community members by removing fiction and nonfiction materials both before and after the United States' entry into the war.

Documents within the libraries both expand upon and at times contradict information contained in Metcalf's files. Burlington Public Library, for example, gradually eliminated acquisition of German-language texts after 1914 in favor of materials discussing current events. While the librarian responded favorably to Metcalf's censorship request, this is never mentioned in board meeting minutes, despite the library's pro-access stance in response to other challenges made immediately following the war. Despite these occasional differences, the response of Iowa libraries supports the work of Wayne Wiegand, who found that libraries' work could be understood in the context of a period of neutrality from 1914 to 1916 and one of more fervent involvement in the war effort upon the United States' entrance into the war. Wiegand also found that this was in keeping with larger cultural shifts in the United States, as official policy and public sentiment moved away from neutrality and toward active involvement (alongside increasing patriotic fervor) as time progressed.[2]

This project used a small-scale approach based upon records created within six Iowa libraries to support Wiegand's findings from a nationwide study of libraries, which sought "to view public libraries' activity during World War I through the eyes of large and small local public libraries."[3] However, this essay provides a much more intimate focus on a smaller number of institutions within a statewide, rather than national, study. Through the examination of contemporary administrative records produced by Iowa libraries, this research creates a detailed portrait of individual institutions and their adaptation to life during wartime. The present paper compares the actions of these libraries using the same timeframes outlined in Wiegand's book. These include public libraries in Burlington, Davenport, Mount Pleasant, Iowa City, Cedar Rapids, and Dubuque. This study examines records created between 1912 and 1920, and thus the present discussion will include libraries before, during, and after the war. This will be followed by a brief mention of postwar library activity.

THE POPULATION OF IOWA

Iowa's population rose almost continuously from the 1830s, when European American settlers first came to the state, through 1915.[4] For example, the population of the state was 2,210,050 in 1905 and rose to 2,358,066 in 1915.[5] During the prewar and wartime periods, the percentage of foreign-born Iowans decreased, while the native-born population increased.[6] However, the number of second-generation immigrants (the children of immigrants) was still high, indicating that while there was not a wave of immigration around the time World War I began, there had been a generation earlier. Those with two native-born parents numbered 1,422,464, while 654,855 others were residents with at least one foreign-born parent.[7] This is in keeping with German immigration nationally, which steadily rose during the nineteenth century, peaking in the 1850s and 1880s.[8]

Despite fluctuating immigration patterns, German Americans made up a large proportion of Iowa's immigrant population. In 1905, the number of foreign-born persons in Iowa who were born in Germany was 110,167. This was 39.08 percent of the total number of first-generation immigrants for this year: a much larger number than any other immigrant groups. The next largest group was the Swedes, who comprised only 10 percent of the foreign-born population. In 1915, the number of Iowa residents born in Germany had fallen to 88,450, or 33.48 percent of the total foreign-born population. Despite this drop, Germans still vastly outnumbered other immigrant groups:

the next-largest group was, again, immigrants from Sweden, who only comprised 9.72 percent of the total.[9]

German immigrants settled in every county in the state by the end of the nineteenth century, although there is a good deal of variation between counties.[10] The census figures showed Des Moines County (home of the town of Burlington) and Dubuque County (Dubuque) as having similar ratios of native-born and foreign-born residents. Dubuque County had a high second-generation immigrant population, suggesting a wave of immigration to the area the generation before.[11] Henry County (Mount Pleasant) had the smallest immigrant population. Linn County (Cedar Rapids) had the largest population, most likely because of workers attracted to Cedar Rapids' manufacturing industry. Because of the possible inaccuracy of Scott County's (Davenport) figures, it is hard to draw conclusions about them, although research elsewhere informs us that Davenport had a large German-speaking population.[12] The census data also showed that Iowa was a well-educated state, with a 99 percent literacy rate, and with 245 "free public and other general libraries" in operation.[13] This high literacy rate and large number of libraries (more than two per county) indicates that the public was both learned and interested in libraries, a theory further supported by increasing circulation and numbers of patrons in the prewar period.

Iowa Libraries before the War

In 1912, each of the six libraries indicated an increased demand for services, mostly in the areas of circulation and the issuing of library cards to new patrons. Meeting minutes and annual reports provide near-constant examples of the increased use of the libraries and the increased circulation of materials. Mount Pleasant Public Library's minutes are typical of all the libraries in showing increases that continued through the end of the war.[14] While it is possible that some of this increase may be due to a growing population throughout the state, librarians used a variety of strategies to actively recruit new patrons, and this may account for the majority of the increase in the prewar period.

E. Joanna Hagey, librarian at Cedar Rapids Public Library, gave talks at local factories in January 1913. The library also ran small lending libraries for factory workers.[15] Like Hagey, Lillian B. Arnold of Dubuque operated a small library for industrial workers, these employed at the Union railcar barns.[16] Arnold and her staff also worked to increase circulation by encouraging new patrons to use the library. In 1914, they distributed over a hundred cards to college students, including members of Dubuque German College. They also issued cards, at fifty cents per year, to those living outside of city limits and to transients.[17]

Almost all the librarians engaged in outreach to surrounding communities in order to attract new patrons. In 1912, Hagey indicated a desire to receive tax support from these communities so their residents could use the library.[18] The Iowa City Public Library began issuing library cards to rural Johnson County residents in 1914.[19] This broadened their service area beyond the city limits and meant that service decisions made by the library would affect a larger number of people. Libraries further extended their reach by actively cooperating with the schools. E. Joanna Hagey arranged to loan books to schools both in Cedar Rapids and in nearby rural areas, as did Dubuque and Burlington.[20]

Helen McRaith of the Iowa City Public Library was the most active in reaching out to younger readers. Staff members were sent to the schools to sign up whole classrooms for library cards, and the librarian placed publicity material and suggested reading lists in shops to guide children's reading.[21] Mount Pleasant Public Library was the only institution not active in seeking new patrons from outside communities or within local schools. It is possible that this was not necessary in a more rural setting, as Mount Pleasant Public Library was likely serving the whole community already. It was also the only prewar library without documentation of a German-language collection, while the five other libraries actively acquired such materials.

From the start of the century until 1914, Burlington's librarian acquired a sizeable German collection, although there are no records of such purchases after 1914. Prior to this, the 1899 finding list showed sizeable numbers of German-language books, spanning ten pages of the collection guide, and fifty-three English-language books about Germany and Germans. Subsequent lists from 1900 to 1910 indicated further increases to the German collection.[22] Carnegie-Stout Free Public Library's records indicate a German-language collection but leave few clues as to its size or circulation.[23]

Iowa City Public Library also maintained a German collection, which the librarian mentioned in 1913: "The demand for German books was so great that it was necessary to procure additional copies of German stories, their use shows that the German collection should be increased."[24] Cedar Rapids' librarian echoed this need: "Twenty-three new German books were ordered, only six of them are on the shelves at present which proves that the books were needed."[25] While German books were in demand at the Cedar Rapids Public Library, an even greater demand came from the Bohemian community. In the same report, the librarian states, "In April of 1913, 202 Bohemian books were taken out, this year 153. Miss Vashek says that so many Bohemian patrons report that they have read all the titles we have. I hope that the books ordered in February will soon be available."[26] The library's frequent use by Bohemian patrons makes it the only library to cater to an ethnic group larger than the German-speaking one.

Nowhere was the need for German books more acute than in Davenport, a town referred to as "the most German city, not only in the State, but in all the Middle West, the center of all German activities in the State."[27] By 1913, Davenport Public Library's German-language collection contained nearly three thousand titles. The next-largest collection, by contrast, was in French and contained only about two hundred items.[28] The German collection was also in higher demand: German-language books circulated 10,897 times in 1912, while French books only circulated 229 times, Swedish 71 times, and Bohemian 61 times.[29] Library staff grouped foreign-language titles by subject with the English books within finding lists, although they also created a separate German-language finding list in 1909.[30]

Even though every library except Mount Pleasant's documented the existence of a German-language collection, there is some evidence of tension between providing foreign-language materials and promoting Americanization. This balance between assimilation and service is summed up well in Cedar Rapids' 1913 annual report:

> Our Librarian calls attention to the need of additions to our collections of books in foreign tongues. I believe the suggestion a good one, though there are those who may question the wisdom of it, holding that all good Americans, of whatever foreign birth, ought to read the literature of their native lands in English translations, and thus perfect themselves in the ability to become more thorough Americans. It is to be remembered, however, that all literature suffers in translation, and the desire to get their classics in the original form is a natural and proper one on the part of those substantial citizens who have had their birth in other lands.[31]

This tension became more acute once the United States entered the war but during the neutral period was set aside in favor of continued focus on drawing patrons into the library, increasing circulation, and expanding collections.

Iowa Libraries in the Period of Neutrality

When the war began, President Woodrow Wilson immediately declared neutrality, urging Americans to be "impartial in thought as well as action." The president focused on domestic affairs, and it seemed many Americans were not interested in actively engaging with the war overseas either.[32] Just as they would after the United States entered the fighting in 1917, libraries supported government efforts, by both avoiding partisan discussion and sharing materials that might promote peace.[33]

Some German immigrants were an exception to the generally neutral climate, as they felt it was important to try to provide some justification for the German government's perspective on engaging in the war.[34] The German-language press, in particular, sought to illuminate the other side of the controversy, as most English-language newspapers reflected the official U.S. standpoint of neutrality.[35] The National German-American Alliance was particularly active in sharing the German perspective during the neutral period.

In March 1916, at their annual convention in Davenport, "it was resolved that the German-American would live up to his oath of allegiance even though 'he may be forced by a partial government with bleeding heart to fight for England.'" At this same convention it was decided the German Americans would do all they could "to see that the next administration will be American— neither pro-British, nor pro-German, but only a truly American administration."[36] The annual convention in Davenport is evidence of a large German American population that was politically active and perhaps even outspoken. While there is no discussion of politics of the German-American Alliance within Davenport Public Library's records, this level of political activity gives us a context for the potentially charged climate in which that institution existed.

It was also around this time that the pamphlets discussing the causes of war, later removed from Iowa libraries, were published. John W. Burgess, a professor at Columbia University, wrote many articles on the subject that aligned with Germany's official stance on Serbia as a power-hungry entity and Britain as "treacherous." In 1914, Burgess authored a pamphlet titled *The Present Crisis in Europe*, which outlined the viewpoint of the war as detailed by the German-American Alliance. It was also at this same time that he authored *Truth about Germany: Facts about the War*.[37] A German immigrant and prominent industrial psychologist named Hugo Munsterberg authored *The War and America* and *The Peace and America* during the neutral period in the hopes of fostering understanding and strengthening the ties between his adopted and home countries.[38]

Munsterberg's loyalty to Germany cost him dearly, as he was alienated from friends, and "thrown out of clubs and put out of academies" in 1916, even before the United States officially entered the war.[39] Overwhelmed by anti-German sentiment, Munsterberg said, "It has always been the aim of my work to secure real harmony between America, Germany and England. . . . You can imagine with how much sadness and disappointment the last months have filled my mind."[40] Munsterberg died in December 1916, a little over a year before Herbert Metcalf sent out the letter that would initiate the official removal of his works.[41] The story of Munsterberg as a figure during the period of neutrality informs us of a brewing hostility toward Germany even before the United States officially entered the war.

While these adverse sentiments are not evident in Iowa library records, a shift from building German collections does take place, caused in part by wartime shortages, which were a great obstacle to libraries seeking to acquire foreign-language texts. Most librarians ordered their German-language books through Leipzig, but a British embargo reduced the number of books exported. Some librarians suggested that the Department of State might be able to assist in an agreement between the two countries that would facilitate the import of foreign books and periodicals to American libraries, but this request was never granted.[42] The impact went beyond German books to affect other foreign-language texts, including those in Bohemian.

In 1916, the ALA did not print a Bohemian bibliography because "it is almost impossible to secure Bohemian books from abroad."[43] This shortage was evident at the Cedar Rapids Public Library, where 1914 meeting minutes indicated a continued increase in circulation, particularly for foreign-language books. In addition, it was reported that Bohemian books increased in circulation from 148 items the previous year to 220 items in May 1914.[44] However, the records do not show many foreign-language acquisitions, indicating that Bohemian and German patrons were faced with a small and heavily used collection of works in their languages.

Burlington Free Public Library's records most clearly detail a shift in collection development away from German-language books and toward books on the conflict overseas. After 1915, the library began offering new sections on "the War" within its quarterly lists of additions. These included books on philosophy, sociology, and history, and a few discuss Germany's role as an instigator in the conflict. In 1916, finding lists also included "National Defense" and "United States and Foreign Powers."[45] While foreign-language books no longer appeared in Burlington Public Library's records, other libraries still acquired them, and records indicated they were in high demand.

Iowa City's German collection was heavily used in 1915.[46] Davenport Public Library's circulation numbers were the most dramatic, with German-language books circulating forty-four times more than the next-highest-circulating group. After 1916, the German collection was no longer mentioned in the annual reports, and the "foreign books" section was removed from finding aids altogether.[47] Similarly, Dubuque and Burlington's libraries no longer mentioned their German departments after 1914, and by 1916 no library, except Cedar Rapids, made any comment about its German collections. In 1917, Cedar Rapids continued to utilize German traveling libraries and to provide German books to factory workers, in addition to books "teaching one to speak English."[48]

Once the United States entered the war, discussions of these collections became less frequent and were replaced with records of patriotic work. Other trends, such as high circulation numbers, continued through the neutral and wartime periods. One table, originally compiled by E. Joanna Hagey of Cedar Rapids Public Library, shows high circulation numbers for a handful of Iowa libraries. It also shows that the libraries all had small staffs and budgets, spread increasingly thin as wartime demands were placed upon them.

Iowa Libraries in Wartime

Libraries participated in the war effort by both providing resources and information and restricting materials seen as counterproductive to war aims. Several libraries removed materials from their shelves during this time. While it is not mentioned in the library's meeting minutes, Burlington's librarian informed Herbert Metcalf that three books and numerous pamphlets were removed following his request, one having been withdrawn from circulation "some time ago."[49] Davenport's minutes indicate that "a very thorough discussion" took place during a special meeting before it was decided to comply with Metcalf's letter.[50] Mount Pleasant's board also removed books, although how many or what titles is unknown.[51]

In some instances, censorship activities are unclear. For example, the donated German books mentioned in Dubuque's accession records were not given de-accession dates.[52] Almost all other books without withdrawal dates are a part of the Allison Collection, still extant in the library.[53] A similar trend appeared in Iowa City's accession records, where many titles by German American authors seem to have been removed in 1917.[54] This in no way provides concrete evidence of censorship, but it does leave some questions unanswered.

Cedar Rapids provides the most interesting example, as that library withdrew books in response to two separate requests. The librarian's report from March 25, 1918, says, "The chief of police sent word to the library that the War

Department had requested the withdrawal of all books on explosives from the library shelves. All that were in have been placed with the pro-German literature."[55] While no letter from Cedar Rapids' librarian exists in the Metcalf papers, Hagey's statement indicates that the library complied with his request. None of the other libraries mentions the War Department, suggesting that this request may have been intended only for Cedar Rapids.

However common, censorship is far from being the only way that libraries endeavored to support the war.[56] Libraries received requests to purchase Liberty Loans, and Mount Pleasant responded most vigorously, with three donations totaling $2,500 by the end of the war.[57] Other libraries donated money as well: in Cedar Rapids, ALA War Library fundraisers were responded to enthusiastically. Both Cedar Rapids and the surrounding communities consistently exceeded their quotas.[58] In the case of Burlington Public Library, the requests for donations were recorded, but the decisions of the board were not.[59]

Libraries also sent books to Camp Dodge, Iowa, for the soldiers. Davenport and Iowa City public libraries both indicated providing donations but did not regularly keep track of the number of books shipped to the camp.[60] Cedar Rapids' librarian recorded the number of donations periodically, which reached more than five thousand books by the end of the war. Each library, except Mount Pleasant, donated thousands of books, but E. Joanna Hagey said the need for more was still dire after a letter from Major Robbins at Camp Dodge saying, "For heaven's sake send us books."[61] Librarians' enthusiastic response to wartime needs extended to other library activities as well.

Libraries provided space for patriotic group meetings and displayed publications on food conservation, Liberty Loans, thrift stamps, and charitable organizations.[62] Cedar Rapids and Dubuque also provided space for Red Cross work, with Cedar Rapids turning over the entire second floor of their building to the organization.[63] In Cedar Rapids, children were recruited either to solicit donations or to donate money as a part of a game.[64] Staff members from Iowa libraries also engaged in war work beyond their institutions. Employees of Burlington, Davenport, and Iowa City all chose to take a leave of absence to work in military libraries in the United States and overseas, and in one case, at the ALA dispatch offices.[65] Staff continued to volunteer after the end of the war: one staff member from Cedar Rapids went to the Camp Dodge hospital library for three months in 1919.[66]

In all records of war work, the tone of the writing is often one of enthusiasm or at least one of compliance. Helen McRaith of Iowa City used almost jubilant language to describe the library's wartime role in 1917:

The libraries are taking an active part in many ways in aiding the government. Never before has the Public Library meant so much to the community in which it is located, as it has this year. People have looked upon libraries as store houses for books but the war has changed the views of many. This library collected books and magazines for the soldiers at the cantonment during the summer and the response was most generous. Three hundred books—a most interesting collection—was forwarded to Camp Dodge. The library acted as a registration station for Red Cross during the May campaign and many new members were secured here. Official directions for all Red Cross knitting have been kept on file and the demand has been great for these. Duplicate copies of these were obtained and circulated. Food pledge cards were signed by many at the delivery desk in November. Posters calling attention to all Government matters are posted in the library.[67]

In only one instance was there any hint of dissenting opinion when discussing war work, and that came from Burlington Public Library's board while discussing a letter for the War Service Committee in September 1917, "asking co-operation in a National campaign to raise $1,000,000 for Libraries for Soldiers and Sailors. Our appointment being $1,788." The request was not met warmly: "The sentiment of those present . . . was not favorable to the scheme."[68] The tone of this sentence is significant, as it suggests a reluctance not voiced in the records of the other libraries in response to requests for such large sums. This widespread compliance was common of libraries nationwide, many of which actively supported the war effort.[69]

This compliance also would have affected individuals both within the towns and in surrounding areas. Older German-speaking Iowans may not have been able to read in English, reducing their ability to access needed information. Finding lists show that all the libraries had drastically decreased, if not eliminated, their acquisition of German-language titles by the time the United States entered the war. After the passage of the so-called Babel Proclamation by Iowa's governor in May 1918, English was the only language one could use legally anywhere but in one's home.[70] This would have placed further restrictions on an already ostracized group and may have placed further strain on libraries that were trying to provide materials and outreach to non-English-speaking groups.

While all relevant records indicate that the libraries retained censored materials in storage, it is never mentioned whether these "pro-German" materials were ever returned to the circulating collections. An examination of postwar library records through 1920 produced no new information about these books: all three libraries that document censorship never indicated whether materials were kept in storage, put back in circulation, or removed altogether. Those later records do, however, document the beginning of a new era for libraries, in which focus on local concerns was renewed and a more critical stance toward book challenges was fostered.

Iowa Libraries after the War

After Armistice, circulation at Iowa libraries continued to grow. Dubuque's library, for example, indicated that in 1920 it had the largest circulation in its history.[71] Records from the other libraries mirror this trend. Libraries also continued to face book challenges, although their responses were more reserved than in wartime. Burlington's board received a challenge from the Anti-Saloon League regarding books containing "alcoholic recipes" but decided to refrain from action until a law was passed and enforced. It also received a request to remove books "too radical on social conditions." It reviewed the list of books but did not consider any of the items in the library harmful.[72] The Cedar Rapids board also received a request from the Anti-Saloon League, but there is no record of its decision.[73]

In some cases, postwar collection development shifted toward social and political issues. Burlington Public Library began including acquisitions under headings of "Socialism and Communism" and "Social Problems." "The War" is still present as a heading in 1919, but new acquisitions centered on autobiographies and books about the peace process.[74] The only mention of foreign-language books in the postwar period was a fledgling collection of romance-language books (French, Italian, and Spanish) in Mount Pleasant and the acquisition of thirty-seven unspecified foreign-language books in Davenport.[75] Even Cedar Rapids, where the librarian pleaded for new German and Bohemian books through the wartime period, holds no record of foreign-language acquisitions after the war.

Instead, E. Joanna Hagey turned her attention toward assisting soldiers returning to the Cedar Rapids area and saw the library as a central space for both providing information and housing enlistment records.[76] Grace D. Rose also assisted Davenport-area veterans, using ALA booklists to tailor acquisitions to their needs.[77] Libraries would continue to attract more patrons from their communities, with each institution reporting record circulation numbers through 1920.

Nationally, librarians sought to continue channeling the energy and achievements brought on by the war. In her summary of the ALA midwinter meeting in 1920, E. Joanna Hagey said,

What aroused heated arguments was the proposed enlarged programs for ALA activities. It is desired that library work undertaken in war time be continued and library service be extended to all branches of the army, navy, and coast guards. Increased efficiency in Americanization; the printing of more books for the blind as at present the number of titles is very limited; extending library privileges to all people even when population is scattered and national certification of librarians were the main topics. All agreed that the plan was praiseworthy. The only stumbling block was the financial support. The committee seemed to think there would be little or no difficulty in raising the required $2,000,000.00. They did not advocate an intensive drive but would allow until the last of May for the collection of funds.[78]

Her report indicates optimism but also the problem of adequate funding that is familiar to librarians today. It points, as well, to the future direction of libraries as they began to move toward expanding services for underserved populations and ensuring access to materials. Out of this new professional climate arose the concept of access as a right, which would be drafted by Des Moines Public Library's Forrest Spaulding and adopted by the ALA in 1939.[79]

CONCLUDING THOUGHTS

Libraries undertook a variety of approaches to providing service in the time period surrounding World War I. Wayne Wiegand informs us that libraries willingly engaged in the war effort both as a part of the public sentiment and as a way to avoid suspicion, and this research supports that viewpoint.[80] However, it does show a divergence among the libraries, in both how eager they were to censor and when they began to do so. It also shows how librarians and library boards altered the ways they framed discourse about the war in response to outside pressures: library reports become increasingly eager to situate institutions within the patriotic zeitgeist, and records began to employ the language used elsewhere. None of the library records referred to any of their materials as "pro-German" until receiving the letter from the Council of National Defense, but all referred to the items they removed as "pro-German" in response to the letter. Furthermore, these items were never mentioned as seditious or even questionable outside of the context of the council's request, suggesting that librarians did not actively comb the shelves for suspicious materials or that they did not view them as problematic beforehand.

The library records also showed variation in German-language collection development. Some libraries began diverting money and attention from German collections as early as 1914. The books donated to Dubuque in this year represent the only mention of their German department, although books in other languages are mentioned later.[81] Similarly, Burlington had no records of German book purchases after 1914. Cedar Rapids, however, continued to mention its foreign-language collections in the wartime period.[82] All six libraries very quickly shifted toward a focus on wartime activities as soon as the war was declared, and each provides a wealth of information about how the war impacted library activities. As with other libraries nationwide, all the librarians here stepped up to perform their duty, and none stopped to ask if the cost was too great.[83]

NOTES

1. Herbert J. Metcalf Papers, 1910–1919, State Historical Society of Iowa (SHSI), Iowa City, Ms 74, folder 7.

2. Wayne A. Wiegand, *An Active Instrument for Propaganda: The American Public Library during World War I* (New York: Greenwood, 1989).

3. Ibid., 5.

4. Executive Council of the State of Iowa, *Census of Iowa for the Year 1915* (Des Moines: Robert Henderson, 1916), iii.

5. Executive Council of the State of Iowa, *Census of Iowa for the Year 1905* (Des Moines: Bernard Murphy, 1905), xvii; Executive Council of the State of Iowa, *Census of Iowa for the Year 1915*, x.

6. Executive Council of the State of Iowa, *Census of Iowa for the Year 1915*, xliii. The U.S.-born population comprised 88.8 percent of the total, while first-generation immigrants comprised the remaining 11.2 percent, or 264,159 (see xliii, x).

7. Ibid., xlv.

8. Marco Froehlich, "From Germany to the United States to Germany: Emigration and Remigration between 1800 and 1914" (master's thesis, Technical University of Chemnitz, 2007), 12.

9. Executive Council of the State of Iowa, *Census of Iowa for the Year 1915*, lv.

10. Dorothy Schwieder, "History of Iowa," *Iowa Official Register*, 1999–2000, http://publications.iowa.gov/135/1/history/7-1.html; Executive Council of the State of Iowa, *Census of Iowa for the Year 1905*, xxxiii–xlviii; Executive Council of the State of Iowa, *Census of Iowa for the Year 1915*, iv–xlviii.

11. Executive Council of the State of Iowa, *Census of Iowa for the Year 1905*, xxxiii–xlviii.

12. Ibid.; Carl Wittke, *German-Americans and the World War (With Special Emphasis on Ohio's German-Language Press)* (Columbus: Ohio State Archaeological and Historical Society, 1936), 157.

13. Executive Council of the State of Iowa, *Census of Iowa for the Year 1915*, xx.

14. Mount Pleasant Public Library (MPPL), "Board of Library Trustees Meeting Minutes, 3/10/1902–6/7/1917," MPPL Archives, Mount Pleasant, IA; MPPL, "Mount Pleasant Public Library Board of Trustees Meeting Minutes, 7/5/1917–3/7/1946," MPPL Archives, Mount Pleasant, IA.

15. Cedar Rapids Public Library (CRPL), "Minute Book, October 1911 thru December 1914," 54, CRPL Archives, Cedar Rapids, IA.

16. Carnegie-Stout Free Public Library (CSFPL), *Carnegie-Stout Free Public Library, Eighth Annual Report, 1911* (Dubuque, IA: Hardie, 1911).

17. CSFPL, "Scrapbook, 1901–1924," CSFPL Archives, Dubuque, IA.

18. CRPL, "Minute Book, October 1911 thru December 1914," 18.

19. Iowa City Public Library (ICPL), "Report of the Iowa City Public Library for the Year 1914," 3, ICPL Archives, Iowa City, IA.

20. CRPL, "Minute Book, October 1911 thru December 1914," 33; CSFPL, *Carnegie-Stout Free Public Library, Eighth Annual Report, 1911*; Burlington Public Library (BPL), "Burlington Public Library Minutes of Board Meetings, 1885–1927," 340, BPL Archives, Burlington, IA. Most libraries did not save their records that showed the number of books circulating through the schools. However, Burlington Public Library did, and these indicate that more than two thousand books a month were circulated through school collections. Additionally, E. Joanna Hagey collected circulation numbers for Iowa libraries.

21. ICPL, "Report of the Iowa City Public Library for the Year 1914"; ICPL, "Iowa City Public Library Record of Board Meetings, Beginning Nov 15 1905 and Ending March 15, 1927," 251, ICPL Archives, Iowa City, IA.

22. BPL, "Burlington Public Library Lists of Added Books, Some in German, 1900–1910," BPL Archives, Burlington, IA; Clara S. Wilson and Emma J. Schmidt, comps., *Finding List of the Free Public Library of Burlington, Iowa* (Burlington, IA: Conrad Lutz, 1899).

23. CSFPL, *Carnegie-Stout Free Public Library, Eighth Annual Report, 1911*, 12–13; CSFPL, "Scrapbook, 1901–1924"; CSFPL, *Carnegie-Stout Free Public Library, Twelfth Annual Report, 1914* (Dubuque, IA: Hardie, 1914), 13; CSFPL, "Accession Records, 35,001–40,000, June 18 1914–October 19 1916," CSFPL Archives, Dubuque, IA. The library scrapbook shows the donation of German magazines to the library, which was increased by a number of sizeable donations from 1911 to 1914, although there is no further mention of the German department, nor are there records stating how many German books the library held prior to these donations. The books from this period are recorded together in acquisition records, although some of the titles are translated into English.

24. ICPL, "Annual Report of the Iowa City Public Library for the Year 1913," 2, ICPL Archives, Iowa City, IA. ICPL also kept accession records from this time, although all titles are written in English, thus it was more difficult to determine which were the German-language books acquired during this year (author names often made it clear). See ICPL, "Accessions 15001–20000," ICPL Archives, Iowa City, IA.

25. CRPL, "Minute Book, October 1911 thru December 1914," 89.

26. CRPL, "Minute Book, October 1911 thru December 1914," 89, 25, 85. The librarian indicates borrowing materials from the Bohemian Library, most likely the Bohemian-language "Reading Society" mentioned in a 1911 history of Linn County. See Luther Albertus Brewer and Barthinius Larson Wick, *History of Linn County Iowa: From Its Earliest Settlement to the Present Time*, vol. 1 (Chicago: Pioneer Publishing Company, 1911), 124. CRPL also employed Miss Vashek, a Bohemian-speaking woman, to assist patrons several days a week. Since the end of World War I, the Bohemian language and people have been called Czech.

27. August Paul Richter, *Geschichte der Stadt Davenport und der County Scott* (Chicago: Fred Klein, 1917), n.p.

28. Davenport Public Library (DPL), "1913 Annual Report," in Annual Reports, 1911–1920, DPL Archives, Davenport, IA.

29. DPL, "1912 Annual Report."

30. DPL, *Autoren-verzeichniss deutscher bucher* (Davenport, IA: H. Lischer, 1909); DPL, "DPL Archive Finding Lists, 1876 1896 1911," DPL Archives, Davenport, IA.

31. CRPL, "Minute Book, October 1911 thru December 1914," 81.

32. James. L. Stokesbury, *A Short History of World War I* (New York: HarperCollins, 1981), 109.

33. Wiegand, *Active Instrument for Propaganda*, 7.

34. Stokesbury, *Short History of World War I*, 110.

35. Wittke, *German-Americans and the World War*, 5–7.

36. Clifton James Child, *The German-Americans in Politics, 1914–1917* (Madison: University of Wisconsin Press, 1939), 107, 118. The German-American Alliance (GAA) was also very active in distributing propaganda to libraries, although no records have been found indicating whether this organization distributed materials to the libraries in this study; see Wiegand, *Active Instrument for Propaganda*, 14. Given evidence of GAA activity in the state (particularly in Davenport), and that books by Burgess (who wrote for the GAA) were removed from some libraries, it is highly probable.

37. Wittke, *German-Americans and the World War*, 9, 23–24; John William Burgess, *The Present Crisis in Europe* (New York: German-American Literary Defense Committee, 1914); John William Burgess, *Truth about Germany: Facts about the War* (New York: Fatherland, 1914).

38. Jutta Spillman and Lothar Spillman, "The Rise and Fall of Hugo Munsterberg," *Journal of the History of the Behaviorial Sciences* 29 (1993): 12; Hugo Munsterberg, *The War and America* (New York: D. Appleton and Company, 1914); Hugo Munsterberg, *The Peace and America* (New York: D. Appleton and Company, 1915).

39. William Stern, "Hugo Munsterberg: In Memoriam," *Journal of Applied Psychology* 1 (1917): 186–88.

40. Spillmann and Spillmann, "Rise and Fall of Hugo Munsterberg," 12.

41. Ibid. Ironically, Munsterberg had written at length in 1904 about his love of American libraries, especially public libraries for their services in educating those outside of academia. See Hugo Munsterberg, "The Public Library in American Life," in *The Library and Society: Reprints of Papers and Addresses*, ed. Arthur E. Bostwick (New

York: H. W. Wilson Company, 1920), 81–86. Fourteen years later, those same institutions that employed the helpful staff and promoted the comfortable atmosphere he enjoyed would remove his books out of fear that they supported German war aims.

42. Wiegand, *Active Instrument for Propaganda*, 11.

43. Ibid.

44. CRPL, "Minute Book, October 1911 thru December 1914," 81, 89.

45. BPL, "Quarterly List of Additions: July 1914," vol. 1, no. 2; BPL, "Quarterly List of Additions: July 1916," vol. 3, no. 4; BPL, "Quarterly List of Additions: October 1916," vol. 2, no. 8; BPL, "Quarterly List of Additions: January 1915," vol. 2, no. 1; and BPL, "Quarterly List of Additions: April 1916," vol. 2, no 6, all located in BPL Archives, Burlington, IA. The July 1914 list was created just prior to the outbreak of war in Europe, and shows only one book on Germany, that being an English-language book about the history of imperial Germany. More important, it included a section titled "books in the German language," which included thirty newly acquired books. This is the last time a section on German-language books appears in the list.

46. ICPL, "Report of the Iowa City Public Library for the Year 1915," 2, ICPL Archives, Iowa City, IA.

47. DPL, "1916 Annual Report," in Annual Reports 1911–1920; DPL, "1917 Annual Report," in Annual Reports 1911–1920; and DPL, "1918 Annual Report," in Annual Reports 1911–1920, all in DPL Archives, Davenport, IA; DPL, "DPL Archive Finding Lists, 1876 1896 1911."

48. CRPL, "Minute Book, January 1915 thru December 1919," 159, CRPL Archives, Cedar Rapids, IA.

49. Letter to Herbert J. Metcalf from BPL's librarian, Herbert J. Metcalf Papers, 1910–1919, SHSI, Ms 74, folder 7.

50. DPL, "Meeting Minutes of the Davenport Public Library," 51, DPL Archives, Davenport, IA.

51. MPPL, "Mount Pleasant Public Library Board of Trustees Meeting Minutes, 7/5/1917–3/7/1946," 16.

52. CSFPL, "Accession Records, 35,001–40,000, June 18 1914–October 19 1916."

53. Susan Henricks, conversation with the author, March 19, 2010.

54. ICPL, "Accessions 15001–20000."

55. CRPL, "Minute Book, January 1915 thru December 1919," 179.

56. Julia Skinner, "World War I Censorship in Iowa Libraries," 2010, https://maps .google.com/maps/ms?msid=215643432987264317974.00048be6d125287d0b40b& msa=0. This is a publicly available interactive Google map that shows information from each of the letters sent to Herbert Metcalf from Iowa libraries.

57. MPPL, "Mount Pleasant Public Library Board of Trustees Meeting Minutes, 7/5/1917–3/7/1946."

58. CRPL, "Minute Book, January 1915 thru December 1919."

59. BPL, "Burlington Public Library Minutes of Board Meetings, 1885–1927," 41.

60. DPL, "1917 Annual Report," 7; ICPL, "Annual Report 1918," 4, DPL Archives, Iowa City, IA.

61. CRPL, "Minute Book, January 1915 thru December 1919," 185, 167.

62. Betty Coughlin, "The History of the Davenport Public Library" (master's thesis, Western Reserve University, 1952), 37–38; ICPL, "Annual Report 1918"; CRPL, "Minute Book, January 1915 thru December 1919," 161–97.

63. CRPL, "Minute Book, January 1915 thru December 1919," 181; CSFPL, "Carnegie-Stout Library Minutes of Board February 9, 1901–September 10, 1917," 298, CSFPL Archives, Dubuque, IA.

64. CRPL, "Minute Book January 1915 thru December 1919," 179, 187. In 1918, Boy Scouts asked door-to-door for donations for camp libraries.

65. BPL, "Burlington Public Library Minutes of Board Meetings, 1885–1927," 415–19; DPL, "Meeting Minutes of the Davenport Public Library"; ICPL, "Annual Report 1918," 7.

66. CRPL, "Minute Book, January 1915 thru December 1919," 204.

67. ICPL, "Annual Report 1918," 4.

68. BPL, "Burlington Public Library Minutes of Board Meetings, 1885–1927," 410.

69. Wiegand, *Active Instrument for Propaganda*, 55–62.

70. Nancy Derr, "The Babel Proclamation," *Palimpsest* 60, no. 4 (1979): 100–101. Citizens, who were encouraged to report suspicious activity, and local patriotic organizations enforced the law. Examples can be found of letters from concerned citizens in the Metcalf Papers, and examples of the activities undertaken by patriotic groups can be found in the bylaws of the Sibley Loyalty League. See Metcalf Papers, 1910–19, Ms 74; Sibley Loyalty League, "Sibley Loyalty League: Constitution and By-Laws, 1918," SHSI, BL 62, f. 9.

71. CSFPL, "Eighteenth Annual Report, 1920," 9.

72. BPL, "Burlington Public Library Minutes of Board Meetings, 1885–1927," 425, 429.

73. CRPL, "Minute Book, January 1915 thru December 1919," 213.

74. BPL, "List of Additions, October 1919," vol. 3, no 2, BPL Archives, Burlington, IA.

75. MPPL, "Mount Pleasant Public Library Board of Trustees Meeting Minutes, 7/5/1917–3/7/1946," 35; DPL, "1919 Annual Report."

76. CRPL, "Minute Book, January 1915 thru December 1919," 213.

77. DPL, "1918 Annual Report," 10.

78. CRPL, "Minute Book, February 1920 thru December 1923," 225, CRPL Archives, Cedar Rapids, IA.

79. Louise Robbins, *Censorship and the American Library: The American Library Association's Response to Threats to Intellectual Freedom, 1939–1969* (Westport, CT: Greenwood, 1996), 154.

80. Wiegand, *Active Instrument for Propaganda*, 5–6.

81. CSFPL, *Carnegie-Stout Free Public Library, Twelfth Annual Report, 1914*, 13; CSFPL, *Carnegie-Stout Free Public Library, Fourteenth Annual Report, 1916* (Dubuque, IA: Hardie, 13).

82. CRPL, "Minute Book, January 1915 thru December 1919," 159.

83. Wiegand, *Active Instrument for Propaganda*, 6.

Locating the Library in the Nonlibrary Censorship of the 1950s

Ideological Negotiations in the Professional Record

JOAN BESSMAN TAYLOR

> The basic question for librarians to face is whether or not, individually or collectively, they wish to exert their influence in defense of freedom outside of the libraries where freedom is being assaulted. I hope we will not stand like chickens, waiting for our turn on the block.
>
> —RALPH E. ELLSWORTH,
> "Is Intellectual Freedom in Libraries Being Challenged?"

Though Ralph Ellsworth, director of libraries at the State University of Iowa, titled his 1948 editorial on censorship in *ALA Bulletin* "Is Intellectual Freedom in Libraries Being Challenged?," his concluding remark is a call to action beyond library walls.[1] Writing during the post–World War II era of McCarthyism, and as an early member of the Iowa Library Association's (ILA) Intellectual Freedom Committee (IFC), Ellsworth describes librarians as carrying "an almost sacred responsibility" to provide free access to publications representing a variety of viewpoints.[2] His essay establishes a metaphor that recurs throughout contemporary professional discussions, one that places a librarian's jurisdiction "in libraries" or as including protection of the expressions of ideas that transpire "outside" the library. As Louise S. Robbins has demonstrated, during the late 1940s and early 1950s the American Library Association (ALA) led the nation's librarians to develop an ideology of intellectual freedom and claim its defense as a central tenet of their jurisdiction. The primary manifestation of this was the autonomous selection of library materials. The ALA's principal activities then included urging state library associations to form IFCs that both formally adopted the Library Bill of Rights (LBR) and persuaded their local library boards of trustees to make their approval of it a matter of record; adopting resolutions against the use of loyalty investigations in the hiring and retention of library employees; and creating policies against prejudicial labeling of library materials. Each of these occupations focused primarily on the protection of happenings inside the library, because creating a clear reputation for defending intellectual freedom was paramount to the establishment of a shared identity of librarianship as a standards-based profession. As Robbins observes, by referencing events "outside of the libraries" Ellsworth "added something new" to the discourse regarding the emerging jurisdiction of librarians, and in so doing both "began to broaden the sphere of concern and influence exerted by the librarians' code to individuals and situations outside the profession" and "challenged them to fight limitations to First Amendment freedoms wherever they appeared."[3]

The ALA's emphasis on the happenings within library walls and the framing of their jurisdiction as primarily revolving around materials selection makes the early activities of the ILA's IFC particularly interesting in that they bring to the forefront the negotiations, both philosophical and actual, of librarians as they attempt to formulate their positions on and roles in promoting the ideal of intellectual freedom. Library association records and library archives provide a lens through which to view the self-conscious attempts of library professionals to document these negotiations. Correspondence included in these records reveals that the very concept of intellectual freedom was in flux as were its perceived boundaries and the extent to which librarians felt authority and obligation to defend it. Even though the IFC of the ILA adopts the ALA's LBR and envisions itself as employing a shared definition of intellectual freedom, application and enforcement of the ideal sometimes differed between national and local contexts. Differences between the viewpoints confided through person-to-person exchanges and those represented in the official documents and organs of professional groups illustrate the need to present a coherent position in a time of political and cultural upheaval. Librarians were cognizant of the importance of the written record not just to make fixed official policies but also as means of reflecting on the process of their creation and communicating with professionals and patrons succeeding them. Outwardly, the library profession was focused on the freedom to read, exemplified by the formal Freedom to Read Statement jointly issued in 1953 by the ALA and the American Book Publishers Council and published widely; but professional activities of individuals—including self-archiving, scrapbook-keeping, and letter-writing campaigns—indicate that inextricably linked with the freedom to read was the freedom and need to write.[4] Through the process of defining their relationship to the ALA's IFC and to the ideal from which they derived their name, members of the committee came to recognize the power special-interest groups could wield through their social pressure campaigns and thus developed a prescient understanding of the reality intellectual freedom pioneer Judith Krug later articulated, "Censorship of any materials, in any guise, eventually affects the library."[5] The shaping of this understanding is made visible through two examples of nonlibrary censorship in Iowa during the 1950s, which, due to their encroachment on intellectual freedom, were either countered by librarians or, by nature of association with the ideal, interpreted by observers as necessarily involving the library. Examination of the documents created by those involved reveals the significance of these events to librarians' understanding of purpose.

The Iowa Library Association's
Intellectual Freedom Committee

The ILA, founded in 1890, formed its IFC in June 1948, but the association did not begin maintaining a folder of the committee's records and correspondence until January 1952.[6] This need for record-keeping is specifically mentioned in the IFC's 1952 program of activities.[7] Many of the twenty-nine action items represented involve writing letters to allied organizations, including the American Association of University Professors (AAUP), other state library associations, and the Legislative Committee of ALA. They also note authoring articles for the *Iowa Library Quarterly*, the official organ of the Iowa State Traveling Library, and ILA's newsletter, the *Catalyst*, in an effort to educate fellow librarians regarding their professional responsibility to protect the freedom of expression.

The ILA's IFC first described its mission to the greater association in March 1952: "The Intellectual Freedom Committee of the ILA is primarily a 'watchdog' committee. The Committee . . . exists to protect our heritage of intellectual freedom. The Committee has defined intellectual freedom, as did the Council of American Library Association on June 18, 1948, in Atlantic City, when they adopted the Library Bill of Rights."[8] As its new chairman, John F. Harvey, librarian at Parsons College, attempts to summarize to David Berninghausen of the ALA the activities from the IFC's inception to its then current state.[9] Though as first chairman he left no files for the organization, Forrest Spaulding's related activities are recorded in accounts of the fifty-fifth meeting of the ILA, at which he presided over a panel titled "The Trustee and the Censorship of Books." The panel addressed the question of intellectual freedom in libraries and "whether or not library boards should exercise censorship or permit groups to do so." Supporting Spaulding's conviction that library boards were in need of education regarding intellectual freedom even more than librarians were, the panel "suggested that the librarian's decision should be final. The board should elect a librarian in whom they have confidence and then let him select the books. The board should defend his choice in public."[10] At the same conference, the ILA adopted resolutions reaffirming its "belief in the Library Bill of Rights as adopted by the ALA" and "our strong belief in intellectual freedom, our interest in an educated America and universal understanding through books and reading."[11]

The chairman of the IFC in 1950–51 was Richard Farley, Drake University director of libraries, who contended with two situations. First, the Iowa legislature seriously considered a loyalty oath for all state employees. After discussing it "at every district meeting," the IFC conducted an active letter-writing campaign in cooperation with the AAUP and the ILA Legislative Committee.[12] In April 1951, the Iowa Senate overwhelmingly rejected the measure.[13] Second was a dispute over the censorship of supposedly obscene materials on newsstands in Dubuque. In his letter to Berninghausen, Harvey states, "A situation arose in Dubuque in which the public library was subpoenaed for books to be examined by the prosecuting attorney concerning their obscenity; a local church organization was attempting to ban such books from newsstands. The library was not harmed here, so the committee did little more than watch the situation."[14] Though the IFC treated it as falling outside its jurisdiction, or at least left little documentation of activity related to it, scrapbooks of the Carnegie-Stout Library reveal that the Dubuque situation attracted national attention and produced many debates concerning the freedom of speech, the place of the library in society, and their intersection.

THE DUBUQUE OBSCENITY CASE

In October 1950, seven local groups, including the Parent Teachers' Association and the Catholic Mothers' Study Club, complained that material sold on local newsstands—twenty-five-cent reprint editions of Caldwell, John Steinbeck, W. Somerset Maugham, and others—were unfit for youth. According to *Publishers Weekly*, in September 1950, Dubuque police seized a large number of reprints at the Norton News Agency. On October 9, a grand jury returned an indictment against James Norton under Section 725.4 of the 1950 Code of Iowa, which declares it a felony to publish or distribute printed matter that "contains" obscene language or pictures "manifestly tending to corrupt the morals of youth." Pocket Books, Bantam, New American Library of World

Literature, and Avon jointly retained counsel for Norton to determine the extent to which the obscenity prosecution was based on these publishers' titles. Norton was arraigned on October 19 and pleaded not guilty. The case was set over to the December term of the District Court of the State of Iowa.[15] However, when John L. Duffy took office as district attorney in January 1951, the case had not been brought to trial. On February 24, he filed a felony docket stating there was insufficient evidence to submit the case to a jury and that "it should be dismissed in the furtherance of justice."[16] Typically this would deem a case closed. However, the March 4, 1951, edition of Dubuque's *Telegraph-Herald* ran the headline "Dubuque Women's Groups Hint All Out War on 'Obscene' Books" with an article announcing a meeting of protest groups accusing the district attorney of negligence. At the meeting, the women planned a social-pressure campaign to rid Dubuque of obscene literature sold on newsstands, a strategy the National Organization for Decent Literature recommended, and utilized its list of disapproved publications as a guide.

After protest of the newsstands was promulgated, Duffy immediately called a second grand jury but decided that before another indictment the jury should learn something of the classics so that a comparison could be made with the modern "objectionable" authors. It was an attempt, as a scrapbook clipping from the Santa Barbara, California, newspaper the *Independent* framed it, "to determine whether classic literature on a library shelf becomes smut when sold as 25-cent pocket editions from newsstands."[17] Duffy ordered police deputies to obtain copies of Rabelais, *The Decameron*, *Tom Jones*, and *Stretch on the River* by Dubuque author Richard Bissell from the city library, the Carnegie-Stout. The deputies asked for the names of the library patrons who had the books checked out for all copies of *Stretch on the River* in circulation. When staff members at the circulation desk refused to provide patron names because it would violate patron privacy, the deputies demanded to see the city librarian of thirty years, May Mehlhop Clark. When she also refused to provide names, Duffy subpoenaed her to appear before a grand jury with copies of the cited works.[18] Clark testified before the grand jury for about two hours on the books of John Steinbeck, W. Somerset Maugham, MacKinlay Kantor, Emily Hahn, Erle Stanley Gardner, and others.[19]

The subpoenaing of the city librarian, as well as two English professors from the State University of Iowa in Iowa City, to testify on the nature and content of books was an attempt to illustrate how exaggerated, arbitrary, and ultimately unfounded were the accusations of obscenity.[20] The county attorney's desire for expert evidence prompted the obtaining of books from the public library in a manner that effectively prompted a reversal of public sympathies. Whereas many citizens would have sided with Duffy's efforts to defend the sale of reprints on newsstands, the media distorted the events so they more closely resembled the type of government actions deemed contradictory to the proper conduct of a democracy. Duffy's actions ignited discussions picked up by local and national newspapers, including the *New York Times*, *Washington Post*, and *Chicago Tribune*; by professional and trade journals across Iowa and the nation; as well as magazines such as *Time*, the *New Republic*, and *Newsweek*. On the one hand were the discussions Duffy intended—discerning literary quality and the differences between works regarded as classics, many issued as reprints and sold on newsstands alongside contemporary works of realistic fiction, and works that would be considered "smut," the distribution of which was punishable by law. On the other hand were the sensationalized articles and resultant editorials and letters to the editor that viewed Duffy's attempts as trying to censor the library itself, epitomized by the main headline of the *Des Moines Register*, which called the event a "Raid on Dubuque's City Library."[21] Many readers resisted this blurring of messages obfuscating the real issues and were compelled to respond. In the Letterbox column of Dubuque's *Telegraph-Herald*, one writer recounts, "The women have no quarrel with the library or its handling of the books. They never mentioned the library in their protest. They KNOW as do all intelligent people that books on the restricted shelves of the library are NOT accessible to children."[22] Discussions were fraught with conflict about the rights and needs of readers and combined concerns about intellectual freedom and the freedom of the press ("I would like to know if that is not censorship like one would find possibly only in a place like Russia"[23]) with skepticism regarding the attempts of dogmatic civic groups to dictate the reading options not only of the children they claimed to be protecting but those of the city's adults as well.

Practices and policies employed by Iowa's public libraries in the 1950s were so ingrained in the assumptions and schemata of Iowans that they functioned as rhetorical devices in the societal debates about intellectual freedom and democracy transpiring outside library walls. Existing opposite the opportunistic newsstand that sold anything to anyone and accepted anything distributors sent and whose cheap prices induced the "wrong" readers, the library is described as a place of restricted access protecting children, of book experts, of intentionally chosen items, and as central to a free and intelligent society. Its institutionalized practices of passive censorship—restrictive shelving and age-determined access—shielded it from overt censorship attacks and inspired patron trust. This paradoxical position enabled librarians to defend the freedom to read even in nonlibrary contexts.

As letters in her correspondence file at the Carnegie-Stout reveal, May Clark was a trusted city employee known for providing resources to everyone, including the enlisted men and their families, nuns at the area convent, the schools for summer reading programs, and patients in area hospitals. As a key expert, she was quoted often during the grand jury hearings, stating outright that she did not consider the books under discussion "salacious, obscene or objectionable." In fact, the library owned "many of the 25-cent pocket book volumes and they have a large circulation. . . . They are strictly the 'popular' type books for which there is great demand—such as westerns and mysteries." While waiting to testify, a member of a protesting group told Clark that she held the library board responsible for the books on the library shelves. Clark immediately responded that she was responsible for them.[24] Carnegie-Stout accession books list a diversity of titles, including a number that would have been rife for objection. To the dissatisfaction of the protesting women's groups and relief of the labor unions, college students, and library workers, among others quoted in the media, the Dubuque obscenity hearings did not end in indictment, so the case was never brought to trial. An inconvenient consequence of this outcome is the absence of case transcripts or official records that might provide greater insight into the claims made by those who testified before the grand jury. Newspaper clippings collected in a librarian's scrapbook and a few notations in a court docket are all that remain as evidence.

On one hand, the ILA's IFC rightly assessed the events in Dubuque as not having harmed the library. In fact, the events rallied support for the library when its collection included the very items being objected to on the newsstand. Citizens expressed trust that librarians would guide such works into the hands of properly prepared adults. On the other hand, the events reinforced passive censorship and permitted librarians to dodge the issues of class implied by protestors' statements that were less about literary quality than perceived differences between the patronages of newsstands and the public library. Nonetheless, the Dubuque events are later cited as a victory for the cause of intellectual freedom and the free expression of ideas. The May 1951 *Library Journal's* "The News" column, titled "No Indictment," acknowledges that though the legal action was not actually an attempt to ban items from the library, the rights of library patrons were at risk both in the potential violation of library policies intended to protect their privacy and through the social stigma placed on certain types of reading. Describing it as "the librarian's story," the column situates the dispute by stating: "It just goes to show what can happen and what can be done."[25] To similar end, the events in Dubuque are later referenced in the statement of national paperback distributor Freeman Lewis filed in the records of the House of Representatives Select Committee on Current Pornographic Materials (i.e., the Gathings Committee): "In the course of our history we have been challenged twice; once in Dubuque, Iowa, where the case against our publication was thrown out, and once in a New England city where the matter has never been brought to trial." He goes on to say, "It is quite possible, however, that minority pressure groups without legal standing and for interests of their own may attempt to prevent you from distributing certain titles. This form of extra-legal pressure is one which I hope you will resist with every means available to you. No greater danger to freedom of the press exists today than the efforts of well-meaning individuals or groups to deny other citizens the opportunity to choose what they may wish to read."[26] Lewis's admonitions are almost identical to those of the ILA's IFC regarding another nonlibrary censorship case, this time in Ottumwa, to which the IFC actively responded.

Rather than interpreted as unthreatening to the library, "the Ottumwa situation," as the IFC referred to it, is regarded as exemplifying its very raison d'être. Exhibiting a developing sense of purpose, the IFC's March 1952 report in the *Catalyst* asserts: "The censorship activities of the Ministerial Association of Ottumwa are in many ways an example of the sort of thing that the IFC was organized to watch and perhaps act on. The acts of this group in Ottumwa seemed to be a clear violation of article 3 of the Library Bill of Rights."[27]

The Ottumwa Situation

In January 1952, the Ottumwa Ministerial Association approached all local druggists and news dealers asking them to remove from their shelves all magazines and books the dealers themselves "would not wish to have in their homes" or they "would be ashamed to be seen reading." Rev. Harold J. Drown, president of the association, signed a letter mailed to nearly forty dealers with a return card attached so dealers could indicate whether they would cooperate fully or were not in sympathy with the effort. Typical of social pressure campaigns, the letter appealed to the pharmacists' sense of guilt and fear while remaining vague in its asking for immediate removal of unspecified items: "Do you have publications for sale that would excite the lust of youth and perhaps plant an idea to do that which you would condemn? If you do will you get rid of these publications? . . . If you believe in your church; if you believe in the goodness of mankind; if you place these above the profit involved, you will take immediate action."[28]

When reporters asked the Iowa Pharmaceutical Association (IPhA) for their position on the ministers' request, the association responded by quoting a resolution passed at the 1951 and 1952 IPhA Annual Conventions that condemned "the publication, distribution and sale of salacious, obscene, and indecent books, magazines and periodicals"; urged pharmacists throughout the state "to cooperate in this objective with other interested groups"; and requested that "publishers and magazine and periodical distributing agencies also join this objective." Dallas L. Bruner, IPhA secretary and editor of its official organ, the *Iowa Pharmacist*, responded to the publicity in a short column titled "Objectionable Periodicals": "It is . . . a matter of paramount importance that retail druggists make every effort to keep objectionable periodicals out of their stores, as a matter of professional and civic pride. To date we know of no list that has been compiled of periodicals considered objectionable, but if such a list is compiled we will welcome the opportunity to make it available to our entire membership."[29] In the March issue of the journal, he clarified the IPhA's position by stating it did not wish to "be placed in the dubious position of instigating a crusade" but that it would "gladly join in appealing directly to the wholesale distributors . . . in an effort to simplify the removal of publications of questionable character before distribution to the newsstands of Iowa." Attempting to deflect responsibility for evaluating reading materials from the druggists but not wanting to appear uncooperative, he concludes, "No retail pharmacist can justify failure to cooperate with this endeavor, either from a professional or a public relations standpoint, and we will expect, and know we will receive full cooperation."[30]

As the first action of the IFC's response, Harvey, claiming to represent the nine hundred members of the ILA, wrote to Bruner concerning the "alleged challenge to intellectual freedom involving the druggists of Iowa" stating that the IFC wished "to go on record as opposing this kind of censorship and banning of books." It believed, Harvey wrote, "in the fullest possible distribution of reading material and the preservation of free channels of communication between writers and readers." After mentioning an enclosed copy of the ALA's LBR, Harvey stated that he hoped "the committee's understanding of this situation is incorrect and that the Pharmaceutical Association intends no such witch hunt."[31]

In his reply, Bruner described the publicity the IPhA received after which it was "deluged with correspondence from organizations all over Iowa telling us they wanted to join our crusade." He described this outpouring as placing them "in an embarrassing situation" in that they had "instigated no crusade." The IPhA's only action, Bruner explained, had been "to caution our own membership" and publicize to it the resolution passed at convention. He seemed flabbergasted that "now from the other side of the picture, you as Chairman of the ILA Committee on Intellectual Freedom are taking the opposite position."[32] In his lengthy subsequent letter, Harvey, too, expressed surprise at being "the only organization opposing your resolution," given that "on other such occasions involving intellectual freedom the ILA has had several organizations on its side." He went on to enumerate the IFC's objections to the IPhA's resolution, beginning with its expressed "desire to censor and inhibit the sale of books and magazines on bases which are not clearly defined, since no clear definition of 'obscenity' is given." He was careful to state that the ILA "is not to be thought of as promoting this particular printed material or any other kind of material, but simply as promoting all kinds of material without discrimination." He then explained the primary assumption underlying the IPhA's resolution—reading "obscene" publications likely leads to lower moral standards and "anti-social behavior." Pointing to the lack of research on which to base claims about "what reading does to people," he reinforced the authority of the IFC as "composed of librarians who are reading specialists." After expressing gratitude for Bruner's "kind and fair treatment" and commiseration with the challenges presented by "certain conservative elements of our communities," Harvey presented him with ALA's Statement on Labeling, which he conceptualized as applying to "the present situation even though it is aimed primarily at another kind of labeling."[33]

Newspaper coverage of the Ottumwa situation framed the "clean-up" effort as a laudable instance of civic cooperation while also hinting that IPhA members were less than comfortable in their compliance. Local newspaper articles with titles such as "Thousands of Books Removed from Newsstands in Ottumwa," "Let's Co-operate," and "Paying Off" highlight the advantage social-pressure campaigns have over those that attempt to establish that materials violate the legal definition of obscenity. Stressing that "there is no asking for official censorship," the methods used in Ottumwa were described as "paying off in invaluable dividends."[34] Use of the term "objectionable" rather than the legally imbued "obscene" and the absence of a list of problematic titles functioned dually to grant power to the ministers' request while at the same time undermining it. Repeated requests from pharmacists for lists from which to operate indicate their resistance to determining what adults were permitted to purchase and read and to the expectation that they be intimately familiar with the titles they sold, even when wholesalers were determining what was sent to each store.[35]

Realistically, the effect of the campaign was a one-time removal of publications, primarily those with "suggestive" covers or those that could not legally be sent through the mail. The March "Report on the Ottumwa Situation" sent by the IFC to the Executive officers of ILA and to ALA's IFC indicates that Harvey visited "half the book and magazine outlets to estimate the extent to which 'salacious' literature was on their shelves" and talked at length with at least one proprietor. He characterized the campaign's results: "The campaign had apparently gone further in some stores than others, however, the range being quite wide and the average store showing much less change than the ministers would like. . . . It is still possible in most of the drug stores which I visited to obtain every kind of reading material which was previously available . . . the situation is on its way to 'normalcy' with the censored literature becoming more easily available each time stock is replenished." Harvey concluded by asking what action the IFC should take on the matter, noting that it "should probably not approach the ministers," since it might merely lead them to further censorial activity. He also mentioned his letter written to the IPhA attempting "to nip in the bud the statewide campaign which, according to druggists in Ottumwa and Fairfield, has apparently not gotten started."[36]

The IFC report prompted a flurry of letter writing, recommending varying degrees of involvement and different interpretations of professional jurisdiction. Opal Tanner, vice president of ILA, immediately replied, "My reaction to the Ottumwa situation so far as we are concerned is to let sleeping dogs lie! As you say, it might stimulate them to action again. The best publicity magazines or books can have is to be banned by some group or library."[37] Berninghausen, retiring as ALA's IFC executive secretary, replies with a short handwritten note, advising, "I would sit tight on the Ottumwa affair until it hits the library," and directing Harvey to send copies of his "excellent reports" to William Dix and Paul Bixler, the newly installed chairman and executive secretary of the ALA Committee.[38] This exchange further substantiates Robbins' observation regarding the ALA's evolving stance on intellectual freedom issues that "professional ideology is not static but changes through professional discourse and internal strife and in response to the social and cultural milieu in which the profession strives to retain its jurisdiction."[39] Berninghausen's reluctance to act on censorship happening outside library walls coupled with his acknowledgement that a deleterious effect on the library was inevitable (he used "until" rather than "unless" to describe its occurrence) must have left Harvey befuddled. Professional contention concerning the extent of a librarian's jurisdiction regarding intellectual freedom was echoed in Dix's reply. Dix prefaced his advice with the disclaimer that he could not speak for the ALA Committee as a whole, but that "we should perhaps be a bit cautious in initiating action in matters which do not concern libraries directly." He pointed out that the ministerial group in other cities had been "one of the staunchest defenders of free communication of ideas" and that one would not want to alienate potential supporters. Even having made such statements, he was both self-conscious concerning their reception and aware of the role that context plays in the forming of protocol: "This may seem to you an unnecessarily conservative reply and you of course must act as the local situation dictates. Sometimes the national view and the local view are somewhat different."[40]

Bixler's response to Harvey's inquiry was less conservative than Dix's, telling him the IFC "acted properly and well" concerning the situation, the letter to the IPhA was potentially helpful in demonstrating that not everyone shared its members' position, and "it would serve no useful purpose to approach the ministers on the situation." He went on to state that if the matter were pushed again, the point should be made that "you do not underwrite the literature nor do you take issue with the opinions about it (after all, the ministers have a right to their opinions and to their expression), but that you oppose censorship of the material."[41] This was precisely Harvey's tack after receiving Bruner's initial reply. The IFC and Bixler's shared modus operandi was not to approach the would-be censors directly but rather to persuade book providers not to be unduly influenced by special interest groups and instead continue offering a diversity of reading materials. They also shared a more expansive view of the librarian's responsibility in confronting acts of censorship than many of their colleagues. Bixler's mediating of his perspective with that of the greater association is evidenced in the June 1952 *Newsletter on Intellectual Freedom*: "A report from the active IFC of the Iowa Library Association indicates concern over attempted censoring of magazines and books sold in drugstores. This is not a quarter from which it is usually possible to work up much enthusiasm for defense—though censorship is censorship anywhere."[42]

After receiving Harvey's final report, Dix commended the IFC for "managing to walk the very tight rope between informing people so that they will be ready for trouble and stirring up difficulties by overactive propaganda."[43] He included the program plan for the upcoming ALA Conference on Intellectual Freedom in New York. The description of the third session, "Pressures—

Wherefrom and How?" indicates that the sponsoring committee intended to address the question "What can librarians do, in addition to their efforts as selectors of books and administrators of internal library policy, to preserve the public's right to examine all points of view and help to maintain free inquiry?" The combination of words used here, "in addition to" and "internal" in relation to library policy, point to professional activities beyond library walls. That librarians beyond Iowa were already recognizing that the objections leveled against formats available outside the library could be brought to bear on those within the library is made apparent in the section providing background of the conference. It begins: "This, of course, is a conference primarily for librarians. Earlier the committee had conceived of it as a series of working discussion groups by those most intimately concerned with problems of free communication. But it became clear that the need and interest among librarians was too great to limit attendance to intimate groups. And we recognized further that the library is not isolated, and that any worthwhile exploration of *its* problems of free communication should be related to the larger principle of free communication."[44]

The conference foregrounded attempts within the library profession to elucidate the relationship of professional imperatives to larger societal principles and the extent to which the professional organizations wanted to go on record regarding any particular position. The ALA's decision not to testify or file a formal statement for inclusion in the proceedings of the Gathings Committee hearings was a major outcome of one such deliberation. Julia D. Bennett, director of the ALA Washington, DC, office, recounted that Gathings Committee members told her that the investigation "would handle the type of material that can be secured at newsstands and from under counters in certain places of business" and that they "did not feel the ALA should be at all concerned with this." The investigation was framed as a discussion about pocket books and magazines in terms of "the covers and obscene materials included." Bennett acknowledged, however, that such a discussion could easily dissolve into a debate about the contents of reprints of popular fiction and nonfiction, given that they sometimes were reprinted with lurid covers having nothing to do with their content. In the event the committee went beyond its scope, Bennett thought the ALA should either testify or present a statement for incorporation in the hearings. Calling it a "tricky hearing" and recognizing that it would "receive great press publicity," she apprehensively anticipated that once published the hearings would "be used by civic groups in working with their local problems." She stressed the need for any testimony on ALA's part to be well worded, as "it may be picked up by the press and used later in connection to the hearings."[45] In response, Bixler authored a statement that he proposed filing into the official records but after closely assessing the testimonies over several days of the hearings, it was decided that the ALA "would do better to remain out of it."[46] Whereas ALA elected not to push its jurisdiction in these highly publicized hearings, the ILA viewed them as necessarily involving "every librarian in the state" and reminded ILA members that "the investigating committee was particularly interested in the so-called 'pocket books' which sell for 25 cents. Probably more of these are sold through Iowa drugstore outlets than any other agency in the state."[47]

In the years immediately following the incidents in Dubuque and Ottumwa, the IFC reported "few instances on which it has been necessary for the Committee to take public action," but continued to take a broad view of the type of incidents that would fall under its purview. In a 1954 memo sent to all district meetings, the IFC reminded the ILA membership: "It is important that the committee be informed *immediately* [if] you become aware that an individual or group is likely to make an attempt to 'investigate' the library, the schools, the news-stands, or any other agency of public information in your community." It concluded with a suggestion that members urge their library boards to go on record as endorsing the LBR if they had not already done so.

The IFC's perspective of the library as just one "agency of public information" among others operating within a community at any given time acknowledges that policies related to censorship, labeling, and intellectual freedom fundamentally affect the lives of all people, whether performing as library patrons or as citizens at large. It honors the ways the library serves as a rhetorical device, depicting not only a physical space but a way of life and representing both free inquiry and resistance to the social stigma often attached to certain types of reading and writing. This understanding of librarians as cultural agents whose policies and public actions respond to diverse needs and values enabled a general acceptance and trust of the library, leading to its unconditional defense. Though brought about through institutional negotiations, the outcomes envisioned were far from institutionally bounded.

CONCLUSION

Whether by keeping a library scrapbook, logging board minutes, passing association-wide resolutions, creating committee archives, writing correspondence to allied groups, circulating organizational newsletters, authoring journal articles, producing annual reports, publishing newspaper editorials, or filing legal testimonies, professional ideologies are formulated over time through communication between members of the profession and with those outside it. Often the records kept by individuals while conducting their work and archived through their professional affiliations include perspectives on fundamental principle negotiations unattainable elsewhere. The records of state professional associations such as the ILA reveal the processes through which state associations form professional identities locally, in relation to their parent organization, and situated in the cultural values of society writ large. Through its efforts to define and protect intellectual freedom and determine the boundaries of the library in doing so, the library profession has preserved and promoted the freedom to read by exercising a strong commitment to the production and preservation of the written word. The cultural record created and preserved by librarians reveals not only the role of the library in the life of the user but also the importance of libraries and the ideals with which they have become synonymous to the lives of all who value participation in a free society.

NOTES

I gratefully acknowledge Wayne Wiegand for directing me to the Dubuque case and May Clark's involvement in it; Susan Henricks, director of the Carnegie-Stout Public Library, for granting me access to the library's historical documents; my graduate assistant, Kalmia Strong, for her assistance in preparing this manuscript; and the State Historical Society of Iowa for funding this research.

1. Ralph E. Ellsworth, "Is Intellectual Freedom in Libraries Being Challenged?," *ALA Bulletin* 42 (February 1948): 57–58.

2. The titles "Intellectual Freedom Committee" and "Committee on Intellectual Freedom" are used interchangeably in ILA's records. For clarity and consistency here, I will use IFC throughout.

3. Louise S. Robbins, *Censorship and the American Library: The American Library Association's Response to Threats to Intellectual Freedom, 1939–1969* (Westport, CT: Greenwood, 1996), 31–34.

4. American Library Association and American Book Publishers Council, "The Freedom to Read: A Statement Prepared by the Westchester Conference of the American Library Association and the American Book Publishers Council," American Library Association, Chicago, IL, May 2 and 3, 1953.

5. Judith F. Krug, "Intellectual Freedom and ALA: Historical Overview," in *Encyclopedia of Library and Information Science*, 2nd ed., ed. Miriam A. Drake (New York: Marcel Dekker, 2003), 1379–89.

6. Minutes of the Executive Board of Iowa Library Association, Iowa Library Association, MsC491, Special Collections Department, University of Iowa Libraries, Iowa City, Iowa (hereafter ILA).

7. Intellectual Freedom Committee, Program for Activities, 1952, ILA.

8. John F. Harvey, "Intellectual Freedom Committee," *Catalyst* 5, no. 2 (March 1952): n.p., copy included in ILA.

9. John F. Harvey to David Berninghausen, February 27, 1952, ILA.

10. "Iowa Library Association," *Iowa Library Quarterly* 15, no. 15 (October 1948): 228–31.

11. Mildred H. Pike, D. S. Humestow, and Evelyn Van Wagner, Memorandum on resolutions passed at ILA conference, October 9, 1948, Mason City, IA, ILA.

12. Germaine Krettek to John Harvey, February 19, 1952, ILA.

13. Arnold A. Rogow, "The Loyalty Oath in Iowa, 1951," *American Political Science Review* 55, no. 4 (December 1961): 861.

14. John F. Harvey to David Berninghausen, February 27, 1952, ILA.

15. "Dubuque Newsdealer Indicted for Obscene Book Sales," *Publishers Weekly* 158 (November 11, 1950): 2136.

16. City of Dubuque, Felony docket filed February 24, 1951, Dubuque (Iowa) County Courthouse.

17. "Do Classics Become Filth in Cheap Publications?," *Independent* (Santa Barbara, CA), March 12, 1951, copy included in Scrapbook 1949–1966, May Clark, Carnegie-Stout Public Library, Dubuque, IA.

18. Dolores Owsley, e-mail message to author, September 4, 2010.

19. "The News: No Indictment," *Library Journal* 76, no. 9 (May 1951): 764.

20. Professors subpoenaed were Paul Engle, founder of the Iowa Writers Workshop, and W. R. Irwin.

21. "Raid on Dubuque's City Library," *Des Moines Register*, March 10, 1951, copy included in the Carnegie-Stout Public Library scrapbook.

22. "Letterbox," *Dubuque (IA) Telegraph-Herald*, March 15, 1951.

23. Michael L. Keeley, letter to the editor, *Telegraph-Herald*, March 18, 1951.

24. Carnegie-Stout board meeting minutes indicate discussions centered on building maintenance, acquisition and preservation of artwork for the library, et cetera. Clark's authority to make selection decisions is supported by the absence of entries pertaining to the content of the physical collections despite the existence of a dedicated book committee.

25. "The News: No Indictment," 764.

26. Freeman Lewis, statement filed in the records of the Gathings Committee, December 9, 1952, quoted in Kenneth C. Davis, "The Lady Goes to Court: Paperbacks and Censorship," *Publishing Research Quarterly* 11, no. 4 (December 1995): 9–32.

27. Harvey, "Intellectual Freedom Committee," *Catalyst* 5, no. 2 (March 1952).

28. "Civic Leaders Laud Book Removal," *Ottumwa (IA) Daily Courier*, January 29, 1952, 14.

29. "Objectionable Periodicals," *Iowa Pharmacist* Seventy-third Convention issue (February 24–26, 1952): 56.

30. "Convention Action on Objectionable Publications," *Iowa Pharmacist* (March 1952): 14, 29.

31. John F. Harvey to Dal Bruner, March 27, 1952, ILA.

32. D. L. Bruner to John F. Harvey, April 4, 1952, ILA.

33. John F. Harvey to D. L. Bruner, April 8, 1952, ILA.

34. "Let's Co-operate," *Ottumwa Daily Courier*, January 25, 1952, 4; "Paying Off," *Ottumwa Daily Courier*, January 28, 1952, 4.

35. Additionally, druggists were implored to sacrifice profit for the sake of "a good town" in a climate where the expansion of supermarket offerings was already compromising their financial security.

36. John F. Harvey, "Report on the Ottumwa Situation," March 22, 1952, ILA.

37. Opal Tanner to John Harvey, March 25, 1952, ILA.

38. Dave Berninghausen to John Harvey, undated correspondence, ILA.

39. Robbins, *Censorship and the American Library*, 67.

40. William S. Dix to John F. Harvey, April 19, 1952, ILA.

41. Paul Bixler to John F. Harvey, April 14, 1952, ILA.

42. Paul Bixler, *Newsletter on Intellectual Freedom*, June 1952, Record Group 69/2/6, box 1, ALA Archives, University of Illinois at Urbana-Champaign, Urbana, Illinois.

43. William S. Dix to John F. Harvey, May 23, 1952, ILA.

44. Program plan for Institute on Intellectual Freedom, June 28–29, 1952, New York, included in William S. Dix to John F. Harvey, May 23, 1952.

45. Julia D. Bennett, "Memorandum on Gathings Hearings," December 2, 1952, Record Group 17/1/6, box 24, ALA Archives.

46. Julia D. Bennett to Paul Bixler, December 9, 1952, Record Group 17/1/6, box 24, ALA Archives.

47. John F. Harvey, "Report of Intellectual Freedom Committee," *Catalyst* 6, no. 2 (March 1953): 3, copy included in ILA.

"Is Your Public Library Family Friendly?"

Libraries as a Site of Conservative Activism,
1992–2002

LORETTA M. GAFFNEY

In 1992, conservative Christian and homemaker Karen Jo Gounaud walked into Virginia's Fairfax County Public Library and was alarmed to find the *Washington Blade*, a free gay and lesbian newspaper, available for the taking.[1] Though the library administration and board initially rebuffed her attempts to have the publication removed, Gounaud proved not so easily dissuaded. After attending a Christian Coalition workshop sponsored by her church on antigay activism, Gounaud and her allies went on to spearhead a campaign to create a separate "adults only" section of the library for topics (including homosexuality) that children could not access without parental permission. Though this effort was ultimately not successful, the activists did convince the library to allow parents complete access to their minor children's library records and to acquire multiple copies of eleven "ex-gay" titles for the library collection. These included Richard A. Cohen's *Alfie's Home*, a children's book featuring a boy who jettisons some confusing feelings in order to become heterosexual.[2]

In 1995, with the help of influential activists and organizations like the American Family Association, Gounaud founded Family Friendly Libraries (FFL), and her strategy shifted considerably. Still committed to protecting children from the perceived dangers of gay-themed materials, Gounaud now set her sights higher, targeting the role the American Library Association (ALA) plays in promoting library policies that protect access and diversity.[3] In particular, it was the Library Bill of Rights' inclusion of "age" among the protected categories of user access that troubled Gounaud and her allies, who believed that such freedom for children's reading and viewing opened the door to a host of "objectionable" materials.[4] In protest, FFL created alternative policies, curtailing children's access and offering taxpayers greater influence in managing library collections. Gounaud fleshed out this alternative vision in the FFL charter, which included five articles: collections emphasizing the "traditional family," parental rights to control all aspects of their minor children's library use, respect for community standards, respect for minors (meaning no sexually explicit or gay-themed displays), and taxpayer participation in library policymaking.[5] This vision and FFL's subsequent activism helped catapult public libraries into the culture-wars crossfire of the 1990s.

This chapter explores why libraries and librarianship became issues in the pro-family movement. Written at the intersection of media studies and library history, it places library challenges within a social movement context, illustrating the symbiotic relationship between grassroots campaigns and national pro-family groups. It examines FFL's history and explains why this organization moved from objections to specific library materials toward a broader critique of library policies and the ALA. After exploring the history of the pro-family movement, I place FFL within the context of this movement during the 1990s. I then trace the history of the organization as it grew from community protest to national prominence. Finally, I analyze both its vision of the public library and its critique of the American Library Association, demonstrating how these activists contested intellectual freedom and raised larger questions about how libraries best serve families and communities. Ultimately, FFL's imagined community was a starkly homogeneous one, its imagined library safe and conventional, and its librarians' most important charge to avoid controversy. This chapter illustrates that the root quarrel in pro-family challenges is not simply an argument about whether or not certain materials belong in libraries but an argument about the purpose of the library and who shall have the right to determine it.

The Pro-Family Movement

FFL's quest to promote "traditional values" and protect children was typical of similar organizations linked in a loose yet powerful coalition known as the pro-family movement. Pro-family activism might be considered a contemporary incarnation of the New Christian Right, a social movement aimed at mobilizing evangelical Christians "into conservative political action." Pro-family activists attempt to sway public opinion and stimulate conservative political activity, whether at the national level—voting for particular presidential candidates or amendments—or at the local level, electing school and library board members sympathetic to pro-family causes. Pro-family organizations engage a large number of issues, but most commonly cluster around cultural contests over abortion, gay rights, and education. No one organization or person speaks for the collective, though there are prominent groups: Focus on the Family, Concerned Women for America, the Family Research Council, and the American Family Association are all highly influential among disparate groups of activists.[6] Pro-family activists are active almost exclusively within the Republican Party; indeed, they provided many of the key votes that helped reelect George W. Bush in 2004.[7]

Though some conservative Christians did participate in anticommunist activism during the 1950s, it was the rapid cultural changes of the 1960s that began to fully ignite religious conservatives' convictions. The sexual revolution, second-wave feminism, and youth resistance to the Vietnam War, in combination with a slew of Supreme Court decisions expanding free speech rights, made many conservative Christians so fearful their values were under attack that they felt morally obliged to get involved in politics.[8] Accordingly, conservative Christian leaders mobilized their flocks by framing activism as the righteous response to an increasingly secular and permissive society. It was no longer enough to condemn abortion or the dismantling of religious liberties as a matter of personal belief; leaders urged believers to do something about it.[9] Eventually, conservative Christians became more interested, invested, and indeed, influential, in politics; they began to identify themselves as "pro-family" and ally themselves with the burgeoning pro-family movement. The term "pro-family" is both good public relations and a kind of truth in advertising. For the family—at least, the heterosexual, two parent-headed family—is exactly what concerns pro-family activists: specifically, the relationships both within the family (between husbands and wives, and parents and children) and between the family and public institutions, including libraries.

Though campaigns to ban and restrict access to "objectionable" books have been a staple of conservative activism, it was the pro-family movement's critique of the public sector during the 1990s that brought libraries as institutions, along with the now suspect professional ethics of librarianship, under widespread public scrutiny. Though libraries could be (and were) sites of community conflict throughout the twentieth century, they still managed to maintain an authority that insulated them from the kinds of attacks on librarianship *itself* that are now commonplace in pro-family circles. For instance, Joan Bessman Taylor's research on 1950s Iowa reveals that even overt protest from librarians against removing "objectionable" books from drugstores did not do much damage to the library or the profession. On the contrary, conservative organizations were often quick to assert that they would have no problem with the same titles in the public library, for they understood the library as a place of restricted access, where librarians would protect children from literature beyond their level of maturity.[10] In contrast to these earlier controversies, contemporary pro-family activists target public institutions themselves as the problem, believing that schools and libraries abuse their professional trust by attacking religion, promoting "liberal" causes such as gay rights, and ultimately denying conservative parents their right to inculcate their religious and political beliefs in their offspring. Libraries increasingly drew the scrutiny of pro-family activists, who saw them not simply as fair game for politics but as places no longer safe for families, run by professionals no longer in touch with communities.

FFL was one of the organizations that helped drive the pro-family movement's attention to libraries and illustrates the productive and cooperative relationship between grassroots activism and national pro-family politics. A small, local organization started by a concerned citizen, FFL eventually caught the attention of more prominent and powerful organizations such as the American Family Association and Focus on the Family. These larger national organizations were able to showcase Gounaud's organization and her cause as an example of a campaign that even a fledgling activist could take on in his (or more likely, her) community.[11] Indeed, Diamond characterizes such library and school controversies as "bite-sized" battles relatively easily won and effective as a kind of boot camp for new activists.[12] Pro-family activism was fueled by thousands of dedicated local activists like Gounaud who, provisioned with some information and resources, began to understand library controversies in a national context, as a call to political arms.

The History of Family Friendly Libraries

A former music teacher and the author of *A Very Mice Joke Book*, Karen Jo Gounaud was a relative stranger to pro-family activism before she took on removing the *Washington Blade* from her local public library. Her own children grown, Gounaud was nevertheless concerned about the *Blade*'s sexually explicit personal ads and advertisements. After mobilizing like-minded community members, joining a group of several hundred Fairfax County activists, and attending a 1993 Christian Coalition–sponsored workshop designed to foster grassroots conservative activism, Gounaud was ready to take her quest to make the library "family friendly" to the next level.[13] Because Gounaud had found her efforts to either remove the *Blade* or restrict its access continually stymied by the policies of the ALA, particularly the Library Bill of Rights and its interpretations, she began to concentrate her energies accordingly. Gounaud believed that unless libraries changed their policies from ALA-based ones to family-friendly ones, children would not be safe and parents and taxpayers would have no control over library collections.[14]

Gounaud began to write and distribute literature promoting this vision, maintaining a list of the activists and supporters around the country who had contacted her for information. Her work soon caught the eye of Phil Burress, a library trustee who wielded a great deal of influence in the pro-family movement.[15] Once a self-confessed porn addict, Burress had been able to put his skills as a former union negotiator to work in forming Citizens for Community Values (CCV), a Cincinnati-based group dedicated to passing local legislation that limited where pornography could be bought, sold, and broadcast. Burress's CCV had also been designated one of Focus on the Family's Family Policy Councils, state-level organizations with varied foci that nevertheless maintain a Focus affiliation.[16] Burress, along with other pro-family movement leaders, encouraged Gounaud to launch FFL as a national organization. In October 1995, the first FFL conference was held in Cincinnati and sponsored by Burress, though Gounaud was still the organization's president and spokesperson. In attendance were about fifty people, including representatives from the Christian Coalition and the American Family Association, as well as members of the library press.[17]

In her opening remarks, Gounaud introduced the fledgling FFL as an organization for librarians who were tired of the ALA and who wanted to "get on with the business of being good, library service people." Good library service amid the ALA was in apparent short supply; Gounaud and Burress each characterized the organization as an elite, left-wing cabal bearing little regard for local communities. Gounaud maintained that the ALA's stranglehold on libraries could only be broken by family-friendly library policies that would protect children and create "more balanced" collections. She also argued that the ALA discouraged librarians from listening to concerned parents, effectively treating those parents as "censorship cases." In addition, Phil Burress accused the ALA of taking the position that "what we see and read doesn't affect behavior and [that's where] we don't agree."[18]

There had been no shortage of library challenges during the 1980s, but the FFL attack on ALA library policies, along with its "common-sense" rather than overtly moralistic approach to library practices, presented a new conundrum for librarianship. After attending the FFL Conference in 1995, *Library Journal* editor John Berry argued for accommodation. In an editorial titled "It Is Their Library, Too!" he wrote: "I have no reason to think FFL . . . is hostile to libraries and librarians. There is no doubt about their hostility to ALA. Still, on the local level I think we can learn from them and help them, just as we help other interest groups." In confining his analysis of the FFL to local theaters, Berry neglected to explore the larger implications for librarianship stemming from FFL's vision of the library. To the extent that he did acknowledge this vision, he seemed to understand it as primarily a clash between rational parental fears and an insufficiently responsive profession: "At ALA and at home, why don't we listen to the likes of Karen Jo Gounaud and FFL? Why not try to help honestly concerned parents guide the reading and viewing of their children?"[19]

Once Karen Jo Gounaud became a darling of the pro-family press and media, including frequent appearances on both James Dobson's *Family News in Focus* and Concerned Women for America's *Beverly LaHaye Live*, the library press grew more defensive. Charles Harmon and Ann Symons saw in FFL's attack on the ALA a larger threat to intellectual freedom, and thus approached the conflict as a problem beyond allaying the concerns of parents. In a 1996 *American Libraries* article titled "But We're Family Friendly Already," the authors urged libraries targeted by the FFL to publicize how they already serve families through a multitude of programs and resources. Ultimately, the authors recognized that it would be necessary to reclaim "the 'family friendly library' moniker from those who would seek to use it to restrict the flow of information and ideas."[20] In 1996, the Public Library Association invited Karen Jo Gounaud as a speaker for its annual conference on the pointedly titled panel "Family Friendly Libraries: Sense or Censorship?" along with John Clark, the leader of a Virginia anticensorship organization. While it was significant that the PLA invited Gounaud to share her views at a national librarian conference, the audience questions and comments directed at Gounaud were openly critical.[21] Ultimately, there would be no reconciliation between the FFL and the ALA.

With the coming of Internet access as a featured resource of many (if not most) public libraries in the late 1990s, FFL discovered an important new front in its battle against the ALA. Raising the specter of children viewing Internet porn in the library, FFL campaigned for mandatory filtering in school and public libraries, vociferously challenging the ALA's antifiltering stance. By the time the second FFL conference rolled around in October 1999, the organization had almost completely shifted its attention from books and collection development policies to the Internet and access policies.[22] Yet despite this shift in focus, the ALA remained the enemy. Earlier that year, the American Family Association had created and distributed a video titled *Excess Access*, featuring Gounaud and Burress. The video accused the ALA of turning a blind eye to children viewing pornography in the public library in the name of intellectual freedom. In the video, librarians are caricatured as dupes of the ALA, following the Library Bill of Rights in lockstep while ignoring community concerns like children's exposure to Internet pornography and sexual predators.[23] Focus on the Family and Concerned Women for America also promoted the video as well as the larger campaign against the ALA and in favor of mandatory filtering in school and public libraries. Pro-family activism ultimately helped fuel the momentum to pass the Children's Internet Protection Act (CIPA), which President Clinton signed into law in 2000. Though the ALA challenged the act in court, arguing that it violated patrons' First Amendment rights, the Supreme Court ruled the law constitutional in 2003.[24]

FFL seemed to lose momentum after the U.S. Supreme Court upheld CIPA; I found virtually no mention of the organization in the library or mainstream press between 2004 and 2006. In 2006, Denise Varenhorst, who had been active in pro-family library activism in Gwinnett County, Georgia, and was the president of Conservative Republican Women, assumed leadership of FFL.[25] It was also 2006 that saw the attempted passage of the Deleting Online Predators Act, and while the legislation was so broad that it remains in committee, the issue of social networking seemed to revive FFL into action. The organization is currently focused primarily on enforcing CIPA in school and public libraries, and, of course, making library policies and collections "family friendly." It continues to oppose the policies of the ALA, particularly the Library Bill of Rights, and the buttons it sells via CafePress read "Power to the Parents" and "Power to the Patrons."[26] FFL still worries about gay-themed children's literature and Internet pornography, but its overarching concern is taxpayer and parental control of library policies. While the organization maintains a relatively low profile, most major pro-family organizations still cite it as a resource for activists interested in taking on their local public library's policies.

The "Family Friendly" Library: FFL vs. the ALA

One of Karen Jo Gounaud's self-professed motivations for founding FFL was a longing for libraries past. In an essay reflecting on her own experience in libraries and her journey to activism, Gounaud writes: "Libraries in my life were always wonderfully imaginative and adventurous, but safe, child-friendly places. Librarians were 'in loco parentis' and partnered with parents in protecting the young. . . . Children's books made way ' . . . for Ducklings,' Mother Goose and Mister Rogers, but never the subjects of homosexuality and inner-city riots. . . . The only 'web' known to kids was safe to browse in a book about a spider named 'Charlotte.'"[27]

Memories of libraries past provide blueprints for their future counterparts; Gounaud founded FFL, in part, to return libraries to their former glory, an ideal state where library materials never challenged "traditional values" and librarians monitored children's reading in order to protect them from knowing too much. To resuscitate this ideal, FFL urged citizens to regain control of their libraries by replacing the policies of the ALA with "family-friendly" ones. An analysis of FFL discourse, however, reveals that this family-friendly library is predicated upon an imagined homogeneity of community values and a narrowly defined service role for the librarian.

Tellingly, FFL often used the metaphor of the "village" to refer to the community at large, believing that each member shares a common responsibility for protecting children. According to Helen Biehle, FFL member and retired history professor, libraries once took this obligation seriously.[28] However, in the wake of 1960s tumult, the ALA led librarians astray by encouraging them to duck out of these responsibilities; therefore, FFL asked libraries to "rejoin" the village by acting as co-protectors of the young. As Gounaud wrote, "it's time for public libraries to rejoin their 'villages.' We must all work together to protect the vulnerable minds of our children and the rights of their parents to expect that protection at our public libraries."[29] Accordingly, FFL imagined the scope of librarians' professional judgment to be anticipating parental wishes and monitoring young readers. Any lack of congruency between librarians' and parents' tastes was a sign not of diverse perspectives but of bad parent/librarian relations; indeed, Gounaud described the parent/librarian relationship as "a broken partnership worth mending."[30]

FFL blamed this broken relationship on the ALA, chiding the organization with labeling parental objections as "censorship," rather than as legitimate involvement in their children's lives: "The people asking the questions and raising the objections are not extremist folk screaming for Nazi-like censorship. They are loving guardians shocked and saddened by unexpected confrontations with librarians. . . . [Let's] give them a little help and encouragement in their efforts to keep the world's gutter from pouring directly into the minds of their kids."[31] That all will agree on the contents of the "world's gutter" is, of course, assumed. FFL also cited the annual ALA cosponsored Banned Books Week as evidence that the ALA seeks to intimidate and ridicule concerned parents. They argued that it is not just a "negative" event but also a campaign fueled by "exaggerated and deceitful misrepresentations of involved parents [who are] simply trying to protect their children from age-inappropriate materials by suggesting more appropriate access and selection policies."[32] Again, any diversity of opinion or judgment about what constitutes "inappropriate" was effectively dismissed.

FFL often cited the ALA's power as the reason community values could not reign in the library; ALA influence could be felt everywhere, infiltrating library systems with its policies, accreditation, and awards. Gounaud wrote that the ALA "controls the education of most librarians, an impressive part of the flow of public state moneys to local library systems affect sales . . . [and] the training of local library boards of trustees who are supposed to be representing the public."[33] Award-winning books, imagined by FFL to be vetted for appropriate content, "[are] not necessarily a safe choice, either. The ALA controls most of the awards, too."[34] While the ALA's stranglehold over the profession absolved individual librarians from blame, it also denied them any professional agency. In his opening address at the 1995 FFL conference, Burress insisted that he wasn't blaming librarians, but he also revealed that he viewed them as automatons carrying out the will of the library board: "Neither the FFL leadership nor I believe librarians are the problem. . . . Librarians simply follow the directions of their board of trustees who have adopted the liberal agenda of the ALA."[35] FFL believed trustees, board members, and librarians ran scared from the ALA, too afraid to speak up and challenge its power.

In addition to its sheer reach, the ALA also troubled FFL because it believed the association wielded private influence in the public realm. ALA authority was described as illegitimate, even illegal, divorced and distant from local communities: "Though the ALA is currently a politically powerful national organization, it is still only a PRIVATE organization whose policies, including the infamous 'Library Bill of Rights' and other related documents, have no basis in law."[36] FFL imagined every public as a local one, its values universalized into "traditional" standards that everyone presumably agreed on. FFL rhetoric privileged the parochial at all costs, attempting to encourage local activism by reminding citizens that the library belonged to them and not the ALA. This discourse of community ownership was intended both to spur citizens to action and suggest that the ALA had seized and usurped the rights of the community. Accordingly, Gounaud reminded activists to "never lose sight

of the fact that you are protecting your children, your community, your tax
money, all rightfully yours to protect and defend. The library system ultimately answers to all of you—not to the American Library Association."[37]

In addition to being characterized as a distant, private organization out of
touch with communities, the ALA was also caricatured as a hard-Left organization that censored conservative viewpoints. In her satirical poem "Ode to
the ALA," Gounaud accused the ALA of First Amendment hypocrisy:

> "Right Wing" is the enemy
> "Left Wing" is O.K.
> That's the First Amendment
> As retold by ALA.[38]

FFL lambasted the ALA for supporting various issues such as nuclear dis-
armament and gay rights, interpreting such stances as further evidence of
hostility toward conservatives. Indeed, Burress argued that the ALA's entire
agenda was hostile to the pro-family movement, "attacking the family, all
issues facing the pro-family movement, our work to preserve pro-family values
and our desire to protect children through parental rights policies."[39] The FFL
found in the ALA's liberal policy orientation "a hostile attitude toward conservative citizens" and believed its own positions were not taken seriously or with
respect.[40] FFL thus skewered libraries that subscribed to ALA policies for a
lack of balance in their collections. One of the suggestions in their written test
for determining a library's family-friendly quotient was to check for balance
in the collection on hot-button topics: "Most hot button issues of our times,
like abortion, euthanasia, homosexuality, etc are heavily weighted on the liberal and left sides of the debates. Conservative materials, especially Christian
conservative materials, with an opposite perspective on those issues are much
harder to find if they are there at all."[41]

Despite this apparent commitment to viewpoint diversity, FFL nevertheless
maintained that libraries should act as nonneutral institutions, promoting certain values over others. One of the values they believed should be promoted
was that of the traditional family, qualified as "mother and father married to
one another raising children together." FFL insisted traditional families should
be protected and supported by public institutions because they believed them
the "proven best" way of raising children and because they envisioned families as the building blocks of society.[42] Upholding the traditional family also
meant giving less time and space to nontraditional families—notably, gay and

lesbian ones. Unquestionably, one of the reasons FFL critiqued the ALA was that it supported gay and lesbian rights, which it understood to be yet another way the organization denigrated the traditional family. FFL believed that its challenges and objections to gay and lesbian materials not only were not taken seriously but were, in fact, censored by the ALA and that this censorship occurred for political reasons. In fact, Gounaud claimed the closer a library was affiliated with the ALA, the more likely it was to promote gay rights.[43]

Ultimately, FFL believed the ALA had abdicated community responsibility by discouraging librarians from leveraging the library's moral influence. Helen Biehle saw this as a radical departure from the profession's roots: "And this is the heart of the change: today the ALA resoundingly rejects this responsibility as naïve and old-fashioned." FFL went on to argue that the ALA was bent on purging (or at least silencing) the librarians in its ranks who might disagree with the Library Bill of Rights, intimidating them into toeing the party line. They believed library schools indoctrinated future librarians into the new creed of rejecting community responsibility in favor of abdicating judgment. As Biehle wrote, the ALA's "official statements ridicule and ostracize librarians who do not comply with this rejection of responsibility to the community, and library schools teach the new doctrine. The acceptance of moral responsibility for children in the library is now called 'unprofessional'; making a responsible moral judgment about materials purchased for the library is called 'elitist' and the librarian who is brave enough to do either is labeled a 'censor.'"[44] Because the ALA seemed to value "free speech" over the protection of children, FFL argued that intellectual freedom had become a hard line that trumped all other considerations and values.

But according to FFL, opposing intellectual freedom did not mean the group embraced censorship. Rather, FFL defined censorship as government censorship of information and prior restraint on what could or could not be said, not the removal of "inappropriate" books from libraries. It claimed that censorship involved political speech, not moral questions about what children should or should not be exposed to. The ALA, FFL argued, had radically (and perhaps willfully) misunderstood the meaning of censorship: "When a citizen objects to a store selling a certain book, or about a library holding a certain volume, this is not censorship. Rather, it is the exchange of ideas and opinions that, in fact, enhances the vibrancy of the American public square."[45] FFL members took deep umbrage at being called "censors" or any suggestion that their positions were extreme. Rather, they believed that what they demanded was "responsible sponsorship," comparing their objections to the routine decisions about collection development that librarians make every day: "That the ALA confuses the censorship of political speech with the setting of moral standards for the purchase and access of materials is a zealotry which holds ideological orthodoxy more precious than the welfare of children."[46] Thus, standards of morality were not only agreed upon but also effectively divorced from considerations of intellectual freedom. Commitments to access and diversity could not, FFL suggested, be considered elements of the community's (and children's) welfare.

Conclusion: The Legacy of FFL

Though it would ultimately fall short of its earlier ambition to serve as a widely represented alternative to the ALA and its policies, FFL's history and writings demonstrate that significant disagreement persists over the role of the public library in American life. Certainly, libraries have long been sites of struggle over cultural values. As Louise Robbins writes of a community civil rights battle that resulted in one Oklahoma librarian's firing in 1950, "when the cultural discourse is contested, the institutions charged with the transmission of culture become arenas in the contest."[47] FFL significantly shifted the terms of that contest and thus left its mark on contemporary library activism. Indeed, as Emily Knox illustrates in her investigation of a 2009 library challenge in West Bend, Wisconsin, all of the hallmarks of FFL activism—including working to change library policies rather than simply challenging materials and promoting the idea of "safe" libraries—are alive and well in recent library controversies.[48]

By bringing libraries and librarianship to the fore of the discussion, FFL and other activists reemphasized the importance of public libraries' service to communities and in so doing brought the nature of that service into question. For FFL, prizing safety over freedom, consistency over diversity, and the past over the future were both a vision of the public library's role and a critique of librarians' professionalism. While FFL may have faded from prominence as an organization, its competing vision of library values—and the imperative of activists to assert those values—has proven a tenacious one. Pro-family activists now step into the cultural fray not simply to determine the library's role but to declare their right to determine it.

Notes

The chapter title comes from Karen Jo Gounaud, "Is Your Public Library Family Friendly?," http://web.archive.org/web/20001031141603/www.fflibraries.org/Basic_Docs/laurasum.htm.

1. Clyde Wilcox, *Onward Christian Soldiers? The Religious Right in American Politics* (Boulder, CO: Westview, 2011), 94.

2. Mark J. Rozell and Clyde Wilcox, *Second Coming: The New Christian Right in Virginia Politics* (Baltimore: Johns Hopkins University Press, 1996), 197, 196.

3. Sara Diamond, *Not by Politics Alone: The Enduring Influence of the Christian Right* (New York: Guilford Press, 1998), 188.

4. Scott DeNicola, "What Lurks in the Library?," *Focus on the Family Citizen Magazine* 9 (September 18, 1995): 2–3.

5. Karen Jo Gounaud, "Family Friendly Libraries Manifesto," *Voice of Youth Advocates* 18 (1996): 363.

6. Wilcox, *Onward Christian Soldiers?*, 8, 10.

7. Dan Gilgoff, *The Jesus Machine: How James Dobson, Focus on the Family, and Evangelical America Are Winning the Culture War* (New York: St. Martin's, 2007), 194–95.

8. Nancy T. Ammerman, "North American Protestant Fundamentalism," in *Media, Culture, and the Religious Right*, ed. Linda Kintz and Julia Lesage (Minneapolis: University of Minnesota Press, 1998), 92–93.

9. Diamond, *Not by Politics Alone*, 114.

10. Joan Bessman Taylor, "Locating the Library in the Nonlibrary Censorship of the 1950s: Ideological Negotiations in the Professional Record," this volume, 173, 174.

11. See Linda Kintz, *Between Jesus and the Market: The Emotions That Matter in Right-Wing America* (Durham, NC: Duke University Press, 1997), for a discussion of how and why much pro-family activism is dominated by homemakers and stay-at-home mothers.

12. Diamond, *Not by Politics Alone*, 174.

13. Rozell and Wilcox, *Second Coming*, 197.

14. Family Friendly Libraries, "A Vision for Family Friendly Libraries," http://web.archive.org/web/20001031182016/www.fflibraries.org/Basic_Docs/vision.htm.

15. For an interview and portrait of Burress, see Skip Tate, "Family Friendly Libraries," *Cincinnati Magazine* 29, no. 4 (January 1996): 23–25.

16. Gilgoff, *Jesus Machine*, 175.

17. "Family Friendly Libraries Attacks ALA in Cincy Meeting," *Library Journal* 120, no. 19 (1995): 12.

18. Family Friendly Libraries, *"Family Friendly" Library Conference: Saturday, October 21, 1995, Cincinnati, Ohio* (n.p., 1995).

19. John Berry, "It Is Their Library, Too!," *Library Journal* 120, no. 18 (November 1, 1995): 6.

20. Charles Harmon and Ann Symons, "'But We're Family Friendly Already': How to Respond to the Challenge," *American Libraries* 27 (1996): 63.

21. John Clark and Karen Jo Gounaud, "Family Friendly Libraries: Sense or Censorship?," Public Library Association Conference, Portland, OR, March 26–30, 1996.

22. Family Friendly Libraries, "Family Friendly Library Internet Guidelines and Regulations," http://web.archive.org/web/20010110162800/www.fflibraries.org/Internet_Docs/interrec.htm.

23. *Excess Access: Pornography, Children, and the American Library Association*, directed by Rusty Benson and Brad Bullock, 21 min. (American Family Association, 1999), videocassette.

24. Marjorie Heins, *Not in Front of the Children: "Indecency," Censorship, and the Innocence of Youth*, 2nd ed. (New Brunswick, NJ: Rutgers University Press, 2007).

25. Family Friendly Libraries, "Family Friendly Libraries Announces New Leadership, Education Campaign," http://web.archive.org/web/20070723114805/http://www.fflibraries.org/March2000_Press_Release.html.

26. Family Friendly Libraries, http://www.cafepress.com/power2patrons.

27. Karen Jo Gounaud, "Grassroots Adventures on an Unexpected Front," http://web.archive.org/web/20010110181100/www.fflibraries.org/Speeches_Editorials_Papers/junecit.htm.

28. Helen Biehle, "Focus: The Seduction of the American Public Library," *Education Reporter* 121 (February 1996): 3–4.

29. Family Friendly Libraries, "Parent Alert: Beware the Public Libraries," http://web.archive.org/web/20010110183900/www.fflibraries.org/Speeches_Editorials_Papers/stlmetro.htm.

30. Karen Jo Gounaud, "Parents and Librarians: A Broken Partnership Worth Mending," http://web.archive.org/web/20010110173700/www.fflibraries.org/On_ALA/ParentsAndLibrarians9-99.htm.

31. Family Friendly Libraries, "Shameful Bedfellows: Cyberporn and the American Library Association," http://web.archive.org/web/20010426100734/www.fflibraries.org/Speeches_Editorials_Papers/wsjffl96.htm.

32. Family Friendly Libraries, "Family Friendly Libraries Books Week Press Release," http://web.archive.org/web/20010422014956/www.fflibraries.org/Books_Week/FFLBooksWeekFlyer.htm.

33. Family Friendly Libraries, "What's Wrong with the ALA?," http://web.archive.org/web/20010110175300/www.fflibraries.org/On_ALA/stlala.htm.

34. Family Friendly Libraries, "Parent Alert."

35. Phil Burress, "Opening Address," in FFL, *"Family Friendly" Library Conference*.

36. Family Friendly Libraries, "A Vision for Family Friendly Libraries."

37. Family Friendly Libraries, "Family Friendly Libraries Test," http://web.archive.org/web/20001031163130/www.fflibraries.org/Basic_Docs/test.htm.

38. Karen Jo Gounaud, "Ode to the ALA," http://web.archive.org/web/20010110172800/www.fflibraries.org/On_ALA/OdeToALA.htm.

39. Phil Burress, "Opening Address," in FFL, *"Family Friendly" Library Conference*.

40. Family Friendly Libraries, "Family Friendly Libraries Setting the Record Straight, 1996," http://web.archive.org/web/20001031152118/www.fflibraries.org/Basic_Docs/record.htm.

41. Family Friendly Libraries, "Parent Alert."

42. Family Friendly Libraries, "A Vision for Family Friendly Libraries."

43. Karen Jo Gounaud, "Homosexual Ideology within the Library System," http://web.archive.org/web/19981202120438/www.fflibraries.org/Schell.htm.

44. Biehle, "Focus," 3, 4.

45. Family Friendly Libraries, "Social Research Brief: Censorship, "http://web.ar chive.org/web/20001017231828/www.fflibraries.org/Education_Docs/SocialResearch Brief-Censorship.htm.

46. Biehle, "Focus," 4.

47. Louise S. Robbins, *The Dismissal of Miss Ruth Brown: Civil Rights, Censorship, and the American Library* (Norman: University of Oklahoma Press, 2000), 161.

48. Emily Knox, "The Challengers of West Bend: The Library as a Community Institution," this volume, 200–214.

The Challengers of
West Bend

The Library as a Community Institution

EMILY KNOX

We do not agree with their disturbing standard of "all materials available to all ages." With this said, let it be known that we vehemently reject their standards, we resent their presence, and we are repulsed by their insistence on holding the door open to sexually explicit, profane, and crude materials to the children in our community. We reject their standards and their principles.

. . . This is a propaganda battle to insure children retain access to inappropriate material despite the law, common sense, and community standards. If you choose to reject your community's request via petition . . . the loss . . . will be to the children you claim to serve and you will no longer be considered a safe library and we will strongly promote it as such.

—GINNY MAZIARKA, Town of West Bend,
Public Hearing Testimony, June 2, 2009

On February 3, 2009, four months prior to giving her public testimony, Ginny Maziarka and her husband Jim sent a letter to the director of the West Bend (Wisconsin) Community Memorial Library. The letter, which was placed in the overnight book drop, requested that the library remove a link on its website that recommended gay, lesbian, bisexual, and transgender books for young adults. Two months later, as a direct result of the Maziarkas' complaint, West Bend city aldermen refused to reappoint four members of the library board.

Challenges to materials in libraries are quite common, and the American Library Association's Office for Intellectual Freedom (OIF)—which monitors challenge cases throughout the country—logged 348 challenges in 2010. The

West Bend case received a large amount of press coverage, included high involvement of the local community, and was politicized, as demonstrated by the city aldermen case. These characteristics make the events in West Bend an ideal case study for examining challengers and the discourse of censorship in the United States. This study focuses on how challengers construct the library as an institution in society through their arguments regarding controversial materials. Challengers constitute a segment of the reading public that seeks to regulate and control what others read. Though not "readers" as commonly defined, they employ their own interpretive strategies when encountering "inappropriate" materials in libraries.

THE ESCALATION OF A CHALLENGE

The saga in West Bend began on February 3, 2009, when the director received a letter of complaint from Jim and Ginny Maziarka, expressing their concern about the library's online young adult booklist. It should be noted that the booklist had been added to the site five years earlier.[1] The library board was scheduled to meet that evening, and the Maziarkas wished to be included on the agenda. Due to Wisconsin law, the agenda could not be changed, and the letter-writers' concerns could not be heard until the next monthly meeting.

On February 13, the library received another letter from the Maziarkas—addressed to the West Bend mayor, the library director, and the library board—requesting the addition of several "ex-gay" books to the collection. Along with the letter, the Maziarkas included a copy of the West Bend library's Request for Reconsideration of Library Materials form and a challenge list of thirty-seven books.

According to the library's policy, the first step of the reconsideration process called for a meeting between the complainant and the library director. The Maziarkas, the library's young adult librarian, and the assistant director met on February 23. The meeting ended without a resolution, as did a meeting with the Maziarkas and the library's director and assistant director on February 25.

On March 3, the library board met to discuss the challenge. However, the discussion had to be tabled and the meeting rescheduled for March 25, due to high interest from the local community. The Maziarkas informed the assistant director they would be out of town that day, and the meeting was again rescheduled for March 26.

In the meantime, on March 13 the Maziarkas sent an e-mail to the library challenging additional materials and suggesting more titles that should be added to the collection. On March 19, the library administration and the West Bend city attorney sent the Maziarkas an e-mail concerning the original challenge list that the library received on February 13. The letter stated that after discussion with the Maziarkas, the city attorney understood that they no longer wanted to have the books removed; rather they should be relocated and labeled as sexually explicit. Since the nature of the request had changed, the original complaint filed on February 13 was considered withdrawn, and, as a result, the March 26 meeting of the library board was cancelled. If the Maziarkas wanted materials to be reclassified, they would have to submit an individual form for each title.

The Maziarkas then decided to form the West Bend Citizens for Safe Libraries and held their own meeting on March 26. Since they would be presenting what they believed to be sexually explicit material, minors were asked to leave the meeting. The Maziarkas read passages from several books, including the frequently challenged *Rainbow Boys* by Alex Sanchez and *Baby Be-Bop* by Francesca Lia Block, and presented a slide show. They also passed around a petition, which was never formally addressed by the board, that called for library policy changes, including reclassifying "pornographic" youth-oriented books and the visual identification of materials deemed "explicit."[2]

In late April at the annual city council organization meeting, the West Bend city aldermen voted to commission the library board. Of the nine board members, four were up for three-year-term reappointments. The council voted down all four. According to a newspaper account of the meeting, one of the aldermen stated that the appointees were not serving the interest of the community and that he "wanted people on the Library Board who think and use a little common sense. I'm concerned about the morality of this city."[3] Finally, on June 2, the library board held a two-and-a-half-hour meeting, during which almost sixty people spoke both for and against the Maziarkas' petition. The library board, which included the four members whom the city aldermen had removed but were still serving out their terms, voted to keep the existing policies regarding challenged materials in place.

READING, LIBRARIES, AND THE FIELD OF CULTURAL PRODUCTION

This study focuses on the challengers in the West Bend case and their understanding of the status of the library in society and how this understanding is shaped by their view of reading practices. Reading is a social practice that has changed over time and encompasses different physical modalities (such as reading silently or aloud) and interpretive strategies. Interpretive strategies can be understood as a set of decisions regarding what one will do with the text.[4] Reading is a powerful, empathetic activity, and individuals often speak of books "changing their lives." I contend that it is fear of this power of texts that informs challengers' behavior concerning materials they consider problematic.

Libraries, in light of their relationship to books, are seen as spaces that must be controlled, since they contain texts that can change one's moral character. The presence of a book in a library collection means that the library and, by extension, the community itself, approves of the words written inside it.[5] As Thomas Augst notes, "one of the primary social functions of the library remains symbolic: the staging of freedom in the local, often mundane struggle of individuals to craft a meaningful identity for themselves amidst routine paths and standard choices for society."[6] Although this view might seem somewhat exaggerated, it is clear from her testimony that Ginny Maziarka and possibly other challengers believe that no less than the soul of the community is at stake.

Libraries are integral institutions in what Pierre Bourdieu calls the field of cultural production. Fields—economic, political, and academic—are generally defined as hierarchically demarcated social spaces. The field of cultural production is unique because it reverses the arrangement of the economic field. Instead of maximizing economic power, people within the field of cultural production often maximize symbolic power by minimizing economic power.

Two important principles operate within this conceptualization of cultural production. First, in the field of large-scale production, those whose work is more subject to the norms of society as a whole generally enjoy more economic success but less symbolic success. Second, in the field of restricted production, those who operate outside middle-of-the-road norms often have less economic success but more symbolic success. The field of cultural production creates a social space in which the (economic) loser wins.[7]

There are distinct homologies between the producers and consumers of these fields. People who produce and consume goods from the field of restricted production will tend to have similar educational and cultural backgrounds, as will those who produce and consume within the field of large-scale productions. One example of these homologous tendencies can be found in modern art. Contemporary modern art is usually created within the field of restricted production, and for a contemporary art gallery visitor to understand the art that is displayed, he or she must be aware of the long history of that which has come before it. This knowledge is only available to those who possess a certain type of cultural capital.

Libraries, however—especially public libraries—are a radically different type of institution within the field of cultural production. The symbolic goods (e.g., books and other materials) accumulated within their collections are not segregated according to the fields of restricted and large-scale cultural production. Libraries' use of space and classification schemes present works that call on different symbolic universes (that is, they appeal to different social groups) in an entirely haphazard manner.

In library and information science there are few studies that examine why people engage in challenge behavior. It is hoped that this one will help libraries provide more effective responses to the entire reading public, including those who challenge library materials. It will attempt to demonstrate through analysis of challengers' arguments that they are engaging in rational, systematic behavior and their actions are closely tied to both the library as a site of symbolic power and their understanding of the practice of reading. This study is driven by the following research questions: First, how do the challengers construct the library as an institution within the field of cultural production? Second, how do the challengers' understandings of the practice of reading inform these constructions?

For clarity, it is necessary to define some of these terms. A "challenge" occurs when an individual or group asks library administrators to remove, restrict, or relocate materials within the library. Challenges do not always lead to banning, that is, the removal of materials from the library's collections. Nor do they always lead to a change in the materials' status (such as restriction or relocations with the library). Individuals who bring challenges, either written or oral, against library material, are engaging in "challenge behavior." Since labeling people as "censors" is controversial, they are collectively called "challengers."

Two types of documents posted to the West Bend Community Memorial Library website were used for this study. The first consisted of letters to the editor, transcripts of voicemail messages, and opinion columns in the *West Bend Daily News*, a local newspaper. The second consisted of transcripts of individual testimonies from the videotaped hearing held on June 2, 2009, before the West Bend library board.[8] This study is part of a larger research project that examines the ideological, rhetorical, and argumentative frameworks in the discourse of censorship and the nature of censorship practices.

THE LIBRARY: A CONTESTED INSTITUTION

The challengers articulated many themes and concepts; however, this chapter focuses on three themes that relate to their view of the library as an institution in society. First, they were concerned that the library be a "safe space" that protects children. Second, they advanced reclassifying and labeling controversial materials within the library in order for the institution to maintain its status as a safe space. Finally, many of the challengers believed that if the library did not move and/or label these materials accordingly, children would be in danger of "stumbling upon" them when they were unsupervised. For each theme, I first present the position of the library profession as codified in the ALA Code of Ethics and the Library Bill of Rights, followed by the position of challengers in the West Bend case.[9]

When it comes to the idea that the library should not only protect children but also be a "safe space" for them, there is a stark contradiction between how librarians and challengers in the West Bend case view the role of the library. As noted in the Library Bill of Rights, all library patrons—including children—should have access to all library materials. Libraries, including public libraries, do not operate in loco parentis. That is, they do not have a legal responsibility to protect children from materials that parents might view as harmful. In practice, this means that most libraries do not place age restrictions on borrowing materials. Even though the collection may be physically separated into different categories such as "Young Adult" or "Adult Nonfiction," anyone with a valid library card may check out any circulating item. Challengers, however, view the library as an institution that has a moral responsibility to protect children from reading materials the challengers believe will be harmful to their development. For them, the local library is similar to a public school or a religious institution, and it should provide both a physical safe haven for children and help parents in the difficult job of parenting.

The challengers in the West Bend case express in four different ways the theme that the library is an institution that should protect children. Three are constructed as active roles the library should assume to ensure children's safety, while one is constructed negatively.

First, as mentioned, some of the challengers see the library as an organization intended to help parents raise their children. Parenting is difficult, and parents should be able to depend on the staff at the library to help them decide which books are best for their children. One challenger states in a letter to the editor:

> While it is true that no one is forced to read a book just because it is available, it is also true that there is no way for a parent to properly supervise a child when the child is visiting the library alone after school. While it is tough to be a good

kid these days, it is even harder to be a good parent. I don't believe we would infringe on our children's First Amendment Rights by restricting access to books whose content may be objectionable, in the opinion of the parent. The parent determines this, not the child, and not the child's friends. Parents rely on the judgment of library staff.[10]

Exemplifying the second positive theme, another letter-writer notes that the library has a duty to maintain decency in its collections.

> Since our library does not hold every book ever printed the board presumably has to set parameters for what materials to acquire and hold. These parameters should reflect the character of our community—what is considered acceptable in New York or San Francisco does not necessarily belong here. . . . While parents should monitor their children's reading, it is not unreasonable to expect the library to uphold a basic level of propriety as well.[11]

It should be noted that these letter-writers use different standards for what might be considered "good" materials. The writer of the first quote believes that *parents* make this determination, and the writer of the second quote believes that the *community* does. Both writers, however, suggest that the library should conform to these standards to protect children.

Third, there is distinct fear that some parents are not adequately involved in their children's lives; in such cases, the library should be willing to protect the neglected:

> I've read a few of the books cover to cover, not just excerpts. These books have very graphic and detailed sexual behavior not suitable for children in grades six through eight. . . . The books in question are directed to both the gay and the straight, but either way the content is too graphic for minors. . . . Should parents be more involved in what their children are reading? Yes, yet many fall through the cracks and those are the children who need protection.[12]

> It's about protecting the innocent children who go to libraries. Yes, it's true that parents should be involved as to what their children are reading and be concerned about the content of what's being fed to their developing minds. What about those innocent children who are 11 or 12, who don't have parents involved in their lives because they are overwhelmed by being a single parent, two parents working several jobs, or those who have parents or caretakers who just

cannot be there because of physical illness, mental illness or death, etc. and choose
the library as a safe place to go?[13]

Finally, many of the challengers see the library as an institution that currently fulfills its role as a protector of children. However, it will renege on its
duty if it fails to remove materials that might be harmful. This view is
expressed in many of the letters, columns, and testimonies:

> I've been pondering the issue of the obscene books in the youth section of our
> library. Should parents have to protect their children from the youth section of
> the library in the same way they have to protect their children from the Internet?
> That seems to be the case and it is very sad.[14]

> Please West Bend aldermen, mayor and library board: Once and for all, do some-
> thing. Join other safe libraries around the country that have learned from the list
> of crimes within libraries and be proactive in protecting our youth. Take the
> action needed so that our beautiful award-winning library will come out of this
> controversy unscathed and highly respected as a safe community-first library.[15]

> Our library policy states that it shall endeavor to acquire materials which are of
> current and permanent value; that meet the high standards of quality and rep-
> resent the best available to meet the community's needs and interests. This is
> a propaganda battle to insure children retain access to inappropriate material
> despite the law, common sense, and community standards. If you choose to
> reject your community's request via the petition; the loss will not be to me, it
> will not be to my husband, [or to] West Bend Citizens for Safe Libraries. It will
> be to the children you claim to serve and you will no longer be considered a safe
> library and we will strongly promote it as such.[16]

As demonstrated by the above statements, challengers think the library has
a very particular role to play in the community. Like a public school, it must
be a safe place for children. Parents must be able to trust that their children
will not be in moral or physical danger when visiting the library alone. Some
believe, contrary to what is written in the Library Bill of Rights or the ALA
Code of Ethics, that the library should help parents in the difficult task of raising children by both providing materials that are virtuous and labeling those
that might prove harmful to children's moral development. Many of the challengers think this task should be accomplished through careful segregation of

the library's collection. That is, the library can be made into a safe space and protect children through proper classification.

The second major theme that appears in this discourse is that of the library as structured space. For example, classification is an area where challengers and librarians differ. Librarians and other information professionals view classification of library materials as a method of providing access. Cataloging and classification of items is approached from a positive point of view—what placement will make it easier for the patrons to find this material? The library's classification system, particularly of fiction, is often physically represented in the layout of public libraries. Regardless of size, public libraries tend to have separate sections for children's, youth, young adult, and adult books.[17] Challengers (and possibly other patrons) view these segregated sections as mental barriers; their presence dissuades people from going to "inappropriate" areas of the library.

Challengers tend to view classification as both prescriptive and performative. That is, if a particular book is located in the young adult section of the library, it is both positive for youth development and a young adult book. There is little acknowledgment that classification is subjective. The a priori segregation of the public library space through the classification described above allows challengers to argue that reclassification of controversial materials is not a form of censorship. Many of the challengers state that there would be no controversy over the books if they were moved within the library.

The challengers in the West Bend case have different opinions regarding where the materials should be located. However, many agree that as long as the books remain in the young adult section they are misclassified. One writes that the library should move the materials "behind the desk":

> I would like to express my deep disappointment in our library's stand on the YA Zone content made available to our youth. I understand there are children who desire to read such materials. There are also children who do not want to read these types of materials or need to know they are available. To have them in plain view for everyone is very inappropriate. No one is saying you can't offer these materials, but those people should have to ask for them.[18]

The use of the expression "in plain view" is thought-provoking and gives some insight into how the writer constructs the controversial materials. One does not have to read the books—simply viewing them might prove harmful. The books should be located not just "behind the desk" but presumably "under the desk," where someone who walks up to ask a question would not be able to see them.

A more common request is for the books to be reclassified into the adult section of the library:

> Please do not allow the Library Board to represent the people of West Bend regarding the inappropriate material in the children's section. It is not anyone's intention to have it removed from the system, but have it moved to the adult section. It is and should be the choice of all parents to decide when their child is ready to view such material.[19]

> The Library certainly has the right to have these books there, but I couldn't imagine my grandchild coming across one of these books. Why is it so difficult to just move them to the adult section and then have other books promoting our family values?[20]

> Let's at least give the parents and kids the resources needed to make parental decisions and wise choices instead of slipping in some porn when no one is looking. A fair warning to what they will find within the library materials by labeling them as containing adult material, putting them upstairs where kids won't see them while browsing the YA section.[21]

Note that the last letter-writer explicitly refers to the physical layout of the West Bend library. The adult section is upstairs, and the young adult section is, presumably, downstairs. Therefore, with reclassification the young adults will not see adult materials.

Another classification issue challengers often address is labeling. For libraries, labeling for content is often quite controversial. For example, during the 1950s, librarians struggled over whether or not communist propaganda should be labeled as such.[22] Officially, the ALA does not support labeling of any kind, but libraries often do not follow this guideline.[23]

As with reclassifying books, many of the challengers view labeling books as "explicit materials" as a simple way to diffuse any controversy. As shown here, some of the challengers ask for both reclassification and labeling:

> Just because Planned Parenthood and the ALA deems these books appropriate, doesn't mean this community has to also. All that is being sought is a simple reclassification and an added "visual identification" for these books. Are hundreds of citizens really just asking too much?[24]

Two of [these] requests were very responsible—move the objectionable books to a
more adult area or label them for a certain age. . . . I would like to see those mature
board members acknowledge young children are not ready for pornography-
type material and still be willing to move or label questionable material.[25]

Labeling is presented as a common-sense approach to ensuring that parents
know what their children are reading. Books are viewed as similar to other
types of media, such as movies or television. Some of the challengers argue
that if these media have warning labels, then so should books.

Any other form of media—movies, TV shows, magazines—they all have
warning labels on them if they have sexually explicit content. Books should be
no different.[26]

These folks have asked you a request. It is perfectly reasonable. We do it with
cigarettes, we do it with pornography. . . . If it was my choice, I would have
asked you to get rid of the books completely. But these folks have asked you
something completely reasonable.[27]

None of the challengers discuss how labeling might be carried out in the
future; many of them view labeling as a solution of least effort for handling
the books causing a problem in the community at the moment. More than
anything else, labeling books as explicit would provide a visual cue for parents
to quickly identify the nature of the books their children are reading. Both
reclassification and labeling are directly related to another primary argument
for the challengers: many of them are concerned their children will blindly encounter materials that they believe are unsuitable for children. They believe the
nature of the library space and its classification will enable people to "stumble"
into explicit material.

The challengers' final argument combines both the space of the library and
the fear of encountering what they believe to be dangerous information. Many
of the challengers refer to a fear that children will "stumble upon" the controversial books if they are not reclassified or clearly labeled as being explicit:

As far as I know, the whole library is still accessible to everybody regardless of age.
Concerned parents simply wanted the books moved out of an area where children might stumble across them. To me, it seems that's just good parenting—
not Nazi book burning![28]

If you haven't informed yourself on the library issue and the contents of the books, go online and take a look at the books. Do you also know why you've never read anything from the books, in the paper or other media? It's because if they print anything from the books, they'll lose their license. Do you really think it's OK to let some 10- or 12-year-old kid stumble over the books in the YA section? I don't! Just move the books to the adult section.[29]

The theme of a sudden encounter is paramount in these arguments. Note that there is an underlying assumption in the challengers' arguments that if children see the material, they will be enticed to read it and then harmed in some fashion. The use of "stumble upon" and "coming across" implies a loss of control over the library environment. This and the presence of stealth controversial materials lead to the feeling that the library is not a safe place. Similar to reclassification and labeling, "stumbling upon" pertains to the actual space of the library. The shelves hold materials that children would not "normally" pick up. But, in trying to locate suitable, non-explicit material, they will see these books and be inevitably drawn to them.

There are, thus, three major themes in the challengers' statements that relate to the library as an institution in the field of cultural production. First, the library should protect children from materials that might harm them. Second, the library should appropriately classify and segregate these materials. Finally, if the library fails to treat these materials as suggested, children are in danger of stumbling upon them. All of these themes relate to the idea of the library as a place and space of safety.

A COLLISION OF FIELDS

As noted, there are two overarching principles in Bourdieu's theory of the field of cultural production. The first concerns the field of restricted production, which produces symbolic goods for producers. The second incorporates the field of large-scale production, which produces symbolic goods for the masses. Many institutions within the field of cultural production, such as museums and theaters, strictly segregate these two types of symbolic goods. The library does not. The public library, in particular, uses a classification system based on subject matter and a secondary one based on the relative reading difficulty of a particular item.

What makes the library potentially dangerous? It arbitrarily collocates differently constructed symbolic goods—from the field of large-scale production and from the field of restricted production—on its shelves. Even though the homology between producers and consumers still exists when one considers the interpretation of a given item, the library as an institution operates as if it does not. It becomes a dangerous place in which the innocent can "stumble upon" materials for which they do not possess the cognitive structures to interpret "correctly."

This is particularly noticeable if one considers the manner in which fiction is arranged in most public libraries. After sorting according to broad genre (mysteries, science fiction, romance, et cetera), books are placed on the shelf according to the last name of the work's author. In any given library, depending on the size of the collection, Jean Auel might be collocated with Jane Austen and Paul Auster. Following Bourdieu's theory, these authors' books operate as different symbolic goods within dissimilar symbolic universes. Auster, for example, is a postmodernist author who operates within the field of restricted production, while Auel writes epic prehistoric romances within the field of large-scale production. People who hold different symbolic, cultural, and social capital will construct and interpret these works differently.

The study demonstrates that the West Bend case is a disagreement over two issues: space and interpretation. The challengers want to remove the danger they perceive in the library space by reclassifying and labeling items they believe will cause harm to children. This fear of harm to children's moral character drives the challengers, who see direct correlations among reading, beliefs, and moral development. If a child reads a book that states that homosexuality is acceptable, then the child will believe that homosexuality is acceptable.

Challengers constitute a particular kind of reading public for libraries—one that not only declares but also tries to implement its own understanding of the role of the library within a community. The arguments made by the challengers as described here present themes that help explain their understanding of the status of the library as an institution in society. The library has a duty to protect children and prevent them from coming across explicit material by labeling and classifying it appropriately. If the library fails to do this, it is no longer considered a safe space and is directly implicated in hindering children's moral development.

Notes

1. Kristin Pekoll, "Stand up! Defending Teen's Right to Read at West Bend Community Library," *Voice of Youth Advocates* (*VOYA*) 32 (2009): 284–87.

2. West Bend Citizens for Safe Libraries, petition, available at https://sites.google.com/site/wbcitizens4safelibraries/.

3. Dave Rank, "Four Tossed off Library Board," *West Bend Daily News*, April 22, 2009.

4. Stanley Eugene Fish, *Is There a Text in This Class?* (Cambridge, MA: Harvard University Press, 1982).

5. The idea of the library as symbol can be explained using Pierre Bourdieu's concepts of symbolic capital and power. Symbolic capital is an asset that operates as an altered and corporeal type of economic capital; its effects come from its suppression of its original source of power. For Bourdieu, symbolic capital is important because it is often misrecognized as something entirely different—common sense, for example. Challenges to materials in libraries can be understood as part of a struggle between competing symbolic systems. Challengers and librarians operate within different symbolic systems, and each group works to enforce its own ideas of how the library should operate and what materials it should have in its collections. Individuals do not see the world as totally structured—they have "space" in which to operate and interact. As Bourdieu states, "this objective of uncertainty . . . provides a basis for the plurality of visions of the world. . . . At the same time, it provides a base for symbolic struggles over the power to produce and impose the legitimate visions of the world." Pierre Bourdieu, "Social Space and Symbolic Power," *Sociological Theory* 4 (1989): 14–25.

6. Thomas Augst, "Faith in Reading: Public Libraries, Liberalism, and the Civil Religion," in *Institutions of Reading: The Social Life of Libraries in the United States*, ed. Thomas Augst and Kenneth E. Carpenter (Amherst: University of Massachusetts Press, 2007), 183.

7. Pierre Bourdieu, *The Field of Cultural Production: Essays on Art and Literature* (New York: Columbia University Press, 1993).

8. Even though the authors and testifiers are easily traceable, I use initials for attribution, to provide some anonymity for those not party to the original written complaint. I coded the documents for common themes using Atlas.ti qualitative data analysis software. Codes originated from previous research and emerged through the study's research process.

9. The ALA Code of Ethics and the Library Bill of Rights are both available on the ALA website, at http://www.ala.org/ala/issuesadvocacy/proethics/codeofethics/code ethics.cfm and http://www.ala.org/ala/issuesadvocacy/intfreedom/librarybill/index.cfm.

10. K.S., *West Bend Daily News*, June 5, 2009.

11. R.M., *West Bend Daily News*, May 15, 2009.

12. K.B., *West Bend Daily News*, April 4, 2009.

13. J.G., *West Bend Daily News*, July 22, 2009.

14. M.W., *West Bend Daily News*, April 9, 2009.

15. D.A.H., *West Bend Daily News*, April 30, 2009.

16. G.M., public hearing testimony, June 2, 2009.

17. These terms are themselves constructions. How does one demarcate "children's" or "young adult" books? The challengers use many different terms—including minors, young people, teenagers, and children—to describe the people who will be reading the

challenged books. All of these classifications have different socially constructed interpretations, which the challengers call on to make their arguments.

18. J.C., *West Bend Daily News*, March 6, 2009.

19. A.B., *West Bend Daily News*, July 15, 2009.

20. Anonymous, *West Bend Daily News*, May 5, 2009.

21. D.A.H., *West Bend Daily News*, April 30, 2009.

22. Louise S. Robbins, "Segregating Propaganda in American Libraries: Ralph Ulveling Confronts the Intellectual Freedom Committee," *Library Quarterly* 63, no. 2 (April 1993): 143–65.

23. American Library Association, *Intellectual Freedom Manual*, 8th ed. (Chicago: American Library Association, 2010).

24. L.E., *West Bend Daily News*, April 22, 2009.

25. P.P., *West Bend Daily News*, June 6, 2009.

26. Anonymous, *West Bend Daily News*, April 28, 2009.

27. T.F., public hearing testimony, June 2, 2009.

28. B.W., *West Bend Daily News*, May 13, 2009.

29. L.B., *West Bend Daily News*, June 4, 2009.

PART 4

LIBRARIANS AND THE ALTERNATIVE PRESS

Meta-Radicalism

The Alternative Press by and for
Activist Librarians

ALYCIA SELLIE

Where have all the flowers (and political leaflets, social protest
pamphlets, movement literature, and fugitive materials) gone?
—RICHARD AKEROYD and RUSSELL BENEDICT,
"A Directory of Ephemera Collections in a
National Underground Network"

Inside the cavernous main reading room at the New York Public Library
on 5th Avenue, away from the clamor of the surrounding streets, I began
to open a dusty manila folder.[1] I untied the surrounding string and looked
down at the top item of the stack: the January 15, 1974, issue of *Top Secret*.
This issue—and every other in the folder—appeared to consist of photocopies
of lined notebook paper, bound by a single staple, now rusted at each top left
corner. On the pages were reproductions of a handwritten text, inscribed in a
sprawling but legible hand. Although *Top Secret* represents the tedious and dedicated work of a massive archival project, it could easily be mistaken for something far less professional or important, perhaps even the ranting of a fanatic.

Top Secret was written by and for an alliance of librarians who were activists, if not fanatics. It brought together news and information to be shared
among librarians committed to a cause that others found too difficult, too
time-consuming, or just too utterly crazy to tackle: collecting alternative
publications.

Ever since R. Crumb's baby buggy filled with *Zap* comics hit the streets
of Haight-Ashbury, the struggle to keep the alternative press present and visible in library collections has been fought by radical librarians. Beginning in
the 1960s, if not earlier, these activist librarians have been arguing about the
importance of collecting, preserving, and sharing materials produced outside

the mainstream. Many have done so using the only outlet available to them—the alternative press.

ALTERNATIVES

As long as authors matter, ideas are urgent, and words want to run like
wild horses, the world needs small, independent publishers.

—CELESTE WEST, "Roll Yr Own"

Literature about the alternative press almost always begins with an investigation of the word "alternative."[2] One particular exploration by Chris Dodge notes the rejection within the word. Dodge importantly asks, "Alternative to What?," and answers: "Alternative means real choice is involved; options, diversity. How much difference is there between *Time* and *Newsweek*? With nearly identical covers (Diana vs. Diana, Monica vs. Monica, ad nauseam), they might as well be called *Tweedledum* and *Tweedledee*."[3]

Alternatives are DIY; they are made by "organizations which are involved with changing, freeing, enabling. . . . Their mission is communication, not commerce." In recounting her experiences talking with independent publishers while putting together the index *Alternatives in Print*, Jackie Eubanks remembered the response of one small publisher in particular. When she asked about the price of his publication, he cried: "Charge? We don't charge!" and then compromised: "Ok, you can put 'Donation' down as price. We wouldn't want anybody who wanted it not to be able to get it." Eubanks recorded that alternative publishers are "as committed to destroying profit" as large vendors are to making it.[4]

"Alternative will mean materials produced by non-standard, non-establishment groups or individuals . . . oriented towards radical/independent politics and culture," wrote James Danky in "The Acquisition of Alternative Materials."[5] Building on Danky's definition, I will use "alternative" here as a broad term that covers many types of publications, all of which vary from mainstream models.[6] Danky writes that while the term "alternative" "can be applied to ultra-conservative/right wing materials, the publications that I center on are from the far left.[7] Here I will explore a small section of radical library publications and locate them within the overall world of alternative publishing, as well as within librarianship.

My focus is serial publications that call for the inclusion of alternative materials in library collections. This is narrower than a study of the alternative press overall; I am looking only at radical publications made by and for North American librarians. Further, I am studying two specific eras of publication:

the radical "underground" press of the 1960s and 1970s and zines produced since the 1990s. Finally, in an effort to understand the wider success or failings of librarians as collectors of alternative materials, I will examine whether librarians have collected and preserved the alternative library literature created by their peers.

Inside Activists and Meta-Radicals

If you want to be a bookstore clerk, go ahead and order exclusively from the national best-seller lists. If you want to be a librarian, make room in your budget for some small press items.

—DOROTHY THEWS and MARY ALICE HARVEY,
"Libraries and the Small Press"

Alternative publications are not easy for most libraries to collect.[8] Toni Samek writes that "because of the profession's heavy reliance on mainstream review media, publishers, and vendors . . . materials produced by the alternative press, and materials that reflect alienated social sectors, are often underrepresented in libraries."[9] Alternative publications—with small press runs, unusual publishing schedules, and antiquated (or unautomated) billing systems—have been historically difficult to fit into library acquisition processes.

In 2001, Sanford Berman published an article titled "Inside Censorship," in which he argued that there are two forms of censorship that happen within libraries. The first, outside censorship, takes place when library materials are threatened or removed from a library collection due to protest from a library patron or group. The second, what Berman called librarianship's "dirty little secret," is *inside*, or self-censorship.[10]

Inside censorship occurs when librarians avoid adding materials to their collection—not because of any policy but because they fear that the material will be challenged or cause conflict or because the items would be too difficult to acquire. Berman says inside censorship restricts library collections through "seldom-acknowledged and hard-to-justify boundaries or exclusions." These restrictions are based on format (comic books and graphic novels, for example, have only just begun to enter into library collections) as well as content (Berman argues that if libraries really followed the standards set forth by the American Library Association [ALA] in its Library Bill of Rights, there would be far more materials with sexual content in the nation's libraries).[11] Alternative periodicals have long fallen victim to inside censorship: encumbered not just with acquisitions difficulties, these publications come in nonstandard formats and offer content that is vastly different from what is presented in the mainstream.

Librarians who battle against inside censorship are engaged in one form of what I call "inside activism." Instead of championing libraries to the greater public or advocating that libraries take a political stance or engage with activist causes in the wider world (both of which might be thought of as "outside activism"), these librarians are working on the social implications of collecting—from within the profession. Inside activists encourage fellow librarians to consider their professional praxis.

One of the most significant ways librarians have tried to convince their colleagues to collect alternative press titles has been through the production of their own alternative papers and zines. By creating works that advocate for other publications, librarians have been involved in a form of advocacy that I deem "meta-radicalism": in which librarians perform inside activism through print, producing alternative publications to advocate for the inclusion of alternative publications in libraries.

Many activist librarians have promoted the alternative press in mainstream publications like *Library Journal* or *Wilson Library Bulletin*—but these articles are not part of meta-radicalism. Rather, meta-radical publications are created in the alternative tradition, outside of the commercial mainstream. Meta-radicalism is contained in the underground papers created by librarians that document the importance of underground papers. Meta-radicalism is found in zines by library workers that promote zine libraries. These are professional publications, but they exist outside of proper library worlds. Created for librarians by librarians, meta-radical papers are political works that revolt against hegemony, resist rote professional activity, and fight against lifeless library collections. They are inside activism by way of the self-published page.

THE 1960s AND 1970s: NEW ISSUES

We can try to be fair but not unbiased. We either speak out and select or else keep quiet. Keeping quiet is just another way of supporting what is going on, which is a political stance.

—CELESTE WEST, quoted in Milton Wolf, "A Conversation with Celeste West"

Alternative publications born in the 1960s and 1970s—those works "heaved up on shore during a decade of social and political turmoil, of changing societal and cultural norms"—influenced contemporary journalism and political life, as well as the roles of librarians and library publishing.[12]

In the 1960s, with the advent of easier and more affordable forms of printing, underground newspapers flourished. Laurence Leamer described this era as a turning point in which publications became liberated from the restrictions of "why *this* story can't run here; *that* picture has to go there; or *that* story has to end here."[13] A small team could self-publish a paper that had formerly been controlled by restrictive systems of editors, printers, and advertisers. These publications were often created in the editors' homes and sold hand-to-hand by their creators on the streets. Well-known titles like the *Berkeley Barb*, the *Los Angeles Free Press*, and the *East Village Other* were so accessible and inviting that readers were inspired to found their own presses; at least a hundred independent papers were in circulation throughout the United States by 1967.[14]

Radicals started publishing their own papers not simply because it was something they could now afford to do, but because they believed their perspectives were not being represented in established media.[15] Across the country, papers were popping up that shared minority viewpoints, from the personal to the political. Gay and lesbian papers like the *Los Angeles Advocate* and *Come Out!* emerged as LGBTQI communities became more visible and radicalized.[16] Feminist presses began to collectivize and publish books, newspapers, and magazines. Radical African American newspapers, such as *Black Panther* and *Muhammad Speaks*, circulated throughout the country.[17] Librarians took note. They began to see their holdings were not measuring up; not only did they lack alternative titles, but their shelves were "nearly bereft of information on black, Hispanic, ethnic, and political publishers."[18]

The underground press was also in conflict with the dominant mass media's assumed objectivity. Alternative publishers began to weave together their "personal lives, journalism and activism" in ways that crossed established boundaries of authority and neutrality.[19] Librarians were also struggling over issues of objectivity in their profession.[20] They began to question whether their detachment from political issues was hindering their ability to serve their communities. They became concerned that librarians' failure to take stands on key issues (such as racism, sexism, and other oppressions) would keep patrons—especially those in minority groups—out of the library altogether.[21]

Many librarians believed the antidote to disconnected library collections was the alternative press. Battling the concept of "balanced" collections—in which acquisition of the mainstream left is equalized by inclusion of the mainstream right—the meta-radicals argued that alternative publications would bring the ideas of minority groups and new thought into library collections beyond the right/left binary. Advocates for alternatives fought diligently against the possibility that every library would hold duplicate collections of materials produced by conglomerate publishing houses. They agonized over the possibility that library holdings would be without connection to local culture or without acknowledgement of each community's unique sociopolitical identity. Many librarians—including Valerie Wheat, Sanford Berman and Noel Peattie— sought ways to bring "libraries to the people!"[22]

REVOLTING LIBRARIANS: THE FIRST WAVE, UNDERGROUND

We were showing what a good time you could have being an
information freak.

—CELESTE WEST, quoted in Wolf, "A Conversation
with Celeste West"

"This is about fighting censorship, and the place to begin is with ourselves," proclaimed Celeste West to the Alumni Association at the School of Library and Information Studies at Berkeley. "I see two main areas of self-censorship in libraries. One is putting up with hierarchical working conditions. The other is book selection." When West gave this speech in 1982, she showed no idealized vision of library work. She told the group gathered for the California Library Association Convention: "You buy largely what the corporate media crank out." West asked her audience to "speculate on the books never written and all the pages omitted because writers know commercial publishers are timid." Then she asked them to donate "just one good staff person, or equivalent, and ten percent of their budget" to the cause of alternative publications.[23]

Although West was continually critical of what she deemed the "literary-industrial complex," this speech was unusual for her: more often, she protested in print rather than behind a podium. West wrote about the connections she saw between the "conglomeritis" of large publishing houses and the homogenization of libraries. She called for the independent press and DIY publishing to rescue diversity in print and within library collections. Her activism inspired many of her fellow radical librarians to put pen to paper and to acknowledge their work as inherently political. One call for entries written for her peers and published in *Synergy* in 1969 read: "Are you a mild-mannered librarian working for a great metropolitan library? Become Superlibrarian: change that old image, message all the media, taste the fruit of your labors. Don't try that old phone booth bit, simply step to the shelves for Sheik Nedzaoui, *Anaga-Ranga*, *Kama-Sutra*, Norman Douglas (pseud. Pilaff Bey), *Liebesmittel*."[24]

Early in her career at the Bay Area Reference Center in the 1960s, West was using underground papers as reference tools with library patrons; much of her time was spent "shaking down alternative magazines, fugitive reprints, and street sheets" to help answer questions.[25] These underground publications inspired much of the content of *Synergy*, which West edited until 1973. She also began her own pioneer feminist press and collaborated on monographs like *Revolting Librarians* and *Booklegger's Guide to the Passionate Perils of Publishing*.[26] The last piece in the latter volume begins:

> An "alternative" library publishing explosion has already happened in the last six years. *Synergy* lit a spark in the doldrums of library literature. *Booklegger* and *Emergency Librarian* carried on the flame. Now there are a number of more specialized publications aiming to fill the vacuum of what is not covered regularly, in depth, or with an awareness by the established library media: women's publishing and resources, prison service, young adult service and issues, non-sexist children's resources, ethnic service and publishing, and responsible, non-racist cataloging. In short, the library profession is beginning to come into the 20th century, and . . . the more radical members seek alternatives.[27]

This reciprocal promotion of sister publications was a part of almost every meta-radical publication of the 1960s and 1970s. One could pick up *Sipapu* and find interviews with the publishers of *Booklegger* or be notified about the next edition of *Alternatives in Print* by browsing the *SRRT Newsletter*.[28]

Celeste West could have been describing James Danky's approach to library collecting when in 1972 she wrote: "Do 'balance' your collection with *pro*-racist, sexist, violence material (on ultramicro-fiche?), but as the ombudsmen of the mediascape, *push* the other, the human-hearted."[29] In the 1970s, Danky was part of a league of librarians dedicated to collecting and cataloging everything from the ephemeral to the contemptible. As part of the Collectors' Network, he helped lead publications of every conceivable color toward a home in a library collection. Working with a community of librarians across the United States, Danky and his cohorts collected, traded, and reviewed alternative publications.

Top Secret was the publication of the Collectors' Network. In it, members shared news and discussed their goals. It documented the collaboration and the hard work of many of the librarians who took part in the venture. The Collectors' Network was a union that achieved more than each member librarian could have done alone, just as the issue of *Top Secret* that I saw as a frail and ephemeral scribbling at the New York Public Library represents much more than can be observed inside manila folders today.

Although West and Danky were only two librarians working within a movement of professionals committed to cohesive collecting, their work highlights the larger goals shared among the meta-radicals. A third figure—whom Sanford

Berman described as "librarian, poet, raconteur, printer, editor, aesthete, social activist, philosopher, essayist, critic, publisher, and eccentric"—also exemplifies the meta-radicals of the underground period: Noel Peattie was the publisher of *Sipapu*, a journal issued irregularly and for many years free of charge for librarians.[30] In *Sipapu*, Peattie excelled at interviews. Over the years he spoke with many alternative publishers—outside of librarianship (from papers like *Oracle*, and *Anvil*, and underground comix like the *Fabulous Furry Freak Brothers* and *Pudge—Girl Blimp)* as well as within (such as fellow meta-radicals Carole Leita, Nancy Shimmel, Jackie Eubanks, and Elliott Shore). Peattie's commitment to alternative materials is clear, even in his early writings. In 1970, he shared that

> nobody is doing exactly what we are doing, to our knowledge. We will describe important papers, as they are born, transmogrified, or killed off; and we do welcome articles of strong opinion. We also encourage, even at some risk, the subscription to controversial (including Movement) papers.
>
> That ethnic and underground papers are controversial, and that librarians have lost their jobs by subscribing to them, there is no doubt. But that young people, especially Third World people, need them, is also true. You can always say "Let them subscribe at home, or buy them in the street; I have a job to protect;" and we cannot tell you to sacrifice your career. But consider, also, that the duty of a librarian is to increase the flow of information, not to impede it, and that self-censorship is the most dangerous form of censorship.[31]

By the time *Sipapu* came to an end in 1995, much had changed in the United States, including within alternative publishing. Peattie sustained his curiosity and enthusiasm for alternative print and freethinking content into the 1990s, when he began to publish reviews of another kind of publication: zines.

THE 1990S AND THEREAFTER:
THE PERSONAL IS A POLITICAL ZINE

The Cold War may be over, Stalinist-state systems long dead, and multinational conglomerates rule the world, but the counterculture and resistance movement are still alive and kicking. They've just moved to another arena.

—DANIEL C. TSANG, "The Alternative Media"

In contrast to the underground publications of the 1960s, which were largely made in editions on presses, zines are usually made in small batches and assembled by hand.[32] In *Girl Zines: Making Media, Doing Feminism*, Alison Piepmeier discusses how zines have a relationship to the body of their creator. Citing Benedict Anderson's *Imagined Communities*, she writes: "While Anderson's newspaper reader has the awareness 'that the ceremony he performs is being replicated simultaneously by thousands (or millions) of others,' zine writers and readers feel community because they know that *not* many others are replicating this act. The imagined community of the zine world is intimate rather than extensive, and linked to the body rather than simply to an imagined other."[33] Jenna Freedman agrees, writing that her zine "reminds me that as I print, assemble, fold, staple, color in and rubberstamp each and every copy of my zine, that inevitably a little of myself—some tiny bit of DNA—goes out with each copy."[34] Today, in an age of screens, apps, and digital publications, zines are important to their creators precisely because they are not Web-based, because they are not blogs. Zines are appealing because they are physical objects that show evidence of personal lives through smells, creases, and other traces of DIY construction.

Whereas underground publications were sold hand-to-hand on the street like contraband, zines are more commonly sent through the mail with a personal note or traded at public events and festivals. While underground papers relied on the more commercial printing technologies of offset and mimeograph presses, zines are most often created on photocopiers. Zines also tend to be smaller: instead of a tabloid- or newspaper-sized work, they are more akin to chapbooks or pamphlets and often are made of a sheet of office paper folded in half and stapled.

The diversity of content within zines is vast. Like the undergrounds, zines include topics that the mainstream media glosses over, avoids, or condemns. Julie Bartel writes that zines "can be about toasters, food, a favorite television show, thrift stores, anarchism, candy, bunnies, sexual abuse, architecture, war, gingerbread men, activism, retirement homes, comics, eating disorders, Barbie dolls—you name it."[35]

Zinesters commonly make their publications at their kitchen tables, just as underground publishers did. But instead of working as teams and sending their publication off to a printer, zine-makers often construct their publications alone and then they might distribute their works to an intentionally small group of readers—perhaps just friends or pen pals.[36] Information about a zine and its creator might be deliberately obfuscated; the date and location of its construction may not appear in its pages, and the author's identity might only be acknowledged through pseudonym. Janice Radway explains that zines "explore the delineation and porousness of boundaries, crossings, connections and com-minglings. Zines are also deeply engaged in conversation with many different discourses appearing in the surrounding culture. Indeed they are so engaged with them that they cite, reference and even ventriloquize a multifarious range of discourses precisely to respond to all of them. Thus, they re-circulate cul-tural discourses at the very moment that they alter them by juxtaposing and combining them."[37] It may seem antithetical for librarians—who are stereo-typically interested in order and organization—to be involved in the chaos of zine-making, but many librarians create zines. Sean Stewart writes: "Some mysterious link exists between zines and librarians. . . . Are librarians drawn to zines because they recognize in these bizarre, photocopied publications the passion for freedom of expression that they themselves so proudly stand for?"[38]

Within the set of zines produced by librarians are works that advocate for the inclusion of zines in libraries. Meta-radicals like Greig Means and Chris Dodge—librarians with and without a master's degree in Library Science—publish zines to promote zine collection and preservation.

RIOT LIBRARRRIAN: ZINES OR BUST

A zine about zine librarians, by zine librarians, for zine librarians . . .
and the people who love them.

—GREIG MEANS, *Zine Librarian Zine*

"At first I thought about forming an association not unlike the ALA, ex-cept exclusively for zine librarians," wrote Greig Means in 2002. "But when I approached a coworker about joining the ZLA, she said, 'What? The Zapatista Liberation Army?' Not wanting to be confused with our freedom fighting comrades to the south, I thought it might be a better idea to do a zine librar-ian zine."[39]

Like the underground publishers of the 1960s and 1970s, zine librarians began to create alternative publications, because they didn't see their interests reflected in the professional literature, and to create community. *Zine Librar-ian Zine* (*ZLZ*) was started by a group of librarians who met at the Under-ground Publishing Conference in 2001. Penny Collins wrote that her desire for *ZLZ* was that it "function as a way for isolated zine librarians to commu-nicate with each other, comparing systems, sharing information and offering advice."[40] More than just a discussion of the inner workings of each collection, *ZLZ* and other meta-radical publications help remind librarians that they are "doing important work. [We're] building communities, promoting free speech, and giving people the tools they need to change the world."[41]

In the same way the meta-radicals of the 1960s fought against the monoculture of the mainstream, zine librarians advocate for the inclusion of materials that go outside the norm and "make serials management look like a piece of cake."[42] Meta-radicals promote zines despite "that the materials are often challenging to acquire and problematic to catalog." Like earlier activists, the meta-radicals declare that these challenges are "no excuse for self-censorship."[43]

While the meta-radicals of the 1960s and 1970s were focused on convincing their peers that the alternative press was important, meta-zinesters focus more on DIY library practices. Because cataloging and staffing are now seen as the main obstacles to collecting alternative literature (and perhaps because of the work done by the earlier meta-radicals), the majority of meta-radical writing on zines focuses on *how* to get zines into a library, not *why*. Step-by-step guides abound, and zine librarians share advice and information via e-mail discussion lists and (un)conferences in addition to within their publications.[44] Reaching outside the limitations of establishment libraries, these meta-radicals form support networks of both accredited and "barefoot," or nondegreed, librarians, and they also reinforce the importance of zine libraries in garden sheds as well as within traditional libraries.

Often even within institutional libraries, zine librarian positions are unpaid, or added voluntarily on top of regular duties—making zine librarianship just as much a labor of love as zine-making. The activism of meta-zinesters tends to be narrower in scope than that of the first wave of meta-radicals, which promoted alternative media in many formats. Most meta-radical zine publications promote zine collecting in particular, not the larger field of alternative materials. Although zine librarians often are interested in the larger significance of collecting the alternative press as a whole, because the work of collecting is often voluntary and additional to their other responsibilities, many zine librarians intentionally constrain the scope of their advocacy and their collections to make their work more manageable (and to obtain approval for their work within their institutions).[45]

Meta-radical zinesters see their work as intensely important, if not always appreciated. Ellen Knutson, a volunteer zine librarian at the Urbana-Champaign Independent Media Center (UCIMC), believes: "If in some small way the UCIMC library makes a difference in giving access to information that is otherwise unavailable to people then I feel like it is all worthwhile."[46] The meta-zinesters who create, contribute to, and advocate for zine collections understand Travis Fristoe's sentiments about participating in zine librarianship:

I continue to volunteer at the Civic Media Center's zine library because it keeps me thinking about the important questions. What do any of our written efforts matter? What is worth archiving? What do zines mean to those outside our immediate circle? . . . Why have I donated my Friday afternoons for the last 5 years to our zine collection? . . . Because we must record the human, the personal and the political voices that are largely silent and silenced in our society. Because if we don't document these attempts at history and culture, who the hell will?[47]

RECEPTION, VIA COLLECTION

"Why, Mr. Peattie, we'd be fired if we bought those things!"

—NOEL PEATTIE, quoted in Bundy and Stielow,
Activism in American Librarianship

In the fall of 1969 and the spring of 1970, S. J. Leon studied the collections of Philadelphia libraries.[48] His survey used a list of titles produced by the Social Responsibilities Round Table of the ALA to compare collections throughout the city. Leon concluded that "the puritanical heritage we read about in our social and cultural histories still lives in Philadelphia area libraries." More important, Leon mentions the restrictions of his survey: "One of the limits of such a study as this is the absence of expansive statements to explain the responses. Are the four libraries that do not have the two plays by LeRoi Jones making evaluative judgments on the merits of these plays? Are they even aware of them? Are they reacting partially to the author's reputation as a militant in Newark's recent ghetto wars? Or are they reacting, perhaps to his anti-Semitic diatribes disguised as poems? All these factors are separable, but only in the minds of knowledgeable collection builders." Leon warns that "sheer statistics have their crudities, and vital half truths are often hidden underneath, between, and around them. Figures don't lie: they merely make half statements much of the time, and much depends on how they are presented."[49] In other words, library records alone ultimately can't tell us *why* an item was added or omitted.

Yet, we lack significant data elsewhere. Any opposition to the alternative press's presence in libraries is as underground as the publications themselves. There is little rebuttal to the work of the meta-radicals—other than complaints about how difficult it can be to acquire and manage alternative publications. Inside censorship has been present and powerful enough to keep alternative materials out of libraries without lengthy discussion or debate. For the most part, librarians have been either too timid or too indifferent to speak out against alternative collections.

With an acknowledgement of the limitations of statistics and data alone, perhaps the best way to measure the effectiveness of the meta-radicals is by examining library records—to see what titles were added to library collections and maintained. Meta-radicals spoke to their fellow librarians. Thus, if their peers were convinced of the importance of alternative publications to libraries, they would have added alternative materials to their holdings.

As I write this, at the end of 2010, more than eight thousand libraries collect *Library Journal*. Roughly 130 libraries that share their cataloging records with OCLC via WorldCat report holdings for *Synergy*. Just ten have *Top Secret*. Because these publications are all serials, these holdings might be dramatically incomplete—each of these libraries may have just a handful of issues of each title, not a comprehensive array.[50]

There are even fewer zines in library collections. The three issues of *Zine Librarian Zine* are held at about sixteen libraries. My own *The Borough Is My Library: A Metropolitan Library Workers Zine* is available at only three libraries, despite its being advertised as free of charge for zine collections.[51]

Despite that there are undoubtedly more copies of all of these publications being read by librarians than what appears in WorldCat, we are presented with a dire picture of library collecting when we see how sparingly alternative library literature has been preserved in permanent collections.[52] These numbers raise many questions: Were alternative publications unappealing to librarians? Was the avoidance of these materials intentional? Have librarians been reading radical publications but keeping them in their home closets instead of in their collections?[53] And most important, if librarians have neglected to collect the alternative publications produced by their own colleagues, how could they claim they did not likewise neglect the wider range of alternative publications?

MEANWHILE, BACK IN THE LIBRARY . . .

If we don't act in our professional capacities as conservators, guardians
of this civilization, we are not librarians. Period.

—CELESTE WEST, quoted in Milton, "A Conversation
with Celeste West"

As I stood inside the New York Public Library and browsed through *Top Secret*, I had the distinct feeling that I had seen the publication before, but I wasn't sure that was possible. I flipped through the stack of issues for a closer look. At the top of one cover page were three letters. Scrawled in pencil, they barely form a word. It would have been easy to overlook this scribble—to think it was some notation of classification. When I finally realized what I was looking at, I was astonished. I knew that few others would have an idea of who had written this note, or about its larger significance.

I worked at the Wisconsin Historical Society (WHS) with James Danky in the early 2000s as I made my way through library school. Russell Benedict once wrote a job description for a student assistant to aid with his Contemporary Issues Collection, which read: "He or she must expect to encounter the absurd, the irrational, the thrilling, and the shocking."[54] This would have been an accurate description of the materials that we received daily in the newspapers and periodicals collection.[55]

Despite that by the time I was at the WHS, the Collectors' Network had been defunct for many years, Danky still maintained a network of his own. He would send items related to the political and religious right to Chip Berlet, Native American publications to the Sequoia Research Center at the University of Arkansas–Little Rock, and boxes of miscellaneous publications to Chris Dodge.[56] The issues Danky sent along were materials that didn't suit the collection or those we had already acquired. Each day in room 225, I would work alongside Danky, sorting the mail. If he encountered a duplicate item, he would grab his pen from his shirt pocket and quickly jot three letters at its top—"Dup."

"Dup." notation on a copy of *Top Secret* located at the New York Public Library. (Photo by Alycia Sellie)

These were the same three letters I found scrawled in pencil at the top of *Top Secret* in the reading room of the New York Public Library, in what looks just like the handwriting I had seen daily for three years.

When I later asked Jim if he remembered sending any duplicate issues to the New York Public Library, he told me that they hadn't ever been on his distribution lists.[57] Although Danky did not send these particular issues—so far as he can recollect—one of his comrades did. Even without the formal Collectors' Network, Danky's persistent work to preserve, share, and forward enabled me to see these materials. Here we have another act of meta-radicalism—from one generation to another. A gift shared from hand to hand—but with a few decades between the sharing, unlike on the streets of San Francisco in the 1960s.

While reading these issues of *Top Secret* has been very important to my own research, it is not difficult to imagine how this creative collecting will have implications for other scholars of print culture. The knowledge that while he was at the WHS Danky was avidly seeking Native American newspapers, labor publications, prisoners' magazines, publications of the religious right, and all kinds of otherwise uncollected tracts is reassuring for future researchers. While some might doubt the need to save and preserve many of the publications that line the shelves in Madison, Danky realizes that each item is awaiting its historian. "For most of the stuff that is acquired," he admitted in an interview in 1992, "the utility won't occur in my lifetime." But he also points out, "If you want to look at contemporary life in America, this is the place to come."[58]

Today, librarians wouldn't be likely to speak negatively about collecting alternative publications; they generally remain silent about the implications of conglomeritis and mainstream collections. This silence is enough to make comprehensive alternative print preservation a difficult goal. There is little movement away from the standard procedures of purchasing materials from a continuously narrower list of corporate library vendors.[59] The prevalence of small and ever more restricted budgets, and the overwhelming array of professional responsibilities and shrinking staffs also sadly limit today's librarian—mentally and fiscally—from extended contemplation of collection development.

Despite the challenges, meta-radical publications continue in print. *Unabashed Librarian*, *Counterpoise*, and *Progressive Librarian* continue the traditions of the revolting librarians that began in the 1960s. Librarians like Kelly ShortandQueer and Jenna Freedman continue to cut, fold, and staple so that

I still find printed publications in my mailbox. Each year I issue my own zine. As I construct my own work, I keep the vision of the revolting librarians close to heart, and I imagine meta-activists to come. In 1977, James Danky asserted, "The social upheavals of the last decade cannot be understood from the pages of the *New York Times* alone."[60] I contend that the history of librarianship cannot be conveyed merely through the study of *Library Journal*.

NOTES

This work is licensed under a Creative Commons Attribution 3.0 Unported License. http://creativecommons.org/licenses/by-sa/3.0/.

1. This chapter's epigraph is from Richard Akeroyd and Russell Benedict, "A Directory of Ephemera Collections in a National Underground Network," *Wilson Library Bulletin* 48 (November 1973): 236.

2. This section's epigraph is from Celeste West, "Roll Yr Own: A Guide for New Publishers, Self-Publishers, and Authors," in *Booklegger's Guide to the Passionate Perils of Publishing*, ed. Celeste West and Valerie Wheat (San Francisco: Booklegger Press, 1978), 21.

3. Chris Dodge, "Alternative to What?," *Counterpoise* 2, no. 2 (1998): 11.

4. Jackie Eubanks, "A.I.P. Adventures," *Booklegger Magazine* 1, no. 1 (1973): 4, 5–6.

5. James P. Danky, "The Acquisition of Alternative Materials," in *Alternative Materials in Libraries*, ed. James Philip Danky and Elliott Shore (Metuchen, NJ: Scarecrow, 1982), 13.

6. Narrower terms that could be used to describe publications that fall within the umbrella of "alternative" might include descriptors of the way that these publications are produced (self-published, small press), their format (broadsides, pamphlets, newsletters), or their content (ethnic press, punk zines, literary mags). Each of these labels could be thought to form a separate branch within the "alternative" tree—which encompasses many variations in form and content—but all grow from the shared roots of the free press.

7. Danky, "Acquisition of Alternative Materials," 13.

8. This section's epigraph is from Dorothy Thews and Mary Alice Harvey, "Libraries and the Small Press," in *Alternative Library Literature, 1984/1985: A Biennial Anthology*, ed. Sanford Berman and James Philip Danky (Jefferson, NC: McFarland, 1986), 86.

9. Toni Samek, "Unbought and Unbossed: Booklegger Press, the First Women-Owned American Library Publisher," in *Women in Print: Essays on the Print Culture of American Women from the Nineteenth and Twentieth Centuries*, ed. James Philip Danky and Wayne A. Wiegand (Madison: University of Wisconsin Press, 2006), 128.

10. Sanford Berman, "'Inside' Censorship," *Progressive Librarian* 18 (Spring 2001): 48–63.

11. Ibid.

12. James Danky and Denis Kitchen, "Introduction," in *Underground Classics: The Transformation of Comics into Comix*, ed. James Philip Danky and Denis Kitchen (New York: Abrams, 2009), 17. This section's epigraph is from Celeste West, quoted in Milton Wolf, "A Conversation with Celeste West," *Technicalities* 2, no. 4 (1982): 6.

13. Laurence Leamer, *The Paper Revolutionaries: The Rise of the Underground Press* (New York: Simon & Schuster, 1972), 34.

14. Donna Lloyd Ellis, "The Underground Press in America: 1955–1970," *Journal of Popular Culture* 5, no. 1 (1971): 105.

15. Or radicals created their own papers because even alternative publishers were ignoring their perspectives. John McMillan documents in his book, *Smoking Typewriters: The Sixties Underground Press and the Rise of Alternative Media in America* (New York: Oxford, 2011), that the domination of white men over the underground press was what inspired LGBTQI folks, women, and people of color to abandon underground presses and create their own papers that operated without deference to white male "leaders." Similarly, the boys' club of the underground comix movement in San Francisco inspired female graphic artist Trina Robbins to promote and publish women's alternative comics.

16. James P. Danky, "The Oppositional Press," in *The Enduring Book: Print Culture in Postwar America*, ed. David Paul Nord, Joan Shelley Rubin, and Michael Schudson (Chapel Hill: University of North Carolina Press, 2009), 269–85.

17. Jacqueline Rhodes, "The Black Press and Radical Print Culture," in Nord, Rubin, and Schudson, *Enduring Book*, 286–303.

18. James P. Danky, introduction to Danky and Shore, *Alternative Materials in Libraries*, vii.

19. Leamer, *Paper Revolutionaries*, 14.

20. Toni Samek, *Intellectual Freedom and Social Responsibility in American Librarianship, 1967–1974* (Jefferson, NC: McFarland, 2001).

21. Samek, "Unbought and Unbossed."

22. Sanford Berman, "Libraries to the People," in *Revolting Librarians*, ed. Celeste West and Elizabeth Katz (San Francisco: Booklegger Press, 1972), 51–57.

23. Celeste West, "The Secret Garden of Censorship: Ourselves," in *Alternative Library Literature, 1982/1983: A Biennial Anthology*, ed. Sanford Berman and James P. Danky (Phoenix, AZ: Oryx Press, 1984), 101–4.

24. Celeste West, "Naked Lunch," *Synergy* no. 22–23 (October–November 1969): 21.

25. Ibid.

26. For more information about Celeste West and *Synergy*, see Toni Samek, "Unbought and Unbossed," 126–55; Toni Samek, "*Synergy*, Social Responsibility and the Sixties: Pivotal Points in the Evolution of American Outreach Library Service," in *Libraries to the People: Histories of Outreach*, ed. Robert S. Freedman and David M. Hovde (Jefferson, NC: McFarland, 2003), 203–18; Toni Samek, K. R. Roberto, and Moyra Long, eds., *She Was a Booklegger: Remembering Celeste West* (Duluth, MN: Library Juice Press, 2010).

27. Valerie Wheat, "The Library Free Press," in West and Wheat, *Booklegger's Guide*, 69.

28. In "The Library Free Press," Wheat listed: *Booklegger Magazine, Collectors' Network News, Emergency Librarian, Hennepin County Library Cataloging Bulletin, Inside/Outside, Librarians for Social Justice, Rocking Chair, SRRT Newsletter, Sipapu, Synergy, Title Varies, Unabashed Librarian, Voice of Youth Advocates, Women in Libraries, Women Library Workers,* and *Young Adult Alternative Newsletter.* My work on this project was possible only because so many alternative library publications identified, promoted, and reviewed other alternative library publications. Mention of alternative library publications would also happen when meta-radicals published in mainstream library publications: Danky and Berman each published reviews of alternative library literature in *Wilson Library Bulletin* and *Library Journal,* for example.

29. Celeste West, introduction to West and Katz, *Revolting Librarians,* n.p.

30. Sanford Berman, foreword to *A Passage for Dissent: The Best of Sipapu, 1970–1988,* ed. Noel Peattie (Jefferson, NC: McFarland, 1989), ix.

31. Noel Peattie, "1:2," in Peattie, *Passage for Dissent,* 10.

32. This section's epigraph is from Daniel C. Tsang, "The Alternative Media: Open Sources on What's Real," *International Journal on Grey Literature* 1, no. 2 (2000): 61.

33. Alison Piepmier, *Girl Zines: Making Media, Doing Feminism* (New York: New York University Press, 2009), 229.

34. Jenna Freedman, "Pinko vs. Punk: A Generational Comparison of Alternative Press Publications and Zines," in *The Generation X Librarian: Essays on Leadership, Technology, Pop Culture, Social Responsibility and Professional Identity,* ed. Martin K. Wallace, Rebecca Tolley-Stokes, and Erik Sean Estep (Jefferson, NC: McFarland, 2011), 154.

35. Julie Bartel, *From A to Zine: Building a Winning Zine Collection in Your Library* (Chicago: American Library Association, 2004), 2.

36. Stephen Duncombe, *Notes from Underground: Zines and the Politics of Alternative Culture* (New York: Verso, 1997), 101.

37. Janice Radway, "Girls, Zines, and the Miscellaneous Production of Subjectivity in an Age of Increasing Circulation," transcript of keynote speech presented December 1, 2000, at the annual colloquium of the Center for Interdisciplinary Studies of Writing, University of Minnesota, Minneapolis, 11.

38. Sean Stewart, "Zines and Librarians: Zines and Librarians: The Phenomenon Explained," in *Zine Librarian Zine 2, Advice for A Young Zine Librarian* (2003): 32.

39. This section's epigraph is from Greig Means, introduction to *Zine Librarian Zine* 1 (Winter 2002): n.p.

40. Penny Collins, "Misfit Theatre Zine Library: Greetings from New Zealand," *Zine Librarian Zine 2, Advice for A Young Zine Librarian* (2003): 26.

41. Greig Means, "Independent Publishing Resource Center: It's Been a Good Year at the IPRC," *Zine Librarian Zine 2, Advice for A Young Zine Librarian* (2003): 45.

42. Travis Fristoe, "Civic Media Center," *Zine Librarian Zine* 1 (Winter 2002): n.p.

43. Brooke Young, "Salt Lake City Public Library: The Public Library Slant," *Zine Librarian Zine* 2, *Advice for A Young Zine Librarian* (2003): 4–5.

44. See the Zine Librarians e-mail list (http://groups.yahoo.com/group/zinelibrarians/), founded by librarian Jenna Freedman, and the Zine Librarians (un)Conference wiki (http://mkezluc.wikispaces.com/ for the events of 2011) for more information.

45. I can attest to this: at the Brooklyn College Library I have created a zine collection instead of an alternative press collection, to make my own voluntary work more manageable for myself. Even though I believe there are many currently published non-zine alternative serials that should be collected in libraries, and I worry over what items are not being collected, I had to choose some constraint for my own collection and, essentially, my own labors.

46. Ellen Knutson, "Urbana-Champaign Independent Media Center: Zine Librarianship: Labor of Love or a Long Slow Descent into Madness," *Zine Librarian Zine* 2, *Advice for A Young Zine Librarian* (2003): 7.

47. Fristoe, "Civic Media Center," n.p.

48. This section's epigraph is from Noel Peattie, "Intellectual Freedom Activism in the Sixties: The Defense of a Professional Standard," in *Activism in American Librarianship, 1962–1973*, ed. Mary Lee Bundy and Frederick J. Stielow (New York: Greenwood, 1987), 48.

49. S. J. Leon, "Book Selection in Philadelphia," *Library Journal* 98, no. 7 (April 1, 1973): 1081–89.

50. In general, if researchers want to see publications but do not have access to this limited number of libraries, they can place interlibrary loan (ILL) requests. Yet, commonly, ILL requests for full issues of print serials will not be granted—requests for specific articles are more common (my own ILL dept was exasperated by my requests for full print runs). The alternative press is also well known for being poorly indexed, so identifying a specific article to request via ILL might pose barriers—even in an age of digitization.

51. It must be noted that these counts might not reflect the true number of collected items—plenty of copies might currently be available in independent libraries or those that do not participate in the OCLC catalog.

52. As one example of librarians having read zines not represented in WorldCat, I have certainly distributed more than three copies of my own zine to my colleagues.

53. After I presented this paper at the conference "Library History Seminar XII: Libraries in the History of Print Culture," a fellow librarian kindly donated her personal collection of *Booklegger, Women Library Workers*, and *WLW Journal* to me for this project—from the bottom of her closet.

54. Akeroyd and Benedict, "A Directory of Ephemera Collections," 236.

55. WHS has one of the largest serials collections in the United States, or just over nine thousand subscriptions when Danky retired in 2007. For more information, see Julie Rigby, "Research File: Documents in Search of Scholars," *Lingua Franca* (Summer/October 1992): 74–75.

56. James Philip Danky, e-mail message to author, August 28, 2010.

57. James Philip Danky, interview by author, Madison, WI, June 4, 2010.

58. Rigby, "Research File," 75.

59. Today, librarians are often focused on digital acquisitions management and are even struggling to maintain perpetual access to online works they have paid for—perhaps another result of conglomeritis and dependence on commercial vendors.

60. James Danky quoted in Patricia J. Case, "Collections of Contemporary Alternative Materials in Libraries: A Directory," in Danky and Shore, *Alternative Materials in Libraries*, 122.

From the Underground
to the Stacks and Beyond

Girl Zines, Zine Librarians, and the
Importance of Itineraries through Print Culture

JANICE A. RADWAY

Recently, as part of an effort to revisit the question of how correlations between literacy and power function, the Society for the History of Authorship, Reading, and Publishing—familiarly known as SHARP—organized its 2010 conference around the theme "Book Culture from Below." The initial call for papers suggested that conference presenters direct their attention beyond the legitimate precincts of book culture and the literate elites who typically inhabit them to investigate "the under-represented and the oppressed."[1] Those generally excluded from book culture were glossed initially as peasants and the laboring classes, but the call observed additionally that presenters might also consider a range of others who have operated without the privileges of traditional literate elites yet have managed, through their "independence and initiative," to adapt the tools of book culture to their own purposes.

This organizing strategy repeats the now familiar post-1968 tactic inspired in the United States by the work of feminist scholarship; labor and working-class history; African American and Native American studies; gay, lesbian, and queer studies; and ethnic studies as well. Indeed, the animating metaphors of "outside" and "below" have done useful work for years by enabling scholars to recover the forgotten or actively erased histories of subordinated populations. Together, the two metaphors guided early research strategies that were designed to redress the bias toward the cultural productions of the writing and reading classes who dominated older forms of political, intellectual, and military history; literary studies; art history; bibliography; and library studies. As a consequence, forgotten texts, popular culture, underground and alternative

literary forms, material culture, folklore, and folklife began to figure significantly within all of these disciplines.

Despite the evident utility of the idea of narrating history from below,
now—after more than three decades of work—this too homogeneous and
spatialized way of conceptualizing power seems more a hindrance than a help
in the effort to trace peoples' literacy practices. To begin with, many have
pressed upon us the importance of attending not simply to the history of
books but rather to the history of print more broadly.[2] This is important
because the dismissed and dispossessed have had to turn frequently to cheaper
and more ephemeral forms, like newspapers and magazines, pamphlets, hand-
bills, posters, and newsletters to make their concerns known. The book circuit
was not always open to them.

More significant, as these oppositional scholarly discourses evolved in
proximity to, and in dialogue with, each other, as well as in the context of
post-structuralist and Foucauldian theories of power, together they began to
challenge the idea that dispossessed subjects or groups can be construed
homogeneously as simple reflections of their particular spatial or cultural origins on the outside. Such scholars have insisted on the necessity of understanding diversity not simply as an external condition of the world population
generally but also as an internal feature of individual subjects and differen-
tiated groups and subgroups. Neither individuals nor groups can be assumed
to be uniform or homogenous, the argument goes. Neither can they be construed as driven by a purity of understanding or purpose born of a place of
origin or point in a fixed social hierarchy. Rather, they must be understood
as internally diverse, the result of conflicted and contested social and biographical histories. Both individuals and groups need to be seen as complex, multifarious, and disparate—one might even say divided and disjunct. So, too,
must the print forms they have created.

This way of conceptualizing subjectivity and the social as inherently fractured is significantly different from any framework that seeks to locate individuals and groups as above or below, inside or outside, elite or dispossessed,
authentically oppositional or unwittingly incorporated. Such a binary formulation construes power as something one either has or hasn't. It tends to ignore
the possibility that there might be multiple forms of power and competing
arenas where control is differently organized, thus leading to contention and
contestation. This simplistic view of power underwrites the supposedly reme-
dial "from below" perspective, because it suggests that dissent and opposition
can come only from outside a dominant social formation. Significantly, this

spatialized view of power excludes the possibility that some privileged individuals participate in print culture from dissident perspectives while others forge alliances across class, race, gender, cultural, and even national boundaries through the very aegis of print culture itself. It also ignores the possibility that dissenting forms can continue to exert their critical effects even after they have been taken up through more mainstream outlets. What is needed is a perspective that attends not to the mapping of fixed positions, whether of authors, readers, or texts, but rather to the itineraries of all three, that is, to the vagaries of their circulation through social formations that are complex, internally fractured and contested, and thus also eternally in motion.

In truth, this perspective *was* represented on the SHARP program, which actually covered more than books and readers thought to have originated cleanly from below some putative elite. Similarly, the conference call's spatialized mode of conceptualizing power was contested in a number of conference presentations and at a roundtable devoted to the theme, where Johan Svedjedal of Uppsala University suggested that "while the concept of below may seem clear-cut at first, it soon dissolves into a series of paradoxes and slippery metaphors."[3] To redress the problems attendant on too heavy a reliance on this familiar metaphor, he proposed that a more complex understanding of power and a more rigorous sociology ought to be applied to book and print culture history. Noting that the concept of intersectionality might be helpful in directing attention to the ways social relations are affected by crosscutting systems of power, he offered as evidence that "most book markets are complex systems with parts that may be labeled both elite and from 'below.'" In expanding his point, Svedjedal observed: "Take an author with working-class background, writing fiction of social protest, but publishing at a prestigious publishing house—his books selling both through the large book-stores, and through book-clubs catering for working class readers. Is he an author from 'below' or from 'above?' It is not easy to say, and presumably his authorial identity will be torn between being one or another." As a consequence, Svedjedal concluded, "the real challenge for the book historian . . . lies in determining the power-relations and social stratifications *in each link in the so-called 'book chain.'*"[4]

With respect to his own subfield, the sociology of literature, and to the history of its efforts to better describe processes of domination and dissent, Svedjedal discussed the worth of various new metaphors ventured by Pierre Bourdieu (the literary field), Robert Darnton (the communications circuit), Adams and Barker (the book cycle), and in his own work on left-wing publishing in twentieth-century Sweden (the book circuit).[5] Whatever the differences

among these various metaphors—and the difference yet again between them
and D. F. McKenzie's recommendation of a sociology of text rather than a history of books—it seems clear that all such efforts at conceptual reorientation
seek to foreground the critical importance of circulation.[6] They highlight the
movement of books, print, texts, and people through a range of institutions,
networks, locales, and interpretive constellations, all of which are divided and
disjunct, crosscut by power relations at every turn and thereby multiply over-
determined. Which is to say, ultimately, that mediating figures like publishers, editors, designers, book-sellers, book agents, reviewers, and—significantly
for our purposes in this volume—librarians all ought to figure more centrally
in the research, study, and narration of what might more accurately be called
the historical sociology of literacy, where literacy encompasses both writing
and reading and the variable institutions and practices fostering relations between them.

Here I would like to explore how such a nuanced understanding of the
subject and the social—along with greater attention to the specific itineraries
of circulation—can illuminate the life of particular texts, especially over time.
I will do so by focusing on the zine production by girls during the 1990s.
In doing so, I want to raise questions about how best to conceptualize the
"underground," that is, "alternative" cultural production and to suggest that
the kind of conceptual spatialization of power embedded in the "from below"
perspective featured at SHARP 2010 can result in too pessimistic, too cynical,
too short-sighted an assessment of the effects of dissenting cultural production
on a social formation. Finally, with the help of the particulars of this case
study, which focuses as well on how girl zines continue to travel in different
cultural venues, I want to draw attention to the complex ways that librarians,
situated at key switch points in the larger culture of print, have an enormous
impact on what gets counted as the cultural tradition, on that which is subsequently made available to others to be selected from, read, and mined for
potentially new purposes.

The foregoing observations derive from my present work on girls and the
handmade publications known as zines that some of them crafted in the 1990s
out of paper, magazine clippings, Sharpies, old typewriters, twine, staples, and
glue. These curious semi-publications—they were intended only for person-
to-person and small-scale mail distribution—are interesting in the context of
the SHARP call for papers for the ways in which they both do and do not fit

its spatialized mode for conceptualizing power. On the one hand, many of the earliest girl zinesters of the late 1980s and 1990s understood themselves a part of the punk music underground.[7] Note the spatialization and hierarchy embedded within the term "*under*ground," which, when used by girls and other zinesters of the 1990s, referred to the punk music scene where participants sought to protest the commodification of rock by producing music from beyond the confines of the corporate record industry. In this formulation, as in others utilizing the notions of outside and below, alternative music was construed as a form of "authentic" oppositional expression, whereas industry-fostered music was dismissed as corporate and commercial and therefore as ideologically mainstream.[8] The zines that issued from within this scene were similarly assumed to be alternative publications, which is to say they were understood as the authentic expression of sentiment and ideas by a youthful population located not only outside but also below the dominant, adult establishment.

Girl zines of the late 1980s and early 1990s were additionally judged alternative by virtue of their critical relationship to mainstream gender norms. Though the relevant history here is complex and only now being elaborated in detail, the practice of what I call "girl zine-ing" is rightly associated with the defiant music of all-girl punk bands like Bikini Kill, Bratmobile, and Heavens to Betsy in the United States, and Huggy Bear in the United Kingdom.[9] These bands were noted for their loud, unruly, deliberately defiant music that foregrounded angry, often screaming, female voices. Those voices and the frenetic, even aggressive, modes of performance that accompanied them challenged traditional assumptions about femininity and protested everyday forms of violence against women. When some of the young women involved in these bands discussed the need for active protest, called for a "girl riot," and then gathered in Washington, DC, in the summer of 1991, they began to talk about the subordinate position of girls not merely within the music scene but beyond it as well. Building on the first girl-oriented zines created a few years earlier by Erin Smith, Tobi Vail, Donna Dresch, Laura McDougell, and Molly Neuman and Allison Wolfe, some of those involved began to call themselves "riot grrrls" and used that term and related language in their subsequently created zines. Shortly after the first meetings, Kathleen Hanna produced *Bikini Kill #1, A Color and Activity Book*; Tobi Vail subtitled *Jigsaw #3* as an "angry grrrl zine"; and Allison Wolfe and Molly Neuman created the first issue of *Riot Grrrl*. Each made an effort to call attention to the everyday surveillance and violence directed against girls and protested the way traditional gender norms constrained girls' agency and sexuality.[10]

As the bands and their zines became more widely known, they generated a
growing fan base of young women who began to communicate among themselves about this new music through their own zines, thus contributing to
the generation of a loose social movement that soon would be termed "riot
grrrl."[11] Cultural commentators from a range of different venues began to
notice riot grrrls because their nonconforming behavior contrasted markedly
with the conduct of the girls who appeared more typically within American
public discourse of the 1990s as silent victims and the targets of intervention
by adults, including journalists, psychologists, social workers, teachers, scholars, and even professional organizations like the American Association of University Women.[12] Riot grrrls, their music, and their zines stood out because
they displayed scandalous, nonnormative performances of femininity and because they refused to comply with traditional expectations that girls present
themselves as objects for the visual pleasure of others or behave as ingratiating
social facilitators rather than opinionated dissenters in their own right.

When viewed as an intervention within a historical context of actively debat-
ing the effects and fate of feminism—indeed 1991 saw not only the advent of
riot grrrl culture but also the Supreme Court confirmation hearings of Clarence
Thomas featuring intense debate about the subject of sexual harassment—
from outside, the writings of adolescent girl zinesters look very much like an
authentic emanation. Indeed they appear a self-evident form of protest against
the easy and familiar ageism and misogyny of the dominant culture. Thus it
makes sense to argue, as many have, that girls turned to zines as an alternative,
noncommercial form, seeking to make themselves present to themselves *as girls*
but also as creative, writing, and reading subjects.[13] Indeed many portrayed
themselves as actively dissenting agents with things to say about the gendered
nature of everyday life and the literate means to do so. As a consequence, they
reveled in unexpurgated, affect-laden writing and celebrated their ability to
communicate with other girls below the radar of adult censorship and beyond
the bounds of normative authority. In so doing, they defiantly reclaimed a
term that in its adjectival forms, "girlish" and "girly," typically associated fem-
inine gender identity with childishness, passivity, and a winsome, nonthreaten-
ing sexuality.

Yet even as it makes sense to underscore the underground origins and outsider stance of the first riot grrrls, it is important to note what seems to have
happened when mainstream culture focused on their activities. Journalists and
traditional trade publishers took up the subject of riot grrrls and their various modes of cultural performance (their music, zines, bodily comportment,

and sartorial style) in part because they appeared so controversial and in part because these mainstream cultural producers were seeking ways to engage younger audiences who seemed to be foreswearing print for MTV. They tried to reach younger, more "hip" audiences by reporting on riot grrrls and their zines in sources like *Newsweek, USA Today, Seventeen,* the *New Yorker, Glamour,* and *Rolling Stone* and by marketing trade-press anthologies of zine excerpts to enthusiasts, fans, and others.[14] Although some of the reporters and publishers were sympathetic to riot grrrls' feminist intentions, on the whole, their actions tended to reinscribe girls and their zines within the zones of the mainstream and the acceptable.[15] Perhaps not surprisingly, mainstream commentators used a range of discursive tactics that contained the significance of riot grrrls by treating them variously as a curiosity, cute and spunky but ineffective, and even an example of feminist outrage run amok.[16]

The rhetorical containment was so vigorous, in fact, that it prompted Kathleen Hanna and some of the original riot grrrls to declare a moratorium on contact with the mainstream press.[17] In attempting to retreat back into invisibility and the underground, they were seeking to preserve their music and zines as sites of authentic dissidence. Even so, it now seems clear that this mainstream media attention attracted more girls to the practice of zine-ing and that while a substantial portion of the zines that resulted repeated and extended the feminist commitments of the first riot grrrl zines, some did not. Instead, younger girl zinesters took up the form of the "per-zine," a type of zine devoted self-consciously to the expression of the personal interests, problems, and opinions of a girl who vigorously insisted on her identity as an individual.[18]

It would therefore be easy enough to contest the location of girl zines as emanations from "outside and below" dominant culture by connecting their celebration of the individual voice to the fact that, as far as we now know, most of the girls who engaged in this form of production, at least within the United States, were privileged by their class and social location. Indeed, most were well educated, white, and middle class. A number of the original riot grrrl band members were college and university students.[19] Yet they were also conversant with discourses of feminism and with the histories of avant-garde art and political dissent in the United States. It is not easy to place them then in relationship to a unitarily conceived dominant culture. Still, when their zines began to be imitated by younger high school girls, it became even clearer that the riot grrrls were largely the children of the white American suburbs. Functioning already as adepts within the world of language, books, and reading, these young women had access to magazines, writing materials, typewriters,

copy machines, and enough disposable income to duplicate their efforts and
to circulate them.

The whiteness and middle-classness of the girl zine community was so
pronounced, in fact, that it eventually generated indigenous forms of protest,
that is, counter-zines from within the girl zine universe, articulating the concerns of young women of color, poor and working-class girls, and lesbian and
queer women. Counter-zines—*Evolution of a Race Riot, Slant, Slander, Quantify, Bamboo Girl,* and others—were effective in rendering visible the political
limitations of girl zines by identifying the traces of race, class, and heterosexual
privilege embedded in even the most openly feminist of girl zine discourse.[20]
Within the hip-hop community, riot grrrls were also often dismissed, as were
punks more generally, for having poached upon and appropriated the real critical stance of music that originated within the black underclass.

Given these many contradictions—not unlike those characterizing Johan
Svedjedal's hard-to-place working-class author—it is difficult to say definitively
whether the zines girls crafted and circulated throughout the 1990s should
be construed as print culture "from below." Nor is it easy to say how truly
"alternative" they were. This is true of underground or alternative music more
generally and of the larger zine scene as well. Commentators on the latter
in particular have debated the authenticity of the sentiments expressed within
zines and questioned whether zines have generated real political activism.
Even Stephen Duncombe, who has offered a sympathetic yet highly nuanced
account of the form, worries about the traces of bourgeois ideology embedded
in the discourse of the zines' largely middle-class creators. At the same time,
he laments the ways the vibrant formal and affective style of zines—like that of
indie and alternative rock itself—was adopted by corporate executives and advertisers seeking to sell their products to the zine generation. Duncombe fears
that through such mainstreaming practices, insurgent zinesters were bought
off, their covers blown, and their outsider redoubt thoroughly occupied.[21]

One can't help but be sympathetic to his concern. From one perspective, this
fate seems to have befallen riot grrrl and the critical impulses that generated
it. Throughout the course of the 1990s, in fact, recording executives, toy man-
ufacturers, apparel producers, and advertisers all recognized that money could
be made from girl culture. Soon riot grrrrl morphed into "girl power" and was
embodied in the figures of the Spice Girls and Britney Spears. Younger and
younger girls appeared at concerts sporting the commercial version of the riot
grrrl look, purchased at Target or Walmart.[22] Similarly, the impulse to create
a zine and connect with other zinesters was channeled into the corporately

managed early social networking sites MySpace and Friendster, gravitated subsequently to instant messaging and texting, and eventually reappeared in transformed fashion on Facebook. It's not surprising to note, then, that Sarah Marcus recently observed that people now write about riot grrrl as a thing of the remote past.[23]

And yet this all-too-familiar story of how a wholly dominant commercial culture incorporated, contained, and bought off an instance of originary, authentic dissent is too simple. To begin with, it simplifies the complexity of riot grrrl itself and the character of the young women involved. They were decidedly middle-class, it is true, but they were also alienated and actively involved in dissent. Furthermore, treating riot grrrl as a unitary phenomenon or musical fad that enjoyed only a transitory life fails to acknowledge that the movement was generated by a host of different people engaging in a range of different practices, many of which had quite distinctive and long-term effects on those whose lives they touched.

Furthermore, even if one agrees that musicians like Kathleen Hanna, Tobi Vail, Alison Wolfe, and Corin Tucker, together with riot grrrl zinesters, *were* displaced by Ginger, Posh, Britney, and their tweeny girl-power fans, one must also acknowledge that, simultaneously, significant numbers of riot grrrl participants continued to work in the music and avant-garde art scenes. Others went on to colleges and universities and even graduate school to build on their early activities as feminist zine writers and artists. Still others pursued forms of political activism as young adults in a range of different arenas. This phenomenon has recently emerged into view as it has become evident that girl zines did not disappear when their creators matured but continued to live on well past the 1990s, not only in the memories of their creators but in archives, books, newspaper articles, artworks, and even academic books and articles like this one. Both zines and their creators have circulated beyond the confines of what was once called the underground, and as they have, they have begun to speak to new audiences and new concerns. My point here is that if we are to understand the significance of the zines created by girls in the 1990s, we cannot look simply to their origins. We must seek to trace their itineraries of circulation through new social regions as well as through time.

Zine-ing in the 1990s was a complex social practice. As such, it involved girls in relation to others, particular materials and discourses, and specific forms of production, duplication, and circulation.[24] To capture the complexities of these relations and the practices that enabled them, I have been trying to devise an approach that would resist nominalizing—that is, fixing—either the zines or the girls themselves on the order of things. What I am attempting to do instead is track the movement of girls and their zines through particular networks, relationships, and communities, as well as time. I aim to trace itineraries of ever-changing processes rather than to map the origins and supposed meanings and effects of objects, people, and texts. Thus, I want to focus not simply on zines but also on the girls who crafted them, as well as on those who distributed, read, anthologized, and wrote about them contemporaneously. I am especially interested in those now-established young women who have continued to circulate girl zines through a range of different sites by means of an equally broad range of practices, including donation, collecting, archiving, academic writing, teaching, and various forms of artistic production. Zine librarians figure centrally in this group.

My current project is titled "Girls, Zines, and their Afterlives: Subjectivity and Sociality in the 1990s and Beyond."[25] It unites textual and visual criticism; a performative orientation to the constitution of texts, subjects, and social forms; and oral history. Though I'm only just embarking on the interviewing process, I want to sketch out three different aspects of girl zine-ing as social practice and performance that have come to the fore in my preliminary investigations. Together, these features suggest that zines are more complex than their roots in dominant, literate, white, middle-class culture would suggest and that their political effects cannot be measured in the short term by asking simply what zines pushed their original writers and readers to do in the world of conventional politics. Despite the privileges of their creators, girl zines strain after forms of subjectivity and sociality that challenge traditional middle-class norms. At the same time, and with the assistance of people I term "zine advocates," it seems possible that they continue to exert disruptive effects in venues their creators could hardly have anticipated negotiating when they were zine-ing as adolescents and young women.

Though girl zines are usually crafted as pamphlets and generally evoke magazines and the codex form, their jumbled, hodgepodge format tends to thwart linear reading. Zines are known for their DIY mode of construction and for their defiance of traditional intellectual property rights.[26] They tend to be presented in collage form, drawing together bits and pieces from books, magazines, newspapers, other zines, letters in the possession of the zinester, her own writings and those of others, images and clip art from a range of sources, and even bits of material culture like glitter, gold stars, tiny toys, thread, yarn, or string. The resulting discontinuities, fractures, overlaps, and contradictions trouble and even thwart the ability to read sequentially from beginning to end. As a consequence, zines call attention to the question of what it means to read. But some go farther still and equivocate more fundamentally about whether they are expressive texts, reconfigurations of discursive conventions, art objects, or new ways of performing subjectivity.

For example, even when a zinester evokes her apparent status as "author" or uses the language of self-expression to present her zine as the emanation of a pre-existing self, the subject the zine performatively constitutes is actually an intersubject composed of materials coming from a range of sources. Coherence and autonomy are only minimally valued in zine-ing. As a result, zines are not authored in any conventional sense, which is to say, it would be unwise to unify the disparate contents of a zine under the sign of a single, individuated name.[27] I think this helps explain why zinesters so often employ pseudonyms, sometimes several, as they produce multiple zines or change them over time. Usually interpreted as privacy devices designed to protect girls voicing nonnormative beliefs or exploring personal trauma, pseudonyms also enable girls to constitute imaginary, porous, unbounded personas marked off as different from their biographical selves. The girl zine subject who is crafted through the practice of collaging is not in any simple way the coherent, individuated, middle-class subject. Rather, she constitutes herself in and through the presence of others who are literally intertwined with her through the juxtaposition and interpenetration of many different textual bits.

I highlight this mode of constituting or performing subjectivity through zine-ing because I believe it is at the heart of the phenomenon as a discursive and aesthetic practice. Apparently alienated and distanced from the immediate local situations within which they found themselves—whether the family, high school, the college social scene, the workplace, or even the streets—these young zinesters demonstrated through their formal practices of composition an intense, exploratory, diffuse, and highly catholic interest in the discourses of others. They did so not by translating and then subordinating the words of others within their own supposedly authoritative voices but by literally incorporating others' words into their own zine performance through the material practices of clip art, cutting, and pasting. As analysts, we could choose to unify the jumbles that result, render them coherent, and explain them away as the effect of a girl's imperfect boundary definition or as an imitative impulse characteristic of adolescent uncertainty and self-exploration.[28] Or we could seek to take this performance at face value as the constitution of what might be called a more choral form of subjectivity, a subjectivity that is demonstrably *inter-*subjective, one that entwines the writer with others through the others' words, including those of newly encountered zinester friends.[29]

This choral mode of performing subjectivity is echoed and extended by the lateral, affiliative, branching mode of circulation characteristic of zine practice. Indeed I think it crucial to underscore the fact that girl zines were not published in the traditional sense. They were not copied in large numbers to be distributed from some central point to a range of anonymous readers unknown to the writer/creator. Rather, they were designed to be directed, one by one, to friends, friends of friends, and ultimately other zinesters and music fans who, having seen mention of a zine in another zine, might write to the zinester in question, offering a dollar or two, a few stamps, or even a copy of her own zine in exchange for the one she wanted. Such a request would prompt the original girl zinester to handwrite the name and address of her new correspondent in an empty space on the back cover of her zine, a space often ornately highlighted by careful framing. This de rigueur feature of the traditional zine format testifies to the importance of correspondence and mailing within the zine universe and marks implicitly the utopian hope for friendship at the heart of the larger practice of zine-ing.

This empty space for the hoped-for addressee found on nearly every zine figures an intense desire to connect literally—and not in the abstract—with actual others, wherever they might be scattered, who might appreciate a zinester's efforts and actually write back in response. Girl zinesters constantly interpolated their imagined readers and implored them not only to write back but also to pass the zine on to others, use it, quote from it, respond to it by creating yet another zine—in short, to weave zines, their creators, and their readers together into a network of mutual, interlocking citation and connection. Girl zinesters envisioned a network of the sympathetic and the likeminded extended through space, beginning with proximate acquaintances first but dispersing ever farther and wider as a result of word-of-mouth and whisper-down-the-lane recommendation.

While it may be true that zine-ing as a practice was meaningful to some as an act of individual expression unfettered by the perceived constraints attending traditional forms of literate behavior, a great deal of formal evidence points to the fact that longing for sociable connection was equally important, if not more so.[30] Such evidence suggests that it might make more sense to associate zines with epistolary practices rather than with the autobiographical activity of authorial expression or even of self-writing.[31] In fact, commentators on girl zine practice have widely noted the importance of reaching out to others.[32] Together, their work has documented that girl zinesters sought to transform their readers into correspondents; their correspondents into practicing zinesters, pen pals, and friends; and their zine networks into alternate forms of sociability. I would add that these networks were not to be grounded in the accident of proximity but rather to be the deliberate, volitional creation of choral subjects stitched quite literally into a tapestry of friendships, affiliations, and connections, a constantly changing social form characterized by extension, dispersal, and dissemination—not merely in space but through time.

I'll come back to the question of zine survival shortly, but first I want to note that in a recent article, Red Chidgey, Elke Zobl, and Jenny Gunnarsson Payne have termed the characteristic mode of zine circulation "rhizomatic."[33] In doing so, they draw on the work of Gilles Deleuze and Félix Guattari and on the adaption of their work by Olga Bailey, Bart Cammaerts, and Nico Carpentier in *Understanding Alternative Media*.[34] The latter employ the Deleuzian term to contest the use of simple binaries like alternative and mainstream or inside and outside to understand the nature of dissenting media production—in much the same way I am attempting here with respect to alternative print cultures. The term "rhizomatic" is helpful because it foregrounds the nonlinear, anarchic, nomadic, generative, heterogeneous, always branching nature of alternative media production, especially that associated with Web-based activity. However, because Chidgey, Zobl, and Payne are describing a contemporary and somewhat different form of zine production—one that connects print, Web-based, and exhibitional forms—and because I'd like to remain closer to the kind of language actually used by girl zinesters, I'm wary of applying it after the fact to the paper zine production and circulation of the 1990s. For the moment, I prefer to term girl zinesters' modes of distribution and circulation "volitional" and "affiliative" for the way they strive deliberately to create new connections, relationships, and friendships as alternatives to those that, by the accident of proximity, involved girls in their families, schools, and local social relations.[35]

Substantial evidence exists to suggest that girl zine-ing of the 1990s was highly successful at creating volitional networks of new friendships and affiliations. Indeed their zines are filled with references to and reviews of other zines, clipped and duplicated excerpts from zines recently encountered, and mention of letters from readers and other zinesters become pen pals and friends. Additionally, as is true within the larger zine universe, girl zines gave rise to the creation of review zines and targeted "distros" (distributors) dedicated to publicizing and facilitating the circulation of zines created by girls. In 1992, for example, while attending a comics convention in London, Sarah Dyer was impressed by the way the alternative magazine *Girl Frenzy* disseminated information about girl bands and girl comic artists throughout Britain. Returning to the United States, she created *Action Girl Newsletter* as a way to inform interested readers about girl bands, comics, and zines. Her work was extended nearly ten years later by Elke Zobl, who created the Web-based *Grrrl Zine Network*, as "an online archive" with a "comprehensive listing of worldwide, multi-lingual, feminist-oriented zines, distros . . . and projects, as well as interviews with zine editors."[36] The website initially included a bibliography, which has burgeoned since then, testifying to the exploding literature on girl zines both in the popular press and in the academic universe.

Taken together, these circulation devices and documentary strategies suggest strongly that girl zines need to be considered as something other than mere ephemera. Clearly, they didn't disappear into stored boxes of teen memorabilia. They have survived, it must be said, through the activities of the many readers, friends, and advocates they generated as they made their way by hand and mail through dispersed networks of like-minded individuals. Those networks clearly extended beyond the confines of girl zinesters' immediate worlds. Just as significantly, however, those networks and the ties they created have persisted over time, ensuring that girl zines now recirculate in new contexts, among new readers, and at the behest of new friends who are putting them to use in the service of a range of different projects. The meaning and ultimate political effects of zines have been extended by this practice. For this reason, it is essential to trace the various itineraries they have traveled and the newly established connections and affiliations they have created as they have continued to circulate at the behest of an ever-expanding network.

Prominent within the network of people devoted to the preservation and ongoing use of girl zines are the individuals I have now alluded to several times, the zine librarians who have campaigned to bring them into one of the central institutions of mainstream book culture, that is, the library. In discussing this phenomenon, however, it is important to note that the archiving of girl zines ought to be placed in the context of larger social developments that helped to make such an activity possible. Since my space is constrained here—and in her essay Alycia Sellie does a fine job of tracing the activities of the progressive librarians and radical archivists who sought to open up libraries to underground and alternative publications in the 1960s, 1970s, and beyond—I simply want to underscore that there is a prehistory to girl zine collection and archiving.

Indeed, in the early 1990s, Chris Dodge, a progressive cataloger at the Hennepin County library in Minneapolis, who was regularly in touch with other underground press advocates, like Sanford Berman and James Danky, began to write regularly on behalf of collecting zines in libraries.[37] In 1992, Billie Aul, senior librarian at the manuscripts and special collections division of the New York State Library, had accepted the donation of Mike Gunderloy's ten-thousand-title zine collection.[38] Gunderloy was the founder of the highly respected zine review *Fact Sheet Five*. Subsequently, as Dodge and others continued to advocate for zine collecting in journals devoted to librarianship, the more general secondary literature on zines gathered steam as well. In fact, the literature seems to have exploded in 1996 and 1997, a phenomenon Dodge chronicled in the *Minnesota Library Association Social Responsibilities Round Table Newsletter*.[39]

The year 1997 saw the appearance of the first full-length book devoted to the zine phenomenon, Duncombe's *Notes from Underground*, as well as the publication of a number of other anthologies.[40] Also in 1997, a number of the first academic articles about girl zines and their connection to the riot grrrl phenomenon were published in the book *Sexing the Groove*, edited by Sheila Whiteley.[41] In addition, the journal *Social Justice* published Julie Chu's still important article, "Navigating the Media Environment."[42]

Thus, it seems clear that very quickly after girl zines made their appearance in the underground scene, they began to circulate in circles beyond the independent bookstores, music venues, adolescent bedrooms, and crash pads that were understood to constitute the literary underground of the 1990s. Librarians, archivists, progressive-minded academics, teachers committed to showing their students that they could be more than passive consumers of mass-produced media, and practicing artists quickly took them up. And many of these figures—though by no means all—were former zinesters themselves. In fact, as girl zinesters of the 1990s matured, a fair number (there is no way to know how many) took up positions in familiar cultural institutions like schools, universities, libraries, publishing houses, and museums. And as they did so, some continued their investment in zine-ing by arguing for its significance as a feminist social practice worthy of preservation, remembering, and careful analysis. And, significantly, in making these arguments, these former girl zinesters necessarily forged alliances with like-minded archivists, professors, journal editors, students, and others whose interests had positioned them to be successfully interpolated by zines as well as by their restive and dissenting young creators.[43]

Within two years of the publication of *A Girl's Guide to Taking Over the World*, for instance, Tristan Taormino donated to the Sophia Smith Collection at the Smith College Library the girl zine collection she had assembled as the basis for the book. Archivists who clearly recognized this dissident form as a significant piece of the history of U.S. women accepted her donation. That same year, Sarah Dyer asked whether the Duke University library would be interested in the zine collection she had assembled as part of her work on *Action Girl Newsletter*. When Amy Leigh, a young librarian, responded positively, the Sarah Dyer Zine Collection was established at the Sallie Bingham Center for Women's History and Culture. In 2003, Jenna Freedman, a zinester and a self-described radical librarian at the Barnard College Library, proposed that Barnard assemble its own collection of zines created by girls. Her proposal was quickly approved, and within a year, the first Barnard zines were exhibited on the shelves, stored in the stacks, and circulated to students.

Freedman has become increasingly prominent among the ranks of zine librarians, maintaining a substantial website of zine resources; producing her blog, *Lower East Side Librarian*; giving papers about zines and libraries at various women's studies conferences and at SHARP and ALA meetings; and collaborating with and facilitating connections among other zine and radical reference librarians.[44] These include former zinester Kelly Wooten, now in charge of the zine collection at Duke; Julie Bartel at the Salt Lake City Public Library, the author of *From A to Zine: Building a Winning Zine Collection in Your Library*; and Alycia Sellie, now at Brooklyn College, who was trained by Jim Danky and is working on a project about zine librarians.[45] Sellie was the founder of the Madison Zine Fest and the creator of the Library Workers Zine Collection at the School of Library and Information Studies at the University of Wisconsin–Madison.

I could go on at some length documenting the way the preservation practices of zine librarians have connected with and facilitated the allied work of feminist scholars working on zines. This writing now gets grouped together as part of the developing field of girl studies, which Elline Lipkin recently mapped.[46] Given the kind of diffusion to which such details attest, it's clear I don't have the space to pursue all those affiliations, branchings, and dispersions here. What I would like to point out, however, in concluding, is that librarians— an educated, professional elite charged with the preservation of the book culture tradition—continue to be instrumental in the complication and questioning of that tradition by further extending the limits of the zine universe and augmenting the networks through which it has been constituted. At the same time, their work is making possible a redefinition of the larger literary field, insisting that any understanding of that field take into account not simply books or even the larger universe of print but also zines and all of the one-off, handmade, self-circulated publications generated by the alternative press.

This brings me back to my starting point, that is, to the question of how to think about the relations between literacy and power. One would be hard pressed to describe librarians—or academics, for that matter—as members of the dispossessed, as outsiders, as participants in book culture from below. Yet, in championing zines as worthy of collection, preservation, and further use, they are significantly extending the reach and effects of girl zine practice, itself the product of young women whose relationship to dominant culture was complicated if not vexed. Although it is possible that the inclusion of zines within libraries might be undercutting and containing their dissenting force, it is equally possible that such a move could be positioning zines and the girls who created them in the 1990s to speak to more than their contemporaries at the time. In fact, it seems evident from the developing literature based on these archival collections that such collections are at least fostering an ongoing conversation among former girl zinesters and their present-day readers about the nature of feminism and its history, especially its fate in the 1990s and beyond. Significantly, an increasingly important part of that conversation is focused on the question of how girl zinesters understood feminism, how they practiced it through zine-ing, and what their activities might mean for those who have come after them.

What the dispersed itineraries of girl zines suggest about book culture, power, and dissidence is that we would do well to foreground processes of circulation, dissemination, articulation, linkage, joinery, and relay in the field of print and book culture studies—and not just at points of distribution where books and related forms find their readers. Rather, we need to attend to these social relationships and connections every step along the way. Subjects are not essentially constituted, fixed one way or the other, by virtue of their origins. Nor are the books and texts they create. Rather, all travel ever-changing paths and are altered by the itineraries they trace and the connections they establish in transit. And the people who foster those connections are critical to what the subjects and the texts they create become.[47] In my estimation, the field of print and book culture studies can go farther in recognizing the significance of the labors of so-called mediators like librarians. That labor needs to be studied carefully and documented more fulsomely if we are to understand the full impact of their activities. In a book history reconfigured to trace itineraries of circulation rather than to locate and map origins, the critically important men and women—librarians, editors, distributors, reviewers, bookstore owners and clerks, and even teachers—all those who organize, hand off, and pass on texts, will wheel into view as the significant figures they are and have been. They have been critical not only to the history of the book and print but also to the history of dissident thought and dissent and, therefore, ultimately to the history of the deployment and contestation of power.[48]

Notes

1. SHARP 2010, Call for Papers, http://www.helsinki.fi/sharp2010/call_for_papers .htm.

2. See, for instance, the mission statement of the Center for the History of Print and Digital Culture (http://www.slis.wisc.edu/chpchome.htm).

3. Johan Svedjedal, "SHARP Panel: Introductory Comments," manuscript, 2010, 4. I want to thank Svedjedal for sharing a copy of his remarks with me.

4. Svedjedal, "SHARP Panel," 4–5 (emphasis added).

5. See Pierre Bourdieu, *Rules of Art: Genesis and Structure of the Literary Field* (Stanford: Stanford University Press, 1996); Robert Darnton, *The Forbidden Best-Sellers of Pre-Revolutionary France* (New York: Norton, 1996), especially 181–97; Thomas R. Adams and Nicholas Barker, "A New Model for the Study of the Book," in *A Potencie of Life: Books in Society; The Clark Lectures, 1986–1987*, ed. Nicholas Barker (London: British Library, 1993), 5–43; and Johan Svedjedal, *The Literary Web: Literature and Publishing in the Age of Digital Production; A Study in the Sociology of Literature* (Stockholm: Kungl. Biblioteket, 2000), esp. ch. 3, "Busy Being Born or Busy Dying? A New Model for Describing Literary Professions," 93–132 (esp. table 6, "Clusters of Functions of Individuals and Institutions in the Book Trade—Traditional," 131–32), and ch. 4, "Something Old, Something New: The Internet and New Combinations of Traditional Professional Functions in the Book Trade," 133–73 (esp. table 9, "Clusters of Functions of Individuals and Institutions in the Book Trade—Digital," 173).

6. It seems that much of McKenzie's work sought to escape the reification embedded in the very concept of the book and even in the idea of the text itself. Within his radically sociological way of thinking, both were rigorously construed as thoroughly social concepts; that is, they were understood to be wholly dependent upon a constellation of social acts and relationships. See D. F. McKenzie, *Bibliography and the Sociology of Texts* (Cambridge: Cambridge University Press, 1999).

7. See Marion Leonard, *Gender in the Music Industry: Rock, Discourse, and Girl Power* (Aldershot, Hampshire: Ashgate, 2007); Nadine Monem, ed., *Riot Grrrl: Revolution*

Girl Style Now! (London: Black Dog, 2007); and Sara Marcus, *Girls to the Front: The True Story of the Riot Grrrl Revolution* (New York: HarperPerrenial, 2010).

8. The concept of the underground and the supporting concept of the alternative has been much debated of late, not only within supposedly underground communities themselves but also by media theorists. See, for instance, Thomas Frank, "Alternative to What?," in *Commodify Your Dissent: Salvos from the Baffler*, ed. Thomas Frank and Matt Weiland (New York: Norton, 1997), 146–61; Chris Atton, *Alternative Media* (London: Sage, 2002); Nick Couldry and James Curran, *Contesting Media Power: Alternative Media in a Networked World* (Lanham, MD: Rowman & Littlefield, 2003); and Olga Bailey, Bart Cammaerts, and Nico Carpentier, *Understanding Alternative Media* (Maidenhead, Berkshire: McGraw-Hill/Open University Press, 2008).

9. In addition to Leonard, *Gender in the Music Industry*, Monem, *Riot Grrrl*, and Marcus, *Girls to the Front*, see Andrea Juno, *Angry Women in Rock*, vol. 1 (New York: Juno Books, 1996).

10. My account of the early days of riot grrrl is heavily indebted to Marcus, *Girls to the Front*, esp. 31–103.

11. On the emergence of the term "riot grrrl," see Julia Downes, "Riot Grrrl: The Legacy and Contemporary Landscape of DIY Feminist Cultural Action," in Monem, *Riot Grrrl*, 12–49; and Marcus, *Girls to the Front*, 75–108.

12. See Carol Gilligan, Nona P. Lyons, and Trudy Hanmer, eds., *Making Connections: The Relational Worlds of Adolescent Girls at Emma Willard School* (Cambridge, MA: Harvard University Press, 1990); Katie Roiphe, *The Morning After: Sex, Fear, and Feminism on Campus* (Boston: Little, Brown, 1993); Mary Pipher, *Reviving Ophelia: Saving the Selves of Adolescent Girls* (New York: Putnam, 1994); Peggy Orenstein, *Schoolgirls: Young Women, Self-esteem, and the Confidence Gap* (New York: Doubleday, 1994); American Association of University Women, *Shortchanging Girls, Shortchanging America: Executive Summary; A Nationwide Poll that Assesses Self-esteem, Education Experiences, Interest in Math and Science, and Career Aspirations of Girls and Boys, 9–15* (Washington, DC: AAUW, 1994); and Joan Jacobs Brumberg, *The Body Project: An Intimate History of American Girls* (New York: Random House, 1997).

13. See Joanne Gottlieb and Gayle Wald, "Smells Like Teen Spirit: Riot Grrrls, Revolution, and Women in Independent Rock," in *Microphone Fiends: Youth Music and Youth Culture*, ed. Andrew Ross and Tricia Rose (New York: Routledge, 1994), 250–74; Julie Chu, "Navigating the Media Environment: How Youth Claim a Place through Zines," *Social Justice* 24 (Fall 1997): 71–85; Sabrina Margarita Alcantara-Tan, "The Herstory of *Bamboo Girl* Zine," *Frontiers* 21 (2000): 159–63; Catherine Driscoll, "Girl Culture, Revenge, and Global Capitalism: Cybergirls, Riot Grrls, Spice Girls," *Australian Feminist Studies* 14 (1999): 173–93; Kristin Schilt, "'I'll Resist with Every Inch and Every Breath': Girls and Zine Making as a Form of Resistance," *Youth and Society* 35 (2003): 71–97; Jennifer Sinor, "Another Form of Crying: Girl Zines as Life Writing," *Prose Studies* 26 (2003): 24–64; Anita Harris, *Future Girl: Young Women in the Twenty-First Century* (London: Routledge, 2004); and Mary Celeste Kearney, *Girls Make Media* (New York: Routledge, 2006).

14. See Farai Chideya, "Revolution, Girl Style," *Newsweek*, November 23, 1992, 84; Elizabeth Snead, "Feminist Riot Grrrls Don't Just Wanna Have Fun," *USA Today*, August 7, 1992, 5D; Elizabeth Wurtzel, "Popular Music—Girl Trouble," *New Yorker*, June 29, 1992, 63–70; Nina Malkin, "It's a Grrrl Thing," *Seventeen*, May 1993, 80–82; and Kim France, "Grrrls at War," *Rolling Stone*, July 8, 1993, 23–24.

15. See Emily White, "Revolution Girl-Style Now!," *LA Weekly*, July 10–16, 1992, 21. White's more sympathetic treatment was reprinted in a number of alternative weeklies throughout the country. It has also been reprinted in *Rock She Wrote*, ed. Evelyn McDonnell and Ann Powers (New York: Dell, 1995), 398–99.

16. See especially Snead, "Feminist Riot Girls"; and France, "Grrrls at War."

17. On this, see Downes, "Riot Grrrl," 30–32; and Marcus, *Grrrls to the Front*, esp. 171–200.

18. It should be noted here that *Sassy* magazine played an important role in informing girls about zines and girl bands in its monthly columns.

19. On the personal and educational background of the early riot grrrls, see Marcus, *Grrrls to the Front*, 31–74.

20. On the question of riot grrrl and race, see Kristin Schilt, "The 'Punk-White Privilege Scene': The Construction of Whiteness in Riot Grrrl Zines," in *Different Wavelengths: Studies of the Contemporary Women's Movement*, ed. Jo Reger (New York: Routledge, 2005), 39–56. See also Alison Piepmeier, *Girl Zines: Making Media, Doing Feminism* (New York: New York University Press, 123–54). See especially Mimi Nguyen, "Asiatic Geek Girl Agitprop from Paper to Pixels," in *Technicolor: Race, Technology, and Everyday Life*, ed. Thuy Linh Tu and Alondra Nelson (New York: New York University Press, 2001), 177–90. Nguyen's zines—*Slander, Slant, Quantify*, and *Evolution of a Race Riot*—were some of the first to highlight the whiteness of the riot grrrl community.

21. Stephen Duncombe, *Notes from Underground: Zines and the Politics of Underground Culture* (London: Verso, 1997).

22. On girlhood and the fate of feminism in the 1990s, see Susan Douglas, *Enlightened Sexism: The Seductive Message that Feminism's Work Is Done* (New York: Holt, 2009). On the relations between riot grrrl and later girl-power discourses, see Maris Meltzer, *Girl Power: The Nineties Revolution in Music* (New York: Faber & Faber, 2010).

23. Sara Marcus, *Grrrls to the Front*, 9.

24. Kate Eichhorn has helpfully discussed girl zine-ing as a set of practices organized around a particular textual community. See her "Sites Unseen: Ethnographic Research in a Textual Community," *Qualitative Studies in Education* 14 (2001): 565–78. I should note that as I was working on the initial presentation draft of this paper, I learned that she is finishing a book about girl zines, zine archives, zine librarians, and their various relationships to feminism. I would like to thank her for sharing a description of her ongoing work with me. For a preliminary description of this work, see her "D.I.Y. Collectors, Archiving Scholars, and Activist Librarians: Legitimizing Feminist Knowledge and Cultural Production since 1990," *Women's Studies* 39 (2010): 622–46.

25. For additional discussions of this developing project, see Janice Radway, "Zines, Half-Lives, and Afterlives: On the Temporalities of Social and Political Change," *PMLA* 126 (2011): 140–50; and Janice Radway, "Zines Then and Now: What Are They? What Do You Do with Them? How Do They Work?," in *From Codex to Hypertext: Reading at the Turn of the Twenty-First Century*, ed. Anouk Lang (Amherst: University of Massachusetts Press, 2012), 27–47. Although there is some overlap between the present discussion and these earlier essays, each develops different methodological, theoretical, and historical points.

26. For a discussion of the way this attitude produces "sabotage and theft," see Duncombe, *Notes from Underground*, 79–86.

27. The two now-classic poststructuralist accounts of "the author" as a historically specific, ideologically contingent theoretical formation are Roland Barthes, "The Death of the Author," in *Image, Music, Text*, trans. Stephen Heath (New York: Hill & Wang, 1977), 142–47; and Michel Foucault, "What Is an Author?," in *Language, Counter-Memory, Practice: Selected Essays and Interviews*, ed. and trans. by Donald F. Bouchard (Ithaca, NY: Cornell University Press, 1977), 113–37. In the former, Barthes notes that "the author is a modern figure, a product of society insofar as, emerging from the Middle Ages with English empiricism, French rationalism and the personal faith of the Reformation, it discovered the prestige of the individual, of, as it is more nobly put, the 'human person.' It is thus logical that in literature it should be this positivism, the epitome and culmination of capitalist ideology, which has attached the greatest importance to the 'person' of the author" (142–43). In the latter, Foucault provides an analysis of how "the author function" works and of how that function is practically managed by certain legitimated overseers of literary discourse. As part of his argument, he notes, "The author serves to neutralize the contradictions that are found in a series of texts. Governing this function is the belief that there must be—at a particular level of an author's thought, of his conscious or unconscious desire—a point where contradictions are resolved, where the incompatible elements can be shown to relate to one another or to cohere around a fundamental and originating contradiction" (128).

28. Once again, Foucault's trenchant analysis points to the difficulties involved in the attribution of authorship not only to an apparently external series of supposedly autonomous texts but also to so-called internal elements or features of them. He writes: "Assuming that we are dealing with an author, is everything he wrote and said, everything he left behind, to be included in his work?" He continues: "If we wish to publish the complete works of Nietzsche, for example, where do we draw the line? Certainly, everything must be published, but can we agree on what 'everything' means? We will, of course, include everything Nietzsche himself published, along with the drafts of his works, his plans for aphorism, his marginal notations and corrections. But what if, in a notebook filled with aphorisms, we find a reference, a reminder of an appointment, an address, or a laundry bill, should this be included in his works? Why not?" (118).

29. My ultimate point here is that, formally, zines highlight their active defiance of the familiar bourgeois literary regime, anchored in the concept of authorship and in its supporting legal finding of a right in and to one's intellectual property. This mode

of composition actively constructs a different form of subjectivity, thus rendering moot the question of its "authenticity" as an expression of a preexisting, singular self.

30. For an excellent discussion of girl zines as a form of life writing that seeks to attend to zinesters' interest in personal expression without seeing zines as the straightforward emanation of a preexisting self, see Sinor, "Another Form of Crying." It is useful to contrast her focus on the creators of zines with Duncombe's more social interest in their modes of distribution and circulation.

31. On this point, see Eichhorn, "Sites Unseen"; and Sinor, "Another Form of Crying."

32. Anita Harris, *Future Girl*, 151–82; Elke Zobl, "Persephone Is Pissed! Grrrl Zine Reading, Making, and Distributing across the Globe," *Hecate* 30 (2004): 156–75; Kate Eichhorn, "Sites Unseen"; Red Chidgey, "Free Trade: Distribution Economies in Feminist Zine Networks," *Signs* 35 (2009): 28–37; Red Chidgey, Elke Zobl, and Jenny Gunnarrson Payne, "Rumours from around the Bloc: Gossip, Rhizomatic Media, and the *Plotzki Femzine*," *Feminist Media Studies* 9 (2010): 477–91; and Piepmeier, *Girl Zines*, 57–87.

33. Chidgey, Zobl, and Payne, "Rumours from around the Bloc," 477.

34. Gilles Deleuze and Félix Guattari, *Anti-Oedipus: Capitalism and Schizophrenia*, trans. Robert Hurley, Mark Seem, and Helen R. Lane (New York: Viking, 1977).

35. When one acknowledges the role the practice of networking played within alternative communities where paper zines flourished from the late 1970s through the 1990s, and then recognizes this practice actually predated the public appearance not only of social networking sites but of the Internet more generally, it seems possible to conclude that, like the Internet, zines were enabling new forms of subject formation and sociability, forms coalescing at a variety of different sites throughout global culture and brought on, perhaps, by increases in mobility, connectivity, and circulation of all sorts. It was this larger historical shift and its consequences that in the two volumes of *Capitalism and Schizophrenia* Deleuze and Guattari sought to diagnose with their notion of the rhizome.

36. See her description of the network in "Persephone Is Pissed," 160–63. See also the website itself, which can be accessed at http://grrrlzines.net/

37. Chris Dodge, "Pushing the Boundaries: Zines and Libraries," *Wilson Library Bulletin* 69 (1995): 26–30.

38. See Julie Herrada, "Zines in Libraries: A Culture Preserved," *Serials Review* 21 (1995): 79–88.

39. Chris Dodge, "The Summer of Zine Books," *Minnesota Library Association Social Responsibilities Round Table Newsletter: Library Alternatives* 10 (Summer 1997): 1–2.

40. Chip Rowe, *The Book of Zines: Readings from the Fringe* (New York: Owl Books, 1997); Seth Friedman, *The "Fact Sheet Five" Zine Reader: The Best Writing from the Underground World of Zines* (New York: Three Rivers Press, 1997); Veronika Kalmar, *Start Your Own Zine* (New York: Hyperion, 1997); and Tristan Taormino and Karen Green, *A Girl's Guide to Taking Over the World: Writings from the Girl Zine Revolution* (New York: St. Martin's Griffin, 1997).

41. Sheila Whiteley, ed., *Sexing the Groove: Popular Music and Gender* (London: Routledge, 1997).

42. Julie Chu, "Navigating the Media Environment: How Youth Claim a Place Through Zines," *Social Justice* 24 (Fall 1997): 71–85.

43. For an early account of the connections between zines and librarians, see Alycia Sellie, "Zines from the Stacks: Self-Published Tracts from Lady Library Workers," *Feminist Collections: A Quarterly of Women's Studies Resources* 27 (2006): 36–39.

44. The website for the Barnard Zine Collection has recently been redesigned; it can be accessed at http://zines.barnard.edu/. See also Jenna Freedman's own website at http://lowereastsidelibrarian.info/ and her new listing of her academic writing at http://lowereastsidelibrarian.info/academic.

45. Julie Bartel, *From A to Zine: Building a Winning Zine Collection in Your Library* (Chicago: American Library Association, 2004).

46. Elline Lipkin, *Girls' Studies* (Berkeley, CA: Seal Press, 2009).

47. On this point, see Kate Eichhorn's new book, *The Archival Turn in Feminism: Outrage in Order* (Philadelphia: Temple University Press, 2013).

48. In the end, then, I'm suggesting that neither librarians nor all these other figures should be treated as middlemen or middlewomen. Nor, really, should they be thought of solely as figures of mediation. If the larger process we are talking about here is one of textual circulation, then librarians and their confreres are absolutely central to its prosecution and ultimate success.

Contributors

JANE AIKIN is the director of the Division of Research Programs, National Endowment for the Humanities. She has held faculty positions at Indiana University, Bloomington, and Kent State University and staff positions at the Association of Research Libraries and the Council on Library Resources. Her publications include *The Nation's Great Library: Herbert Putnam and the Library of Congress, 1899–1939* and (with John Y. Cole) *The Encyclopedia of the Library of Congress: For Congress, the Nation, and the World.*

JAMES J. CONNOLLY is a professor of history and the director of the Center for Middletown Studies at Ball State University. He is the author of several books and articles about U.S. urban, ethnic, and political history. At present, he is collaborating with Frank Felsenstein on a book titled "What Middletown Read: Print Culture and Cosmopolitanism in an American Small City."

FRANK FELSENSTEIN is the Reed D. Voran Honors Distinguished Professor of Humanities at Ball State University. His publications include *Anti-Semitic Stereotypes: A Paradigm of Otherness in English Popular Culture, 1660–1830* and *English Trader, Indian Maid: Representing Gender, Race, and Slavery in the New World.* He and James Connolly are completing "What Middletown Read: Print Culture and Cosmopolitanism in an American Small City."

LORETTA M. GAFFNEY is an adjunct professor and postdoctoral fellow of information studies at the University of California, Los Angeles. Her dissertation is titled "Intellectual Freedom and the Politics of Reading: Libraries as Sites of Conservative Activism, 1990–2010."

ROSS HARVEY is on the faculty of the Graduate School of Library and Information Science, Simmons College, Boston, and has held positions at universities in Australia, Singapore, and New Zealand. His research and teaching interests include the history of the book. He is currently working on the history of nineteenth-century newspapers in New Zealand and Australia.

EMILY KNOX is an assistant professor of library and information science at the University of Illinois at Urbana-Champaign. Her research interests include intellectual freedom and censorship, the intersection of print culture and reading practices, and information ethics and policy.

JOYCE M. LATHAM is an assistant professor in the School of Information Studies at the University of Wisconsin–Milwaukee. Her research focuses on intellectual freedom in the information professions, both historically and contemporaneously.

KATHARINE LEIGH is the head of Cataloging and Metadata Services at Ball State University Libraries. She has worked in libraries for more than seventeen years, starting as a page in the reference department at the Oshkosh Public Library. She holds a BA from Luther College, an MLIS from the University of Wisconsin–Milwaukee, and an MS in political science from Illinois State University.

CHRISTINE PAWLEY is a former professor and director of the School of Library and Information Studies and a former director of the Center for the History of Print and Digital Culture at the University of Wisconsin–Madison. Her publications include *Reading on the Middle Border: The Culture of Print in Late-Nineteenth-Century Osage, Iowa* and *Reading Places: Literacy, Democracy, and the Public Library in Twentieth-Century America*. She is currently working on a history of Progressive Era women's institutional involvement in print culture, tentatively titled "Organizing Women: Print Culture and Community Power in Early Twentieth-Century America."

ELLEN M. POZZI is an instructor of school library media/literacy at William Paterson University in Wayne, New Jersey. She is finishing her dissertation on Italian immigrants and the Newark Free Public Library in New Jersey at the turn of the twentieth century.

JEAN PREER is a professor emerita in the Indiana University School of Library and Information Science at Indianapolis. In her publications, she explores topics combining library science, history, and law. Her essay "Promoting Citizenship: Librarians Help Get Out the Vote in the 1952 Presidential Election" won the 2007 Justin Winsor Prize awarded by the Library History Round Table of the American Library Association. She is the author of *Library Ethics* (2008), honored as the 2009 winner of the Greenwood Publishing Group Award for Best Book in Library Literature.

JANICE A. RADWAY is the Walter Dill Scott Professor of Communication and a professor of American studies and gender studies at Northwestern University. She is past president of the American Studies Association and former editor of *American Quarterly*. She is the author of *Reading the Romance: Women, Patriarchy, and Popular Literature* and *A Feeling for Books: The Book-of-the-Month Club, Literary Taste, and Middle-Class Desire*. She is currently working on an oral history of girl zine production in the 1990s, titled "Girls, Zines, and Their Afterlives."

LOUISE S. ROBBINS is a professor and director emerita of the School of Library and Information Studies of the University of Wisconsin–Madison. Her research has focused on the history of libraries in the McCarthy period, with particular focus on censorship and intellectual freedom. Her *The Dismissal of Miss Ruth Brown: Civil Rights, Censorship, and the American Library* has won both the Willa Award from Women Writing the West and the Eliza Atkins Gleason Award for Best Book in Library History from ALA's Library History Round Table.

ALYCIA SELLIE is the media and cultural studies librarian at Brooklyn College. Her current projects include the Readers' Bill of Rights for Digital Books, which works against digital restrictions on electronic reading, and *The Borough Is My Library: A Greater Metropolitan Library Workers Zine*, which launches annually at the Desk Set Biblioball. Her library and scholarly work is discussed on her website, http://alycia.brokenja.ws/.

JULIA SKINNER is a doctoral student in information studies at Florida State University. Her research interests include the evolution of public libraries during the first half of the twentieth century.

JOHN STRAW is the Assistant Dean for Digital Initiatives and Special Collections in the Ball State University Libraries. He has been in the archives and library profession for thirty-two years, holding positions at Indiana University–Purdue University in Indianapolis, Virginia Tech, and the University of Illinois at Urbana-Champaign before arriving at Ball State University in 1998.

JOAN BESSMAN TAYLOR is an assistant professor in the School of Library and Information Science at the University of Iowa. Her current project is tentatively titled "Talking in Circles: Contemporary Reading and the Social."

WAYNE A. WIEGAND is the F. William Summers Professor of Library and Information Studies Emeritus at Florida State University and the president of the Friends of FSU Libraries. He is currently writing a book tentatively titled "'A Part of Our Lives': A People's History of the American Public Library."

Index

AAUP. *See* American Association of University Professors

abortion, 15, 187, 194

access to information. *See* information access

accessions. *See* collections; homogenization and homogeneity; records and record-keeping

"The Acquisition of Alternative Materials" (Danky), 218

Action Girl Newsletter (zine), 250

Adams, Thomas R., 239–40

adult education, 116–18, 121–23, 130–31, 133

advocacy, 15, 112, 125, 221–22; "inside activism," 220, 227; meta-radicalism as, 220; "outside activism," 220; silence and, 220, 221, 231. *See also* American Library Association; librarians: advocacy of

The Advocate (LGBTQI magazine). See *The Los Angeles Advocate*

African American people and issues. *See* race

Aikin, Elizabeth Jane. *See* Aikin, Jane

Aikin, Jane, 78–93

Akeroyd, Richard (zine librarian), 217

ALA. *See* American Library Association

Alexander, Jeffrey, 27–28

Alfie's Home (Cohen), 185

"alternative," defined, 217–18, 232n6, 239, 255n8

alternative press and publications: 15, 217–20, 223, 224, 225, 226–28, 233n15, 235n50, 241, 250–51, 255n8; "authenticity" and, 238–39, 241, 242–45, 258–59n29; extremes on left and right and, 23, 221, 230

Alternatives in Print (meta-radical publication), 218, 223

American Association for Adult Education, 117. *See also* adult education

American Association of University Professors (AAUP), 170–71

American Book Publishers Council, reaction to obscenity suit, 169

American Family Association, 187–89, 191. *See also* Christian Right; "pro-family" movement

American Federation of Labor (AFL), 114. *See also* labor, organized

American Indians. *See* Native Americans

Americanization, 10–11, 104, 105, 106, 111–12, 113, 119, 155, 162; attitudes toward, 114, 126n13

American Legion, 14, 121, 136, 139, 140–41

American Library Association (ALA), 4, 10, 13, 24, 117, 131, 138, 140, 162; Code of Ethics, 13, 205, 207;

Print Culture History
in Modern America

James P. Danky, Christine Pawley,
and Adam R. Nelson
Series Editors